wake up
and change
your life

How to survive a crisis and be stronger, wiser, and happier

ANDREW G. MARSHALL

MARSHALL METHOD
PUBLISHING

The case histories in this book are based on couples with whom I have worked in my marital therapy practice (their identities have been changed to protect confidentiality and sometimes two or three cases have been merged together) and individuals who wrote to my website.

If readers have a medical complaint, it is important that they consult their doctor.

Marshall Method Publishing
London • Florida
www.marshallmethodpublishing.com

Library of Congress Cataloging-in-Publication Date is available through the Library of Congress.

ISBN: 978-0-9929718-2-3

Cover and interior design: Gary A. Rosenberg • www.thebookcouple.com

Printed in the United States of America

10   9   8   7   6   5   4   3   2   1

To my friend Kate,
who has changed more than anybody I know

CONTENTS

Introduction

In the last thirty years, I have counseled over 2,000 people—ranging in age from early twenties to mid-seventies. Since starting my practice in London, I have worked with couples and individuals from every continent. Despite the different backgrounds and dilemmas, there has been a common thread. Everybody was struggling with **change**. In some cases, it was thrust upon them by their partner. Sometimes, it was an outside event—like the death of a parent or seeing their last single friend get married—that prompted them to take stock. For others, something reasonably trivial like their children asking why they couldn't be nice to each other, or an inconsequential argument about where to keep the trash bags had spiraled out of control (yet again) and helped them realize they couldn't go on like this. Whatever the trigger, their lives weren't working and something needed to change.

Over the past four years, I've been focusing on why some people find it relatively easy to change (although maintaining the progress is still hard) and why others remain trapped in the same old patterns (despite years of self-development work). I've isolated the ideas that promote change and keep people positive despite the inevitable setbacks, and the skills needed to negotiate a way around any blockages. So I have a really positive message: you can change—and with your determination and the tools I'm going to teach, you *will* change.

WHY I DECIDED TO WRITE THIS BOOK

There's no shortage of books offering advice or personal testimony about change, but this one is different. I'm interested in **lasting** rather than superficial change. That's why I'm going to dig deep, explain why change is hard and how, despite our best intentions, we often slip back into the same rut again. I've drawn on ideas from a wide range of sources—psychology, philosophy, religion, and business sciences—to engage with big questions: what it means to be human and how to live the good life. However, at the same time, I am intensely practical and used to delivering real change on the ground, week in and week out, and helping my clients cope when it seems they're taking one step forward and two back.

Each chapter is built around a particular maxim. Think of these as like neural shortcuts to a huge body of knowledge that I've boiled down into a simple sentence—rather like icons on a desktop to connect you to a particular way of looking at the world or a new skill. As we lead busy lives with lots of demands on our time and many distractions, I recap each chapter's maxim in a box called Green Shoots—along with other key ideas. I've also pulled all these maxims together at the end of the book to help you keep them conscious, to overcome old habits, automatic thinking, and unhelpful messages from the past or our general culture.

My main focus, being a marital therapist, is changing your relationships: with yourself, your partner, parents, siblings, friends, and work colleagues. However, the ideas are equally helpful if you're going through a twelve-step program and need to reassess your life and find a way forward without the crutch of drink, drugs, gambling, eating disorders, etc. I promise to be as down to earth as possible and explain everything in clear and simple terms. On the odd occasions that I use terms from psychology and philosophy, it will be so you can take these ideas away, if you wish, to read more and further develop your understanding.

I decided to write this book because some of my clients asked for a summary of what we had undertaken together, so they could refer back. Although many of the ideas and exercises are scattered across my other titles—as I have addressed specific problems—there was not one single place where I'd laid them all out together. Furthermore, my understanding and practice is always developing—thanks to the learning from my clients, other therapists and fellow authors—and this book allows me to review and pull everything together. It's also the book I wish I could have read as a nervous eighteen-year-old being dropped off by my parents at university; in my early thirties when I was "let go" from a big job and thought my career was over; and finally in my late thirties when my first partner died after a long illness. In effect, we all have to face change, but it can be an opportunity as well as a threat.

HOW TO USE THIS BOOK

This book works in two ways. First, it offers reassurance that it is possible to change your life. Second, it provides the building blocks for a new future. Therefore, you can read this book in one go or focus on one chapter and one maxim at a time. It will take a while to work through all the ideas, incorporate the fresh thinking, and try out the new concepts. If I was seeing you in my practice, I would need at least eight weeks to cover everything, and most probably more. So please don't beat yourself up if it takes time to change or if you find yourself slipping back. Everybody has bad weeks. Don't worry, I have plenty of support for when you're in transition from your old life to your new.

Some ideas will strike a chord and be really helpful, others won't be for you. Take what you need and discard the rest. In many ways, it's a sign of progress when you start to pick and choose—rather than swallow my advice wholesale. After all, you're the world's expert on what's right for you.

It's also fine to put the book down and come back when you're in a better place. As I often say to people, 'You're facing a huge crisis and sometimes when you feel the most stuck, you're about to take another step forward.'

Finally, I'd like to thank my clients for allowing me to share their journeys. I have changed names to protect identities, altered trivial details, or sometimes merged two or more cases together.

Andrew G. Marshall
www.andrewgmarshall.com

CHAPTER ONE

Understand the Complexities of Change

You've had this huge wake-up call and something needs to change. Perhaps after years of being the provider, your family treats you like a giant cash machine and there's been too many withdrawals; or your children are about to leave home and you're wondering what next? Alternatively, it's your partner who has sparked the crisis, she or he is threatening to leave or has had an affair, or is behaving so badly that you don't know what to expect from one day to the next.

However you've reached this crisis point, it's clear that ignoring the problem is not going to work (however tempting that might be) and you can't turn back the clock, so there's only one real choice: change. I know change is frightening but here's the good news. It can be change for the better. At the moment, my claim that you can come through this crisis stronger, wiser, and happier seems frankly impossible—that's part of being in crisis—but I have strategies to break the journey into manageable chunks and tools to help you find a way through the minefield ahead.

Perhaps you know where you want to go but you're not sure which way leads to the Promised Land. Maybe, you're panicking and taking a couple of steps in one direction, getting overwhelmed, running back, and then setting off down another path—only to have second thoughts and double back. Alternatively, you're being dragged in a dark direction, with every fiber in your body saying no, but it seems like you've no choice. Finally, you might be sitting on a fallen tree calmly weighing up the options but unable to come to a decision. How do you know what's right for you? What impact will your decisions have on everyone around you? How can you make the best of a bad situation? And even if you come up with clear goals, how do you get from here to there?

We have a complex relationship with change. If we're in control then we're all for it. We're only too happy to upgrade our car or move to a bigger house in a nicer neighborhood. However, even positive change includes loss. We'll miss our friends and, even if we promise to keep in touch, it will never be the same. Perhaps we did our courting in the old car or there's a stain on the upholstery where one of the children was sick and somehow it seems we're letting go of our memories too. Even with change that is good for us—like losing weight, getting fit, and becoming even more gorgeous—it can bring up all sorts of uncomfortable feelings. What if we still don't like ourselves at our target weight? What if our partner still doesn't really notice us?

On the other hand, if the change is being imposed, we will dig in our heels. We complain "it's not fair" or "that's not what I signed up for"; or go on the attack, "after all I've done for you" and "how can you be so selfish?" We don't want our job relocated to the other end of the country. We don't want to get divorced. We don't want our parents to die. We want our old life back, thank you.

I've spent thirty years helping couples and individuals cope with change — some of their own making, but more often it was thrust upon them. I've also had to deal with all sorts of changes myself. I've lost jobs that I put my heart and soul into. I've lost people that I loved dearly. Despite the pain on the couch in my counseling room and in my private life, I have a positive message. Change doesn't have to be so scary; you do have choices, and this fork in the road could be the making of you. If you feel stuck or there's a gun being held to your head and you're being told to change—or else—I can help too. You still have choices, although they don't feel particularly attractive at the moment, and you certainly don't have to just "accept the situation." As I will explain, there are a whole load of new skills that will not only get you out of this hole but also transform your life.

SIX MYTHS ABOUT CHANGE

One of the problems with trying to break with the past are the unhelpful and misleading myths about change. Not only do they leave you feeling helpless and hopeless but encourage you to beat yourself up for being weak-willed when you get stuck. So what are these six myths and how can you combat them?

Wanting it badly is enough

Perhaps this is the most pernicious myth of them all: if you're positive and really put your mind to it then you can do anything you want. Like all myths, there is plenty of truth behind this idea but only up to a point.

Julia, forty, had a shock when she discovered that the majority of the texts from her husband's assistant were not about work. She did some digging and found out that they were meeting up after work, taking the occasional long lunch together, and sharing secrets. Her husband, Philip, forty-three, claimed that "nothing had happened," but under pressure admitted to hand holding, kissing, and cuddling. "After many rows and accusations, because I couldn't believe the evidence in front of me, I calmed down and asked him why he didn't text me—beyond about when he'd be back home or whether he'd picked up our sons—and why he couldn't tell me his intimate secrets," Julia explained. "I got an even bigger shock than uncovering their 'friendship,' because Philip told me I didn't listen to him. I was just about to open my mouth to contradict him and realized that would prove him right."

Julia certainly wanted to change and she had all the incentives in the world: stopping her husband from crossing over from an emotional into a full-blown affair and protecting her three sons from the fallout of a divorce. However, determination alone was not enough.

"On many occasions I was able to listen calmly, but equally lots of the things Philip said made me angry, blow my top, and say hurtful things," said Julia. "He would either accuse me of judging him or just walk away. Later I'd apologize and promise to try harder but I don't think he bought it."

There is another side to the "wanting it badly is enough" myth, which was feeding Philip's skepticism. If the change is proving harder than expected, it's because you don't really want it. Therefore, Philip was not only doubting Julia's ability to change but whether Julia truly loved him.

Challenge the myth: The problem with a simplistic idea of change is that it takes no account of the complexity of decision making. Of course, you are making hundreds of *conscious* decisions every day—for example, to interrupt your partner or let him or her finish, and to walk to work or take the bus. Therefore, if you really want to change, you will improve your relationship by listening. If you really want to get fit, you will walk to work.

However, you are making many more *automatic* decisions—which happen under your radar —and these are also impacting on your behavior. For example, you are less likely to listen if you are tired and stressed, but these states don't happen by accident; they are the results of lots of other decisions—which might have once been conscious—but have now become automatic. For example, your regular bedtime will have been set years ago (maybe even before you had children) and you have taken on too many responsibilities and overfilled your days.

When I dug deeper with Julia, some of her stress and tiredness were down to decisions that hadn't even been consciously taken but seeped in from the greater culture. She wanted her children "to have every opportunity possible" and therefore her day involved juggling one son's archery against another's baseball and "supervising" all of their homework. Her belief that "moms should be on top of everything" had been effectively inherited from her own mother who hardly ever sat down and relaxed.

What's the alternative: Congratulate yourself on your decision to change. It is a really positive move but it's only the first step. When things go wrong, it's not because you're weak-willed or not truly committed, but that you need to become aware of and challenge some of your automatic decision making.

It's not fair to ask people to change

Some people believe in this myth so strongly that they upgrade it. Not only is it unfair to ask your partner to change but it's wrong. In effect, you are asking them to be someone else and therefore not true to themselves.

"Julia has really strong opinions, she knows what she wants, and she goes after it," explained Philip. "It was something that I admired about her when we first met. So what right have I got to change her?"

I have a lot of sympathy for this viewpoint; after all, part of falling in love is accepting the other person—warts and all.

Challenge the myth: First, you are not asking your partner (or being asked by your partner) to change their personality, just their behavior. In effect, it is possible for Julia to both know her mind and listen to other people's opinions. It wouldn't make her a different person, just easier to live with! Second, you're asking rather than demanding. Your partner can look at your request, decide if it is reasonable or not, and make his or her mind up.

"It's not something that I'm being forced to do, but I've looked at my behavior through Philip's eyes and I don't like everything I see," explained Julia. "However, it feels like he's put a label around my neck—'she's bossy'—condemned me and not even given me a proper chance to respond.'

What's the alternative: It's OK to ask your partner to change—as long as it's not followed by a threat. Equally, if you're the person who wants to change, it's OK for your partner to be skeptical—to question your motivation, ask questions about how it will work, and discuss your progress. It's good to talk because you will learn more about each other and begin to challenge the unspoken myths about change.

Change is possible but we soon slip back into our old ways

There's lots of evidence to back up this myth—most probably from your own life. You decide to eat healthily, get more exercise, or cut back on your alcohol intake but after a great start, you're "treating" yourself to a bar of chocolate, finding excuses for not going to the gym, and you've worked so hard that you "deserve" that bottle of wine (and what's the harm in opening a second). In effect, you can change—but for how long?

For Julia, the crisis of Philip crossing the line with his assistant had proved the motivation for changing, but it offered lots of challenges, too.

"He had agreed that they would keep their discussions to office hours and on a strictly business basis," said Julia as she sat down in my counseling room. She had arrived looking angry and he was crestfallen. "The other night, I became suspicious of his typing. It had the rhythm of a back and forward messaging rather than writing a report or something like that. So I challenged Philip and I was right. They were at it again. I just lost it and tried to throw his tablet down the toilet.'

"She wouldn't listen to me when I said it had started innocently. She sent me a reminder of a meeting, I asked about whether the MD had confirmed and we sort of slipped."

Both Julia and Philip had discovered just how hard change can be.

Challenge the myth: Transitioning from your old way of operating to something different is always going to be tough. As I always say to my clients when they slip: "If change was easy, we'd all be doing it all the time." However, it doesn't mean that change is impossible—just that you'll need support while you're replacing bad habits with good ones.

Instead of catastrophizing or giving up, it is better to learn from the setback, make alterations to your plans, and prevent further relapses. For example, Philip decided it would be better if he could arrange for his PA to work on different projects and Julia decided to learn some emergency techniques for coping with extreme stress (see later in the book). Ultimately, there are always more skills to learn and fresh ways of looking at a problem that could support rather than undermine your changes.

What's the alternative: In thirty years as a marital therapist, I've never met anyone who changed without setbacks. So don't come down too heavily on yourself if you've joined the world's least exclusive club. I'm only concerned if you don't learn anything from your mistakes and therefore keep on making the same ones over and over again.

People can't change

There are lots of folk sayings: "you can't teach an old dog new tricks" and "a leopard can't change his spots." Of course someone can *appear* to change but, the myth goes, not deep down. In effect, they are just "rearranging the deck chairs on the *Titanic*." No wonder we get depressed and defensive when someone points out our failings (because if we can't change, they are not just criticizing our behavior but our whole personality too).

Nancy and Lawrence were in their late fifties and had been married for thirty years but Nancy had always felt excluded from Lawrence's life. "I don't know the names of his team, what his work involves beyond in the most general terms. He's often out socializing but I'm never involved," explained Nancy. It had always been an issue, but Nancy had an engrossing job that involved traveling all over the country. "With retirement on the horizon, I'm increasingly concerned about the future and that he's always going to be disappearing somewhere, being secretive, and never letting me close."

"You're being stupid, I like spending time with you," replied Lawrence. "It's just that I have a busy job with lots of demands on my time and, yes, some of that involves socializing, but only with clients."

During the first few weeks of their counseling, they did start spending more time together—which helped—but nothing fundamentally had changed.

"There's no real conversation. I feel alone because you don't tell me what you're thinking and if I ask about your day, you cover it with a pleasantry."

"I want to forget about the office, not bring it home."

"When are you going to let me in?" Nancy pleaded.

"Not when you're angry with me."

"I don't know why I bother," she snapped back.

Not only did Nancy believe Lawrence couldn't change and be more open, but Lawrence feared that Nancy would always be anxious and nothing he gave would be enough for her.

Challenge the myth: So widespread is this myth that clients often ask me despairingly: "Can people change?" I always reply in the affirmative: "If I didn't think change was possible, I would find something else to do with my time." My job is rewarding precisely because change is possible, and that it's normally hard won makes my clients' progress that much sweeter.

What's the alternative: If change is difficult, it is best to have clear goals and a way of monitoring progress. For example, spending more time together can be measured and reviewed each month—but if the goal is "opening up more" how will you know if it's been achieved? Instead of hard evidence, you will be at the whim of your moods (which will fluctuate).

Change needs to be big

If you're facing a big problem—for example, your life no longer makes sense anymore—then you will need a big change. You should move to the city or downsize and find somewhere in the country. You should leave your job and sail around the world, become your own boss, or get breast enlargements and drop a dress size.

Nancy decided that they needed a joint project: "something we can share together." While most people would have renovated one house together, Nancy believed in the "greater the challenge, the greater the reward" and wanted to buy a row of three small houses—in Italy. "They will be both a bolt hole and a revenue stream as vacation rentals," she explained.

Not only can big changes bring big problems—like supervising builders in a foreign language—but the risk is that you take all the underlying issues or unhelpful behavior somewhere else. Despite the new job or the new look, you remain the same person with the same insecurities or self-worth issues. Worse still, when your big solution fails to transform your life, you either plump for another big change (and risk your life descending into chaos) or sink further into depression.

Challenge the myth: When you improve a little bit each day, eventually big changes will occur. It won't happen tomorrow, or the day after, but slowly but surely you will begin to feel better. What's even better is this kind of change is more likely to last—because you've developed helpful habits, and habits stick.

Therefore, I was keener on Nancy and Lawrence sharing their evening meal together and talking over their respective days or choosing a TV box set to share than buying property in Italy (although they enjoyed a fact-finding trip together). In the words of Lao Tzu, the ancient Chinese philosopher from the sixth century BC, "A journey of a thousand miles must begin with the first steps."

What's the alternative: It is fine to have a large goal, but it also helps to have some smaller ones along the way. For example, if your goal is to prepare for retirement, you could experiment by doing something new at the weekend together. Furthermore, achieving a goal—even a smaller one —will give you a boost and underline your commitment to change.

Ultimately there are only two options when facing relationship problems

In many ways, the previous five myths feed into this one and turn a difficult situation into a crisis. Let me explain. If it's not fair to ask people to change, and even if you did they would either backslide or never really change anyway, so you're left with just two options: "put up and shut up" or "splitting up."

Therefore, even though you're fundamentally unhappy, feel unheard, or unloved by your partner, there's no point complaining. So you just bury the pain or tell yourself "that's my lot." As you can imagine, there's only so long that you can continue down this road without getting depressed or exploding. However, many people try to solve their relationship problems with "put up and shut up" for years on end.

Eventually, the fourth myth about change kicks in; i.e. the solution has be something big because the pain is so big. Therefore, the only option is a temporary separation, finding someone else or asking for a divorce (but not necessarily in that order).

Challenge the myth: There is an important alternative to "put up and shut up" and "splitting up": it's called "working on your relationship." For example, you could ask for what you need, you could explain when something is hurtful, you could talk about why your sex life has lost its spark, you could make each other more of a priority, you could develop habits that feed your relationship, and you could address some of the anger between you. As you will discover, I've a whole book of alternatives to "put up and shut up" (which is an option to be used sparingly) and "walk away" (which is really only a last resort).

What's the alternative: Changing your behavior can have a knock-on effect on the people around you, but more importantly your confidence will grow and you'll start to feel more empowered.

HOW TO CHANGE YOUR LIFE

If change is difficult and requires sustained effort, it is important to break everything down into manageable stages and make certain the plan is truly comprehensive. I often explain my method by using the analogy of driving. To reach our destination safely, first we are going to look under hood, discover any faulty wiring or malfunctioning parts, and do the necessary repairs. However, we also need to check your driving habits, improve your skills, and your knowledge about road safety. In effect, I'll be working at an unconscious (what's under the hood) and conscious (what's on the road up ahead) level.

At the heart of each chapter, and each stage of the journey ahead, is a maxim to help shape your attitudes and encapsulate a new skill to promote change. The idea goes back to the sixth century BC and Pythagoras—perhaps one of the ancient world's most influential philosophers —who had a profound understanding of the irrationality of human beings and how it was not enough to engage with just our intellects. He believed insights need to sink into our brains and, in effect, become part of our nervous systems. Therefore he boiled his teachings down into memorable bite-size chunks so philosophy could be a way of life rather than just a set of theories. The initiates at his monastic community in southern Italy would repeat these maxims to themselves or perhaps sing them together. The same idea of packing a lot of meaning into a sentence is also present with Eastern religions in mantras and with Christianity in the Book of Proverbs. It is also backed up by modern neuroscience, which differentiates between the neocortex, the thinking part of the brain (which learns skills and gains knowledge quickly), and the automatic limbic brain responsible for emotions, motivation, and long-term memory (which needs ideas repeated and practiced to create new brain circuits which will slowly become the default options).

The concept is best summed up by Epictetus (AD 55–135), who was a Greek sage and philosopher, when he explained what is needed for a man to make lasting changes: "It is not easy to come to a judgment unless he should state and hear the same principals every day, and at the same time apply them to his life."

As repetition is the key to change, I will introduce and explain a

14

maxim at the beginning of each chapter, give an example of it in action at the end, and repeat it in the bullet points that summarize each chapter. For easy reference, I have also gathered all the maxims together at the end of the book.

FIRST MAXIM

In the first enthusiasm for transforming your life, it is easy jump to conclusions and either make the wrong diagnosis of what needs to change or put together a plan that doesn't fully meet the challenges ahead. Therefore, the first maxim is all about preparation:

I need to explore and understand, before I can act.

Ultimately, it doesn't matter what changes you are looking to make—whether to your relationship with yourself, with your partner (or potential partner) or to your behavior (like your temper, drinking, overeating etc.) —you need to go through these three stages: explore, understand, and action. When I ask clients to guess how much time and energy needs to be devoted to each part, they normally divide them up into more or less even chunks. However, I stress the importance of the first two parts—with exploring feeding into understanding and back into further exploration—and leave action only taking up about five percent.

EXPLORING THE PROBLEMS OF BEING HUMAN

Have you ever watched a small child running down the road? You know they are going faster than their legs can carry them, and a few seconds later they fall over. There is a slight pause and then the child starts crying from the pain, the frustration, and humiliation of falling over. Hopefully, their parents are only a few steps behind and will scoop them into their arms and soothe their tears away—because small children don't have the inner resources (and their brains aren't developed enough) to comfort themselves.

As we grow older, become more independent and go off to school, we need to begin to self-soothe because even the most involved and committed parents cannot protect us from every harm or ease all our pain.

Perhaps that's just as well, or we'd never learn to do it for ourselves. Hopefully, the gap between being frightened, upset, and hurt, and being picked up is going to be small. However, the less soothing that we received as kids, the bigger the gap. I call this gap our inner void and it is the source of much of your current pain and confusion.

Unfortunately, some parents don't know how to soothe properly. They try to make their son or daughter instantly feel better by giving them a candy and thereby mask the upset with a sugar rush. Alternatively, they tell their children to "be more careful" or even give them a smack for being naughty, or they're too busy doing something else to notice. Other parents try and reason away the pain: When Frankie, thirty-five, was a child, her father would cycle her to the bus stop for school. "I was so busy watching this beautiful bird floating through the blue sky that I stopped concentrating. I was about six and pedaling along on my tricycle and I looked over my shoulder as the bird flew over and I fell off. There was quite a lot of blood and many tears. My father stopped cycling and came back to me. 'What's the point of crying? Does it change anything?' And I thought, 'How wise. Tears *won't* change anything.'" On the one hand, Frankie's father was intellectually right. But on the other hand, his daughter grew up into one of the most emotionally repressed women that I've worked with. I often wondered what would have happened if he'd just given Frankie a hug instead of advice.

So how can you recognize when your inner void has come into play? It will either make you feel profoundly uncomfortable or trigger the side of yourself that you dislike the most and will go to great lengths to avoid. For some, it surfaces as an incredible sense of emptiness: having so many problems that nothing or nobody will ever be able to solve them. These people tend to close down, stare into space, and be prone to depression. Alternatively, they can keep themselves so busy that they have no time to think. For others, the overriding emotion is fear and they have to run away, lash out, curl up in a little ball, or fall asleep (and thereby shut out the world). Therefore, the key emotion can be anxiety. The heart racing faster, sweating, being unable to settle to anything. These people feel constantly judged, criticized and believe nothing they do will be good enough. The final option is to be incredibly angry: "It's not fair" or "How dare you?" Overwhelmed by their feelings, these people throw things, make hurtful remarks, or behave spitefully.

Whether you are prone to feeling empty, fearful, anxious, angry—or a combination—it is as though your adult self (or the pretence of being grown-up that you present to the world) has been stripped away and you feel or start acting like a small child again.

HOW CHILDHOOD EVENTS FEED OUR INNER VOID

It is not just how our parents soothed or failed to soothe us that affects our inner void but random quirks of fate and the general powerlessness of being a child.

Birth order

Although every parent claims not to have a favorite child, studies at the University of California had found that sixty-five percent of mothers and seventy percent of fathers have exhibited a preference—in most cases for the eldest. However, there is also a marked basis toward cross-gender favoritism. Psychologist Catherine Salmon, who wrote up her findings in the journal *Human Nature* in 2003, says: "Overall, the most likely candidate for the mother's favorite was the first-born son and for the father, it was the last-born daughter. You would think fathers would favor their sons, but there is a tendency for them to dote on their little princesses." Once the patterns are established, they are awfully hard to break but can sometimes be offset by what is called domain specific favoritism. For example, a father might play golf with his middle son and this becomes their time together and compensates for less attention at other times, or a mother would bond with her daughter on joint shopping trips. Some sons and daughters will unconsciously or deliberately pursue interests to win some extra paternal or maternal love.

Of course, there are advantages to being first born and getting your parents undivided attention (but you have to cope with the jealousy when your brother or sister arrive and perhaps the pressure of setting "a good example" to them) or being the youngest and getting looked after by not just your mother and father but your older siblings too (but you have to deal with not being taken so seriously). Being a middle child can be difficult and many complain of having problems finding their role in the family (but others enjoy being able to slip under the radar). There are also advantages and disadvantages to being an only child: "I often wished I had a brother or sister to spread the load because I felt a terrible burden to perform," explained Samantha, thirty-one. "The focus was all on me doing well and Mom could be very critical if I didn't excel, and of course there were subjects in which I did better at school than others. On one hand, it was great that she was so involved—and ready to go off to the library to find books for school projects. On the other, she would have a very detailed postmortem about why I didn't get an A." The stifling nature of being the focus of all her mother's attention was intensified by her father working away during the week, and so from Monday morning to Friday night it was just the two of them. "Although, they both love me very much, I feel terribly guilty if I disappoint them—even now. It's the same at work, I can't stand letting people down. It's this horrible sinking sense in the pit of my stomach."

"The message that I got from my parents was that I was 'too complicated'," said Belinda, fifty-three. She was the oldest of three children and, when I drew up her family tree (a therapeutic diagram to reveal family dynamics), I was struck by how her father was closest to the middle child and how her mother had a special relationship with the youngest.

"It must have been tough," I said to Belinda.

"I never felt good enough and I find it hard to deal with criticism," she explained. "I did a workshop once where everybody had to choose a special power and I wanted to be invisible."

It made sense when Belinda told me that she wasn't actually her parents' first-born child. They'd had a son who died from cot death. Finally, I realized why her parents might have bonded better with her younger siblings.

"What must it be like to lose a child? You must be terrified that it will happen again?" I asked. "Could it be that your parents could only relax when you'd survived, and that allowed them to bond better with their next two children?"

Ultimately, it is impossible to know the true impact of the death of Belinda's older brother. However, drawing up the family tree helped

Belinda understand her parents better and not take their closeness with her other siblings quite so personally.

Whether you were a winner or a loser in this struggle with your siblings, there will be a long-term psychological cost. Clare Stocker, a research professor at the University of Denver, has shown that less favored children will sometimes turn their disappointment into aggression not only outwardly (toward the preferred brother or sister) but inwardly too (into private emotional turmoil).

How this feeds your inner void: You might feel "not good enough" in comparison with a favored or more successful sibling, or your parents unconsciously gave the message that you were only "acceptable" if you were a "high achiever" or "good." Nobody can meet those targets all the time and therefore you sometimes feel a fraud or expect to be unmasked at any moment.

Meanwhile, if you were the golden child, you might have been unprepared for the wider world that did not instantly sing your praises or fall at your feet, or maybe you have had to grow up with a burden of guilt about all the preferential treatment.

Growing up different

We depend on our parents for food, shelter, and emotional nurturing. We literally have no choice but to go along with their rules—however crazy or bad for us. It can be especially difficult if you don't or can't fit into your parents' view of the world. Perhaps you were a bookish clumsy child in a sporty family or an emotional child in a practical down-to-earth one. Alternatively, the realization that you were different might have come later when you went to school and compared your family to others. For example, you could have been the only Jewish child in your class or your parents earned significantly less than your friends' parents. Whatever the cause, you felt uncomfortable, different, and out on a limb.

Jackie, thirty-eight, came from a family that preferred to sweep anything unpleasant under the carpet. She described her mother as "see no evil" and her father as "speak no evil" and her brother went onto join the diplomatic services. Unfortunately for Jackie, she could not keep quiet when she saw injustice in the family or when somebody was taking advantage of her mother's good nature.

"I was the black sheep, the troublemaker, and a failure," said Jackie. "Even when I was a child, I'd be the one to say the unsayable. I remember one Christmas when my father's brother—who later admitted to a cocaine habit—kept leaving the table and coming back even more wide eyed. Everybody else was trying not to notice his erratic behavior but I piped up, 'Uncle Sean, why do you keep going to the toilet?'"

"So what happened?" I asked.

"I was told off for being rude and, when I sulked, I was sent up to my bedroom."

Jackie played a useful role in her family. Her truth-telling allowed her parents to release some of the tension that builds up when something is not addressed—but without having to face the real problem. However, she was left to cope with her internal struggle alone: "I wanted to fit in but I had to be true to myself too."

How this feeds your inner void: Even when you grow up—and meet people with similar values—you can still find it hard to accept compliments. Partly because positive feedback is often unfamiliar but mainly because the people you most want to impress is your first audience: Mom and Dad.

Sometimes people who grow up feeling different are not truly comfortable in their own skins until they reach middle age and start to accept themselves for who they are, rather than who their parents would have liked them to be. If you felt different for class, race, or religious reasons, you might have developed two personalities: one for home and one for the outside world. No wonder you have trouble knowing where you fit in either place.

State of parents' relationship

When there is a crisis, the natural reaction is to protect the children. Unfortunately, when it is a marital crisis, all too often the parents are so engrossed in fighting that they forget the needs of their children (or imagine their son's or daughter's interests are the same as theirs).

Karen, thirty, came into counseling because she had trouble forming long-term relationships because of the negative role models from her parents. Almost as long as she could remember, there was tension and aggression in the house, and her father would throw things—normally at the wall—when he lost his temper. "I can't have been much more than seven at the time but I remember my mother telling me: 'One day I'm going to split from your Dad. Is that OK?' It felt like she was asking my permission. I loved Mom and wanted to say yes, but I loved Dad too," said Karen. When her parents did divorce, her father used her as a confidant and a go-between. "He'd ask me, 'Do you think Mom will take me back?' or 'Is there any hope?' and one night when I stayed at his apartment I woke up to find him slumped over my bed sobbing. I didn't say anything, just pretended to be asleep." To make matters worse, there was a long drawn-out custody battle too.

There is nothing wrong with parents arguing in front of their children, if they can do it constructively—by this I mean, expressing opinions without getting personal, hearing each other out, and looking for a resolution. In fact, it is healthier than nasty atmospheres or pretending everything is OK (when it isn't) because constructive arguing gives children a positive lesson that you can love someone and still disagree. Unfortunately, many parents show their children what doesn't work: screaming, storming out, point scoring, holding grudges, and trying to wear each other down with angry silences.

How this feeds your inner void: When we are small, we do not have the intellectual capacity to put ourselves into other people's shoes. We are the center of our world and everything revolves around us. Therefore, if your parents divorced when you were under ten, it is not uncommon to believe they wouldn't have split if "I'd been good" or "better at school" or "more lovable." Even older children—who might intellectually know their parents divorced for other reasons—can get stuck in the bereavement process and imagine "If only ..." and come up with all sorts of personal failings which prevented them from saving their parent's marriage or their parent's coming back together.

In addition, your parents' arguments will have left you feeling very vulnerable. If they drew you into their rows, this could have been mixed with a strange sense of power. At times, it might even have felt like you were the parent and they were the child (and therefore you were forced to grow up too quickly).

Parents' long-term illness

Every parent wants to do the best for their children, but circumstances beyond their control or their own bad choices can leave some far short of this goal. Greta, twenty-six, had a difficult childhood. Her mother had mental health issues and was finally diagnosed as a manic depressive and had to be sectioned (for her own safety) on a couple of occasions.

"I never quite knew what mood my mother would be in. She had a terrible temper and would fly into rages—so I kept out of the way as much as possible," she explained. Meanwhile, her father, who admitted, "I fell out of love with Mom and fell in love with my children," had a drinking problem. "He was unpredictable: morose when he was drinking but lovely when he was sober," Greta explained. Her parents divorced when she was ten and her mother would say terrible things like, "I'm going to die and your father will come back."

Meanwhile, Greta would try and keep the peace and soothe over any difficulties between her parents.

"When one of them asked me to tell the other something, I'd edit the worst bits out and on one occasion I deliberately 'lost' a note my mother sent, via me, to my father as I knew it would cause trouble," she told me.

Finally, Greta's father got help for his drinking and entered a recovery program and her mother received the treatment she needed, but by this time Greta had left home.

Despite all these handicaps, Greta grew up to be a successful business-woman with a large circle of friends, but she found it hard to form long-term loving relationships.

How this feeds your inner void: Especially in our teenage years, we all want to be just like our peers and be "normal" but this is harder if your parents are different from everybody else's. Many people who grow up with an erratic parent, or parents, feel unable to bring friends around to the house—for fear of what might happen. Some will become people pleasers (desperate to keep everything nice) and often sacrifice their own needs.

Parents' death

Losing a parent when you're still a child has a lasting impact—especially as our society finds it hard to deal with loss and grief. James, thirty-eight, lost his mother when he was only twelve. "Looking back as an adult, I realize that she'd been ill for a long time but it was hidden from my sister and me. Even at the end, when my mother drifted in and out of consciousness, and I asked if she'd get better, she told me, 'We'll have to wait and see.' It was the last thing she ever said to me." Despite the trauma, life carried on seemingly as normal. "My grandmother told us that we had to be strong for our father's sake and, again, looking back, he took the loss very hard, but we never talked about it and just got on with things. My sister buried herself in her school work, but I disappeared into a dream world—I'd be forever getting into trouble for losing my bicycle or something else."

In some ways, Sarah, thirty-three, had been better prepared for her mother's death from breast cancer. "Nothing was hidden from us and we visited her in hospital several times. I remember watching her cut her hair short when I was about six or seven and thinking it was a game." Her mother died when she was eleven. "We had a lot of support from my grandmother and aunts." However, her father remarried shortly afterwards. "My sister and I were really excited about the wedding but we never really liked our stepmother." When I probed deeper into what made Sarah dislike her, there were a few surface complaints, "she's selfish" and "takes offense at the slightest thing," but the real reason was deeper:

"How could he replace Mom so quickly? I love my Dad and I wouldn't say a word against him and it must have been difficult but...." Her voice trailed off.

"If Mom can be replaced, so can you?" I asked.

"It certainly felt like a betrayal and I suppose that's made me very wary of letting down my barriers and allowing people to get close."

How this feeds your inner void: You have a fear of being abandoned and so protect yourself by pretending (to the outside world and sometimes yourself too) that you don't care: "Nothing can touch me." On the surface, you seem self-contained and reasonably happy but you have shut yourself off from what you crave the most: to be nurtured, cared for, and reassured.

Childhood abuse

Although the degree of damage depends on the type of abuse (physical or sexual), the frequency, and the relationship between the abuser and the abused, there is always a profound impact on the child and a deepening of his or her inner void. Margaret, fifty-six, had been sexually abused by a friend of the family when she was about seven and, when she was a bit older, molested by a cousin. "I don't really have a clear idea of what the friend of the family did but I think it involved me fondling him. I knew it was wrong and he threatened me that if I ever told he'd come around and kill my parents," said Margaret. "With the cousin, it was more aggressive sexual play. He tried to pull down my panties and I did tell my parents— but I didn't say anything about the family friend until very recently."

"What stopped you?" I asked.

"I didn't want to hurt them because I knew, rightly as it turned out, that they would be devastated that they hadn't protected me."

Many children who are physically or mentally abused by their parents minimise what happened or don't even see it as abuse. So instead of specifically enquiring about abuse, when I'm doing my history-taking interview, I ask how people were disciplined as children. Under these circumstances, people happily tell me about beatings with a stick, sons being made to put on boxing gloves and "fight" against their father, and mothers who refused to talk to their daughters for weeks on end.

How this feeds your inner void: Many abusers blame their victims for the abuse and, even if this is not made explicit, children who have been abused often feel responsible, in some shape or form. No wonder, they feel "bad" or believe that they "deserved" the mistreatment.

GAUGE THE SIZE OF YOUR INNER VOID

When first made aware of their inner void, many people panic and imagine that they are "a hopeless case" but, in most cases, they are doing really well under difficult circumstances. At the other end of the scale, some people had a basically happy childhood but wonder why life today is so hard or complicated. To provide some perspective, I have devised a short quiz with some targeted advice at the end. Don't linger too long on the questions, just go for the best match for how you're feeling *most of the time* rather than in your darkest hours.

1. Thinking of your overall well-being during the past year—away from any crisis that prompted you to pick up this book—how would you describe your thought patterns?

a) I generally have positive thoughts.

b) I catch myself thinking positively and sometimes feel guilty or superstitious, which undermines my good mood.

c) I often run myself down.

d) I have a more or less constant negative monologue listing all my failings and mistakes.

2. Thinking about any immediate crisis in your life, how well are you coping?

a) I'm stressed but generally manage to maintain my equilibrium.

b) I'm sort of coping but only with a lot of help from friends or family.

c) I often feel overwhelmed, find it difficult to ask for help, but somehow hold things together (at least for the majority of the time).

d) I'm sleeping badly, my appetite is all over the place, I'm withdrawn or have outbursts of anger. Basically, I'm a complete mess.

3. **Moving onto your work, over the past year, how motivated and positive have you felt?**

a) I am satisfied at work. I have good relationships with my colleagues and, most of the time, it feeds my creativity.

b) Every job has its ups and downs, but I generally find a way to gain satisfaction from my work.

c) I sometimes enjoy work but generally feel that something is missing.

d) I don't feel appreciated and my career doesn't seem to be going anywhere.

4. **Still staying with the past year, rather than any immediate crisis, how would you describe your work/life balance?**

a) I keep reasonable boundaries between work and home and take all my annual leave.

b) Generally, I work too hard but I've been making an effort to leave earlier.

c) I find it hard to draw boundaries and my partner or friends often complain about wanting to see more of me.

d) I rarely see my friends and sometimes can't find time to exercise, because work overwhelms everything.

5. **Thinking of your relationships in general (either with your partner, family, or friends), which statement would best describe your feelings?**

a) I feel truly loved.

b) We have good times together but could be getting more out of the relationship if we supported each other more.

c) We've been treading water and I often feel criticized.

d) I rarely feel loved.

6. Returning to the current crisis, how have you been feeling over the past few days and weeks about your partner/boyfriend or girlfriend?

a) I can see how my behavior has been feeding the crisis and I'm doing my best to fix it.

b) My partner's complaints have some validity, but either I don't know where to start or feel completely overwhelmed.

c) Sometimes it feels like the world, other people or circumstances are against us. Nothing I do seems to make any difference.

d) Constantly under attack. It's completely unfair.

7. Thinking of your goals—both in the immediate and medium term—how would you describe your situation?

a) I have clear goals and feel reasonably confident of achieving them, all I need is to know how to get started.

b) I know what I want but I'm frightened I'll muck it up. I'll need a lot of outside help.

c) I lack the confidence to articulate my goals or fear they'd sound really stupid.

d) It's hard to identify what I truly want.

Total up your answers:

Read the category where you agreed with the most statements and then the category where you had the second most matches. However, it is useful to look at other profiles, too, as it will help you understand the traps that other people fall into (and maybe yourself in darker moments) plus the mental tricks that help by-pass self-defeating behavior.

MOSTLY A: You have a shallow inner void and your internal dialogue is, on the whole, positive and optimistic. In addition, your relationships are good because you have mastered a key skill: the ability to put yourself in other people's shoes and consider how your behavior might be effecting them. Being a "glass half full" person is normally an advantage. For example, studies of survival rates among cancer patients under sixty has shown that pessimists are more likely to die within eight months than optimists who expect to get better. However, the human race as a whole has a tendency to underestimate the chances of job losses, our partner being unfaithful, and even our life span (sometimes by twenty years or more). So when we're told, for example, the divorce statistics, we imagine that our marriage will be one of the ones that endure. Even if we are less hopeful about the general situation (for example, a study in 2007 found seventy percent thought families were less successful than in their parents' generation), we still remain positive about our own lives (in the same survey, seventy-six percent were optimistic about the future of their own family). With this optimism bias hardwired into the way we think, it comes as a horrible shock when our lives don't follow the expected path and we come face-to-face with a personal crisis, a tragedy, or are ambushed by our partner's problems.

Breakthrough Tip: Instead of becoming pessimistic—which feels like a betrayal of your personality—take on board another aspect of optimism: searching for an upside. For example, "I might have lost my job but it provides the time to concentrate on my marriage" or "My flight home might have been canceled but I'll have a chance to try that restaurant that was booked up before." In other words, the bad event is made bearable by transforming it into "a blessing in disguise."

MOSTLY B: You have a relatively shallow inner void. You try to think positively but can slip into being judgmental at times of crisis and become discouraged and deskilled. Your relationships are generally good but sometimes you hold back and play safe rather than allowing yourself to be truly intimate with your partner. It could be that this "don't rock the boat" approach has contributed to your current crisis.

Breakthrough Tip: Everybody worries about what bad events might happen to their families and themselves. However, true optimists spend longer thinking about positive outcomes and fill in more details (for example, how great the sex on vacation will be, how they will feel when they lock the bedroom door behind them, and the look of satisfaction on their partner's face when they climax) than imagining bad ones ("We'll never have sex again" and "Our marriage is doomed" and "I'll never find anyone to love me"). So double check your inner-dialogue and if you find yourself catastrophizing—expecting the worse—put up a mental STOP sign. Next, don't ruminate on what went wrong—"Why did I do that?" or "I should have done that instead"—but free yourself from the past by saying: "It was the best decision at the time" or "I did my best with the information I had." Finally, you are ready to concentrate on what will make things better today or increasing the likelihood of your desired future scenario.

MOSTLY C: You have a relatively deep inner void and would probably describe yourself as a practical pessimist: "There's no point expecting the best of people or things to turn out well because that way I'm rarely disappointed." Unfortunately, your gloomy predictions nearly always come true—because if you don't think you will succeed, you don't put your heart and soul into something and, without true commitment, it's harder to reach your goals. In addition, you have ambivalent self-esteem and don't think you have much control over life. In relationships, you wonder why people don't notice you and attend to your needs. However, by learning a few simple communication skills, you can make a fundamental difference to the quality of your relationships. And by learning to be a qualified optimist, you will be more likely to succeed. The combined effect will begin to heal old hurts and reduce your inner void down to more manageable proportions.

Breakthrough Tip: Try asking your partner for what you need—rather than hoping for him or her to somehow know. Make it something small, specific and repeatable: "Could you pick me up from the station as it's raining?" Respecting yourself enough to ask for what you need is the first step to feeling better. In order to feel more optimistic about your chances of success, you will need a few successes under your belt. So instead of concentrating on the big picture (for example, saving your marriage) break it down into smaller chunks (for example, having a nice weekend together). Remember, small achievements will boost your self-confidence, encourage medium-size goals, and ultimately build into something of which you can be truly proud.

MOSTLY D: Your inner void often feels wide and deep. So it is no surprise that you think in a negative way, don't expect to have your needs met and suffer from low self-esteem. Your biggest fear is that if people discovered the real you, they would think less of you or not really like you. Keeping people at arm's length, or trying to be what you think they want, is exhausting; no wonder you sometimes find relationships hard to cope with. Fortunately, it's possible to change the way that you think and begin to view events in a more positive light. For example, instead of, "That's it, I've got a huge inner void, I might as well close the book now," you could swap that pessimistic thought for something optimistic: "I'm likely to learn the most."

Breakthrough Tip: Start by looking for one thing to be grateful for every day. Even something small—like a really good cup of coffee—will begin to lift your mood and slowly you will notice other positives. If this proves too hard, consider booking a health check-up with your doctor, as you may be suffering from depression or anxiety and need more help through your current crisis.

SHAME

One of the most destructive feelings lurking at the bottom of many people's inner void is shame. It is particularly toxic because shame is the opposite of feeling loved and accepted. As I've explained, we are completely dependent on our parents both emotionally and physically and have to do our best to fit in not only in order to survive but to get the love we need to thrive. So imagine what would happen if someone felt that there was something so abhorrent, disgusting, or stupid about themselves that it made them essentially unlovable.

"I was the little boy with a big secret," said Rob, forty-nine. "I suppose I knew from about four or five that I was different, but I couldn't put my finger on how. Perhaps the feelings were dim, perhaps I always knew but just didn't want to know. Anyway, there was this little boy that lived down the street and I really liked him—not in the way that other best friends 'liked' each other. I wanted more but I didn't know what." Unlike children from ethnic or religious minorities who might have trouble fitting into the wider community but feel secure at home, young gays are worried that their differentness might cause them to lose their parents' love. "It might have been that I wasn't interested in ball games, like my younger brother, or maybe my father sensed something and shrunk away from it, but I definitely had a sense that he was disappointed in me. My parents always said I could be anything I wanted to be, but I knew they were talking careers and not my sexuality. And why would I want to be gay? They were the butt of playground jokes, comedians on the TV with limp wrists who made my Dad seethe with anger, or they got beaten-up in gritty late-night plays (that I watched only after my parents had gone to bed)." Like many young gay men, Rob did everything to fit in, he tried to "man-up" and pretend that he was like everybody else. In other words he buried his shame.

"I was close to my mom—perhaps she wanted to protect me—and she'd praise me for being so helpful and good at cooking. By ten, I could pipe frosting to a professional standard, I started to win competitions and more praise. How I longed for approval! But it wasn't from my father (who might have applauded but looked embarrassed at prize-giving) and it all felt fake because if they'd known my secret ..." Rob couldn't put into words what might happen but I knew it would involve shame.

31

Although growing up gay—especially in the days when most gay men were in the closet and there were no role models—is a clear-cut and easy to understand reason why someone might feel shame, I think everybody gets a dose in some shape or form.

Naomi is thirty-five and her parents are evangelical Christians. Her problems started when she went to secondary school: "It was like everybody else got a memo about how to fit in and be popular but I missed it. Girls can be cruel and I was bullied for not watching the right TV shows (they'd clash with Bible study group) or loving the cool pop stars (who my parents and the church considered Satan worshippers)." Things got considerably worse, around fourteen, when Naomi lost her faith but couldn't tell her parents: "They would have been mortified and I didn't want to hurt them. So I would go to church week after week, going through the motions but inside feeling a fraud. There would be all this talk about believers and nonbelievers and how the first would be raised up—Hallelujah—and the second cast down into a fiery pit. The minister would fix his eye on the congregation as if he could see into our hearts," she said.

"What did you feel?" I asked.

"A fraud. I was being punished at school for what I believed, but the irony was that I didn't."

"So you had a dose of shame at school and in church ..."

"Evangelicals are big on shame."

"And your parents?"

"They thought I was a good girl."

"But your heart was full of darkness ..."

"And shame," said Naomi.

Both Rob and Naomi's parents did not stop loving them when they found out about their sexuality or lack of faith, but their younger selves were not mature enough to grasp this possibility. They had to struggle alone with their shame and find ways of coping with it. However, in a strange way, Rob and Naomi had an advantage over everybody else. Their source of shame was straightforward and had a name (gay or atheist), but the nagging sense that we are somehow not good enough—and the shame *that* breeds—is hard to put our finger on. So our shame is buried deep in our inner void and never talked about.

HOW YOUR CHILDHOOD SHAPED YOU

Draw up a list of all your best qualities down one side of a piece of paper and on the other put down all your failings. When you've finished ask yourself:

- Which side has more entries?

- Which side was easier to compile?

- What positive messages did you receive as a child? How might these have fed your self-esteem?

- What does this say about your inner void?

- What negative messages did you receive as a child? How might these have added to your perceived failings?

- How could you challenge the reliability of these negative messages?

- How many of these messages are out of date?

For example, James, whose mother died when he was twelve, had written that he was "only average" for one of his failings. When I pointed out that he ran a successful small business, he changed it to "average intelligence." So where did this message come from? James had been to a private school where the pupils were streamed into three levels. "I was not one of the really bright kids who took some of their exams a year early and I wasn't one of the dunces. Year after year, I'd be in the middle stream." But did that make him average? "I had a year off from my middle ranking university and worked in a holiday camp," he said, "where most of the guests and the staff had few or no academic qualifications. It made me realize what a privileged and unusual education I'd received." So, measured against his peers, James might have been average, but against the rest of the population, he probably ranked somewhere in the top two or three percent. This message from his childhood was seriously out of date but was still shaping James's opinion of himself and feeding his inner void.

WHAT ELSE FEEDS OUR INNER VOID

I don't want to give the impression that you should blame parents for your inner void. Partly because blame is not a particularly helpful emotion (after all, our mothers and fathers are struggling with the legacy from their own parents), but mainly because there are many other factors that contribute to our inner void. For example, there is the frustration and complexity of life in general. Just following the rules at school, studying hard, and going off to university does not necessarily mean a well-paid job, a loving partner, and beautiful children. Between our expectations or dreams and cold hard reality, there is always going to be another gap, and our inner void grows deeper and wider.

In many jobs, there is also a gap between what people do and the end product. Instead of being craftsmen baking a loaf of bread or making a chair, we're a small part of a much larger process. Instead of giving a service directly to a customer, we might be shuffling data somewhere in the back room or in a call center fielding enquiries with no on-going relationship with the client. This inability to hold the fruit of our labor in our hands or see the smile on our customers' faces is profoundly alienating and this, in turn, adds to our inner void.

Finally, there are the smaller everyday annoyances of traffic jams, tradesmen who don't have the vital spare part, store assistants who are busy talking to their friends, and the convenience store running out of our favorite cookies. If we haven't learned sensible coping strategies, it is easy to imagine the frustrations are in some way personal or that "we've failed" or "we're not good enough" and this provides a drip, drip, drip of negative feelings into our inner void.

FIRST MAXIM IN ACTION

By now, you will have a better sense of the complexity of the journey ahead and why so many plans to change are derailed. I've focused on looking under the "hood of the car" in this chapter but the first maxim works as a new skill too. So how could you use "**I need to explore and understand, before I can act**" in everyday life?

Simon and Alina were in their midfifties and had been together for just four years—after both being married to other people for twenty years. Their courtship had been passionate and fulfilling, but day-to-day living together had not been straightforward and they would alternate between bliss and complete despair.

"I get my hopes up that I've finally found someone who will understand and with whom I'm going to be happy," explained Simon, "but they get dashed when we start rowing. The black moods that descend on the house is like a small death."

Alina nodded bleakly in agreement: "We don't even seem able to sort out the smallest disagreement."

For some reason, their TV had not recorded the next episode in the detective series that they had been watching together. When Alina became confused about the plot, she decided to read her book instead.

"I've got nothing against you following it," she explained. "I'm perfectly happy reading."

"So watching TV—that's another thing we don't do together," Simon complained.

"We're in the same room," soothed Alina. "Isn't that enough?"

"That's another one of my interests that you tolerate—like rallycross driving—rather than entering into the spirit of things, just for once."

"So I'm to blame! Why didn't I guess?"

Somehow, they had changed from the couple who were most likely to hold hands on my couch—and when I first met them I'd had this extraordinary sense of two people growing and changing—into one of the angriest (and all in the space of ten minutes).

When an argument moves like a wildfire through a dry forest, I always suspect that people are rushing to act – rather than staying with exploring and understanding.

"Why have negotiations about how to solve the problem broken down so quickly?" I asked.

"Neither of us like arguments, so we try and find a solution as quickly as possible," Simon explained.

"I thought we could do different activities in the same room," said Alina, "but my generosity—because I could just as easily read in bed—was not acceptable."

"I'd thought that we could use the 'previously on ...' summary at the start of the show to get a sense of what we'd missed and if you were confused that you'd watch the missing episode on one of the catch-up services and then we could continue together."

"Hang on, I didn't know that," said Alina.

"And I didn't know that you'd rather read somewhere quiet."

In effect, they had been so busy trying to sell their solution—for perfectly loving reasons—they had not really listened to each other. In effect, they were trying to act before they had explored, and certainly before they had understood.

"So why should this argument prove so combustible?" I asked. As we'd spent the last few weeks covering this topic, I hoped they would know this answer.

"I think nobody is ever going to love me enough because my mother didn't have much time for me," said Simon.

"My mother blamed me—wrongly—for my father leaving, and I expect everything to be my fault."

With this understanding at the forefront of their minds, they could finally move to action and find a solution for the missing TV show that worked for both of them.

GREEN SHOOTS

- The gap between falling over and your parents picking you up—both literally and metaphorically—can create a well of dark and troubling emotions.

- When a crisis feels overwhelming and deskilling, it has probably awakened something buried deep in your inner void.

- The first maxim to change your life is: "I need to explore and understand, before I can act."

CHAPTER TWO

Stop Going Backward

When you're standing at a crossroads, or facing a difficult and painful time, it is only natural to want to find a way forward—almost any way will do! However, in your determination to escape, you can easily go backward and confirm your partner's worst fears ("You always do that" and "That's why this isn't going to work") or your own ("I can't change" or "What's the point"). So the aim of this chapter is to help you orientate yourself and to develop an inner compass to decide what is the right and wrong direction for you. I'm going to start by looking at the strong emotions that you're experiencing at the moment and helping you to understand them.

MYTHS ABOUT FEELINGS

What are feelings? I'd like you to stop reading for a second and think. It is a deceptively simple question but one that throws up lots of unconscious material. So think about the sentence below and add the first three thoughts that come into your head. (If you come up with more than three that's brilliant; put them all down.)

Feelings are ...

1.

2.

3.

My clients give all sorts of different definitions. For example, feelings are: "important," "difficult to pinpoint," "can hurt," "can consume your every thought," "compulsive," "difficult," "natural," "sometimes best kept to myself," and "easy to express when happy." There are no right or wrong answers. However, lots of people believe in one or more of the following myths about feelings:

Feelings need to be controlled

For many people feelings are dangerous and need to be kept firmly in check with reason or their intellect. They will tell themselves "Don't make a fuss" or tell their partner "You're exaggerating" and insist on "getting everything into proportion."

An example would be Maggie, forty-seven, and Frankie, forty-three, who'd been married for seven years but had not resumed sex after their daughter was born five years earlier. Maggie had been trained from a child, by her domineering mother, to control her emotions; she thought feelings should be "expressed at the right moment" and it often took several hours of talking to her partner for her to work out what she really felt. Meanwhile, Frankie had been to a very academic school where the unspoken message was feelings could get in the way of "reaching your true potential." When we did the exercise, he wrote that feelings were "hard to control" and "not optional" (although I had a strong sense that this was a regret to him) and that "unhappy feelings were more noticeable than happy ones."

Why this myth is so potent: There is always some truth behind every myth. Sometimes, you do need to control your feelings and walk away. However, people who believe this myth are frightened that if they "give in" to their emotions, they'll be stuck with the feeling forever. For example, "I will tumble into depression and despair or be constantly angry."

Downside: It is exhausting to be constantly managing your feelings and worst still the underlying problems remain unchallenged and unchanged. After several years with neither Maggie nor Frankie talking about their absent sex life, and controlling their feelings of distress and aloneness, Frankie believed that Maggie didn't care about him and decided that he could no longer live without love, so left home.

Feelings need to be obeyed

At the opposite end of the scale, feelings are directions to be followed to the letter. These people will tell themselves "better out than in" and feelings are "a window into my soul" or "honest" and "don't hide from them."

For example, Rebecca, fifty-three, would often be besieged by anger and bitterness about her husband's affair—even though it had happened three years previously, he had stopped all contact with the other woman and done his best to answer all her questions. "He'll do something thoughtless and I'll be gripped by this sense of injustice and rage. 'How could he?' 'After all I've done for him!' Out pours all the frustration and fury, I have to tell him what I think or I'll burst with indignation."

Why this myth is so potent: There is an underlying belief in our society that if you don't express your feelings somehow you are not being true to yourself or worse still, risk being controlled by your partner.

Downside: Not only can small and medium feelings—like irritation or being fed up—be whipped up into wrath and rage but it becomes harder to differentiate between minor issues (that might spark a row) and fundamental problems (that are driving the underlying unhappiness). It is also easy to start catastrophizing or become abusive. For example, Rebecca would say things that she would later regret: "Our marriage is over, he's broken it beyond repair. He's scum, the lowest of the low"—and other things she was too embarrassed to repeat in my counseling room.

Sometimes, I find people tip over into the second myth (and take feelings as directions) after years believing the first myth (and controlling feelings by minimizing and rationalizing).

Feelings need to be ignored

With these people, feelings are either blocked out by walking away, doing something engrossing (like work or playing computer games), or putting them in a box and mentally closing the lid. They are likely to say that feelings are "complicated" or "can lead to bigger issues if expressed" or "overrated" or "dangerous."

39

self-absorbed, the "me" society

For example, Rebecca's husband Jerome, aged fifty-five, had been ignoring his feelings: "There's no point in saying anything because I'm always one step away from an argument I can't win. Even the smallest disagreement will link straight back into my affair."

Why this myth is so potent: We all want to be loved but if we have inconvenient feelings, we might upset people and they won't even like us. So why not pack them away and ignore them?

Downside: You don't know what you want or what you truly feel. Worse still, you can't switch off your feelings completely so they leak out as being irritable and cranky with other people. This was certainly what was happening with Jerome and prompting the upset with Rebecca that he was going out of his way to avoid.

SECOND MAXIM

So if controlling, obeying, and ignoring your feelings have profound downsides, what is the alternative? Perhaps, at this point, I should share how I finish the sentence "Feelings are ..."

In my opinion, *feelings are clues about how to behave.* You'll notice I've used the word *clue* rather than direction. In a sense, you're like a detective trying to make sense of all the evidence and your feelings are an important element in reaching your conclusion. Therefore, my second maxim is:

What is this feeling trying to tell me?

Just like a good detective considers all the possibilities, rather than going for the most obvious answer when he or she arrives at the crime scene, I'd like you to take your time, too. You need to balance your short- and long-term needs (or you'd give in to passing desires that would cause lasting suffering). You will also need to consider the impact on everybody else—particularly those that love you. Ultimately, to make a **wise** decision, you need to consult both your heart and your head. (We'll talk more about your head in Chapter Three.)

KEEP A FEELINGS DIARY

It is difficult to know what your feelings are trying to tell you—especially in a crisis—if you have spent years not listening to them or living on autopilot (and therefore not properly aware of your emotions). That's why the Feeling Diary is the most important exercise in the book and why, although it's fine to pick and choose from the rest of the exercises, I strongly recommend setting aside the time for this one. It will help you get to know yourself better, create new, helpful habits, and provide a way of monitoring your progress.

When I'm setting up this exercise with clients, I often ask them to brainstorm as many feeling words as they can come up with. Some people immediately go blank and can't name more than a handful of feelings. To give you a head start, here are the Top 40 feelings (of 2,500) tracked on internet blogs and social-networking sites between 2006 and 2009.

1. Better	15. Lost	28. Wrong
2. Bad	16. Tired	29. Fine
3. Good	17. Old	30. Important
4. Guilty	18. At home	31. Empty
5. The same	19. Stupid	32. Hurt
6. Sorry	20. Ill	33. Terrible
7. Sick	21. Weird	34. Lucky
8. Well	22. Lonely	35. Loved
9. Down	23. Safe	36. Special
10. Comfortable	24. Different	37. Worse
11. Great	25. Best	38. Close
12. Happy	26. Horrible	39. Uncomfortable
13. Alone	27. Confident	40. Depressed
14. Sad		

It is also important to differentiate between an emotion and a thought. Lots of my clients think putting "I feel" before a sentence makes everything that follows into a feeling. For example, "I feel it would be nice to have a boyfriend" or "I feel I'm never going to sort out my life." These are not feelings but thoughts. Of course, there are feelings involved but they are unspecified. In the first case, the feeling could be lonely or sad or even hopeful. In the second, the feeling could be angry, depressed, despairing, or resigned.

- Decide the best way to keep your diary. Some people buy a notebook and others make entries on their smartphone or tablet. At the top of a page put the date and divide it into three columns. In the first column, put the time of the day. In the second put the feeling or feelings. In the third, put the trigger—which could be an event (for example, your partner being late home) or a thought (for example, it's not fair that I have to do the majority of the childcare).

- In week one, try and be more aware of your feelings and, when you've a quiet moment, or at the end of the day, jot down which feelings you've experienced. I ask clients to come up with at least eight a day.

- In week two, look at the patterns. What kinds of feelings are you recording? Sometimes I find clients are only writing down the uncomfortable feelings and overlooking the pleasant or neutral ones. With other people, all their feelings are in the middle of the scale: OK, fine, down, etc. So think, what is your diary missing? It could be, of course, that you're not experiencing these emotions. However, it is more likely that you are not really aware of them and therefore not actively recording them. Spend the second week making a special effort to notice and include any missing feelings.

- In week three, look past the top level of your feelings. Often under "frustrated" or "irritated" there are other stronger emotions.

Most people, when pressed, will come up with a couple of other layers. For example, 'sad' might be the most recognizable emotion but often hidden underneath there is "tearful" and "grief" (which are actually less stuck than sad—because tearful only lasts for a while and grief is a natural part of working through a problem and moving on), while beyond "content," there may be "chirpy" or "happy" (which are much stronger positive emotions).

- Most people find that just recording their feelings makes them calmer and more centered. They also tend to notice the positive emotions more—rather than taking them for granted.

- Keep the feelings diary for at least a month.

There will be more about interpreting your feelings diary and how to use it to make the right changes for you in the next chapter.

STOP USING NEGATIVE WAYS TO FILL YOUR INNER VOID

Not so for Tolle, Singer, Yogananda

If you don't listen properly to your feelings, which are rather like an inner-compass, you are not only less likely to know if you're heading in the right direction but also unlikely to recognize when you've reached a crossroads. You'd think, therefore, it would be relatively easy to persuade people to embrace the maxim "What are my feelings trying to tell me?" but there is one major problem.

What if the feelings are telling us something that is too horrible to contemplate—even for a moment? For example, "You're not good enough" or "You're stupid and you'll never get it right" or "Nobody is ever going to love you."

There is no end to the destructive messages stored in our inner voids and, as you can imagine, we'll do anything to avoid or manage them. Unfortunately, these coping strategies cause more problems than they solve —that's why I describe them as negative ways of filling your inner void.

They fall into five categories—Perfectionism, Denial, Outsourcing, Acting Out, and Self-medicating—and can be used singularly or in conjunction with each other. However, I'm going to look at them one by one.

Perfectionism

There are two scenarios where parents unwittingly create perfectionism. The first is where they want the best for their children and push them to excel. There's nothing wrong with high standards, but sometimes children can interpret this message as "I'm only OK if I'm top of the class, prettiest or win the race." As an adult this is interpreted as: "I'm only acceptable if I do everything right," "get the best deal on a secondhand car," "know more than everybody else round the dinner table," or "have the best behaved children" because the alternative is to be a "failure" (and nothing is worse than that). The second scenario is where parents have made their children—normally unwittingly—feel shame. Returning to Rob, the gay man from the previous chapter: "I had to be the best at cake decorating and I'd spend hours at home practicing. Looking back, I suppose I knew I had to create something beautiful to cover up the ugly truth about my sexuality. That's the reason why it's always gays who know about makeovers, interior design, clothes, hair—I don't think it's that we've got some gay gene that makes us good at these things—just a need to distract from the truth and make everything look 'nice,' at least on the surface." Rob came into counseling after his latest relationship had failed because, despite being a pastry chef of a top London restaurant, he felt worthless and suffered from low self-esteem. As he talked, it became clear how important it was to Rob to be the best.

"So you have to earn the most money and work in the most acclaimed restaurant?" I summarized.

Rob nodded.

"But don't restaurants come and go out of fashion?" I asked. "Aren't there trends in what judges or the people who award stars are looking for? It doesn't mean that the customers aren't enjoying your food?"

Rob looked at me glumly. I could tell he agreed with me intellectually, but my words offered little comfort. Next we discussed Rob's relationships.

"It'll start off fine, lots of passion and wonderful weekends in far-flung resorts, hours on the telephone, but somehow it goes flat, he's inconsiderate or too wrapped up in his work," Rob explained.

"It's no longer perfect?" I asked.

Rob nodded again.

"Or somebody else is more beautiful or one of your friends is more in love?"

"I know it sounds stupid but if I don't get a review from a critic or have a love life that could be anything less than wonderful, I feel this cold sinking feeling inside and I push myself harder or decide there's something wrong with my relationship."

"And when the relationship ends, the shame about being a 'failure' will be so great that you'll need to prove yourself all over again?" I suggested.

"I'll have a one-night stand or a wild fling and end up feeling even worse."

Although Rob's perfectionism has been an asset at work, it made him a nightmare to live with (he always had to have the most stylish and neatest house) prone to affairs (because there was always somebody who appeared "better") and sought relationships with extremely beautiful or dangerous men (with whom he had little in common but had great sex).

In general, perfectionism can fill up your inner void but only if you get everything "just so" and are rewarded with an A plus or a standing ovation.

Downside: Perfectionists are always overcompensating to try and block out the messages running down much of their effort. Unfortunately, this makes it hard for them to accept criticism (even if it is constructive). They also suffer from what I call "crash and lash," so when something goes wrong they tend to lash out at other people. Alternatively, they will have a "f*** it" moment. For example, Jane, fifty, wanted to have a "perfect" last Christmas with her ex-husband and their two children before he married his new fiancée: "She was flying home to be with her own family but the bad weather meant the airport was closed and we all spent Christmas together. I hated seeing her in what used to be my kitchen, the children were sulky, and she wore this low cut top that didn't seem appropriate." When it couldn't be the picture perfect vacation that Jane had imagined, she didn't just make the most of a difficult day. "I thought f*** it, I'll go around to the neighbors and get horribly drunk. Everything's already ruined. And it was, because when I came back I caused a horrible scene."

Central Task: To stop seeing everything in black and white terms and hold both the positive and negatives of a situation at the same time.

Denial

When I take a childhood history and uncover something horrible—for example, being sent away to boarding school at six—some clients brush away my sympathy, minimize the impact of events, or close down the conversation altogether with a shrug of the shoulders.

There are a variety of strategies tied up with denying. These include rationalizing away the problem ("My parents had no choice because there were no good schools nearby"), turning it into an asset ("It made me self-reliant") or simply ignoring the impact altogether ("It didn't do me any harm"). These people generally work long hours or are ruled by habits.

One of my favorite fables is about a man on a horse galloping down a road. He was going so fast, it appeared to the onlookers that he must be going somewhere important. So one of them shouted up to the rider: "Where are you going?" The rider replied: "I don't know. Ask the horse." I like this fable because it's really about us. All too often, we don't know where we're going or why. The horse is our habits pulling us along, powerless to resist. We ask friends when we meet: 'How are you? Keeping busy?' As if speed and activity are more important than destination; as if we were in control of our habits—while, all too often, our habits control us and stop us from noticing that we have a gaping inner void.

A typical example of someone who denied his difficult and painful feelings is Philip, thirty-two, who had been married to his partner, Cassie, for seven years. When I asked both of them what they wanted from counseling, Philip answered:

"Nothing really. I'm here because she wanted me to come. Everything's fine."

"You're not happy in your job," Cassie countered.

Philip worked as a solicitor.

"Everybody goes through tough patches: a hard nut client or the senior partner putting on pressure. Nothing out of the ordinary," he explained. His parents had been rational—"keep your head down" and "get on with it" —and he had learned from their example.

When I turned to Cassie, I wasn't surprised to discover that she felt unloved, unsupported, and had given Philip an ultimatum: come into counseling or I'll leave.

Although denying his inner void—and his need for intimacy—had allowed Philip to "keep the show on the road," it had only worked up to a point. His marriage was in crisis and even then he still found it hard to engage—because he would not only have to listen to Cassie's feelings about being unloved but to his own fears about being not good enough too.

There is another variation on denial where people push themselves so hard at work or fill every corner of their social life that the only time they stop is when completely exhausted. In this way, they have no energy to argue with their partner or a ready-made excuse for just vegetating in front of the TV. If they are single, they are too tired to register just how much they don't like their own company or how empty a lot of drinking and partying can be.

Downside: There are three main risks associated with denial: depression, breakdown, and a midlife crisis. In many ways, depression is a natural response to a problem. If your life doesn't add up, it is good to stop, look inside, and make changes. Unfortunately instead of listening to their inner void —and that something needs attention—people who use denial to cope with adversity just press on regardless. In many ways, Philip was already suffering from low-level depression when he started counseling but it risked tipping over into something more serious when Cassie moved into the spare room (and ended all sexual contact which had been his only outlet for closeness). Fortunately, he used our sessions to open up and talk. Sadly, many people leave it too late.

Christopher, forty-two, had been unhappy in his marriage for almost ten years—since the birth of his second child: "My wife is so wrapped up in the children, I often feel that I'm only there to pay the bills and play Daddy when required. If I complain, I get my head bitten off or treated like a naughty school boy." He had tried to solve the problem by telling himself "I expect too much" and shut down his inner void by working hard. It had kept the show on the road but left him feeling like a drudge and old before his time: "I can see nothing but work, bills, and responsibility." It was no surprise that he had "escaped" into an affair with a woman seventeen years younger and was torn between returning to his wife or, as he put it, "running away and starting again."

Central Task: To get in touch with your feelings and listen to what they have to say—however painful.

DEALING WITH UNPLEASANT FEELINGS

If you distance yourself from unpleasant feelings—either by denying them, hiding behind perfectionism or distracting yourself—you are not alone. We are so determined to avoid shame that it does not come anywhere in the Top 500; feelings and feeling ashamed —which is more about our behavior rather than who we are—is only the seventy-eighth most common emotion. However, unpleasant feelings are part of being human and it is healthier to embrace rather than suppress or run away from them. So how do you avoid feeling overwhelmed? Many clients fear that if they allow themselves to feel these feelings they will be trapped there forever. So I give them this exercise:

- Imagine your emotions are like a river and you're sitting on the bank watching the water flow past.

- What sort of river is flowing past? A mountain stream bubbling over rocks or a broad calm estuary about to reach the sea?

- When you feel something unpleasant—like sadness, disappointment, or regret—don't do anything. Just sit on your bank and observe what you're feeling.

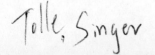

- You'll be surprised to find that most emotions don't last long and that another one—often something more pleasant will float past.

- Think about how long it takes for something to pass—seconds, minutes, or hours?

- If you've already started your feelings diary, you can consult it to discover how long each of your recorded emotions did last. Even the strongest feelings pass and something else comes along. You have the evidence in your diary.

Acting out

When children have problems at home—for example, parents' divorcing—they often "act out" their problems by being disruptive in class or take their anger out by bullying smaller or weaker pupils. Adults act out by losing their temper with the wrong person or the right person but over something trivial, driving too fast, or plotting revenge. In all the drama, the original upset is forgotten or transformed from shame (about some personal failing) into righteous anger ("He cut me off in the traffic"). In many ways this is the opposite of denial because there is no shortage of feelings—but equally unhelpful because nothing gets sorted.

Jackie, thirty-three, came into counseling after her marriage broke down after only six months (and before that none of her relationships had lasted more than six weeks). When I drew up her family tree, I was surprised to discover that she came from a very solid family and parents who had been childhood sweethearts. What could have made her choose a man whose father had already reached his fourth marriage?

"My father worked very hard to give us a good standard of living and I didn't want to disappoint him," Jackie explained. "Except it was tough, I was always in my sister's shadow because she was academic and could get all the grades without any trouble. I wondered if I'd been adopted because my younger brother was bright too and when it got too bad, I'd plot to run away from home—but I never did."

Although Jackie's father wanted the best for her—and not to have to scrimp and save like he did—he was also very controlling.

"There were only three good universities in the country and they were all within commuting distance from home, so I had to go to one of them," she explained. "Although my careers guidance teacher had suggested something caring—like a teacher or nursing—he'd said I needed a proper profession and I should study economics and go into the city."

Because Jackie loved her father dearly and didn't want to let him down (or make him ashamed of her), she followed the career path that he'd set out. In fact, she had not "rebelled" until she lost her job in finance and "ran away" to work as a ski instructor. The short-lived relationships—which had revolved around lots of drinking and the sort of men her father would not have approved of—had been typical teenager acting out. Her husband was cut from similar cloth. It had taken her several years of "living for the moment" but she had finally enrolled in nursing college and started a job that she loved. Instead of rebelling against her father, she had decided to follow her own life path.

Downside: It is very easy to be distracted from the real problem and sidetracked into displacement activities. This is particularly common when couples are getting divorced and channel their guilt about splitting up (and letting their children down) into becoming "super" parent or a "better" parent than their partner. Before Tracey and Mike, both in their late forties, divorced, they had no trouble deciding what was best for their thirteen-year-old daughter. However, when she injured her ankle doing gymnastics, they had row after row. "In the past, he would have let me decide when it was OK for her to start gradually doing sport again," said Tracey. "After all, I took her to the doctors and saw the consultant—while he was busy working and enjoying his new life." By this, she meant seeing his new girlfriend (who was significantly younger than Tracey). "But now he's super Dad, he screams down the phone at me. 'I'm currying favor' or 'I'm being reckless with her health.' Perhaps, if he was here on the ground, he'd be able to judge." No wonder the row about the ankle went around in circles; Tracey and Mike were using it to act out their anger toward each other.

Central Task: To distinguish between deep feelings that need to be acted on and passing emotions that are like bits of scrap paper blown about by the wind.

DECONSTRUCT AN ARGUMENT

Take the most recent argument with your partner or, if you're single, with your parents, friends, or work colleagues and look for signs of acting out.

- Think about what sparked this particular row, what each of you said, and the general flow of the argument.

- What triggered the argument?

- What helped resolve the dispute?

- What hindered?

- If you had to apportion responsibility between you and the other party, what would be the portions: 50/50 or something else?

- How would the portions shift if you changed the focus from this *particular* row to the pattern of *all* your rows?

- What is the contribution of each party to the pattern of rows?

- Are you making symmetrical contributions? For example, both of you are mind reading or interrupting each other.

- Are you making complementary contributions? By this I mean, do your behaviors reinforce and sustain each other. For example, one party shouts and the other retreats.

- Thinking about just your own behavior, what would you like to do differently next time you have a disagreement?

Outsourcing

Instead of taking responsibility for their own problems, people who use this strategy expect someone else to come to their rescue (and then get angry if they don't rise to the challenge) or use other people to prop up their self-esteem (and then criticize for not giving enough compliments). Whereas once their parents would have picked them up, dusted them off, and soothed, it is now the turn of their partner to regulate their emotions.

Miriam, thirty-seven, had had a difficult day. The children had been playing up. The traffic was bad and the air conditioning in the car had broken down. So when she finally picked up her husband from the railroad station, after a week-long business trip, she was in a foul mood.

"It's difficult to wait and the traffic wardens had chased me away twice, so I had to keep circling," Miriam said, turning to her husband Gregory, "and you didn't help. Hardly a smile or a thank you."

"What do you expect, the atmosphere in the car was horrible. I just kept my head down," said Gregory.

"Perhaps if you'd been nicer, I'd have calmed down and we could have had a nice weekend."

The couple were on the point of breaking up but were having one last attempt to rekindle their love for each other. Unfortunately, picking up Gregory from the station—which was supposed to be a nice gesture—had sparked a weekend of warfare.

"So you were angry with the traffic wardens, the children, and the garage for not fixing the air conditioning, what did you expect Gregory to do?" I had a picture of a hurt little girl and her parents leaning down to help, so I answered my own question. "Kiss and make it better?"

In many ways, Gregory was expecting Miriam to regulate his feeling, too. The business trip had not gone as well as expected, signaling problems had delayed his train, and he was tired too:

"I was looking forward to getting home and having a little TLC, to help me unwind and forget about all the pressures."

Of course that's part of the unspoken contract in every good relationship, we want to help or cheer up our partner when he or she is down. However, we're not there to "magic" their problems away.

At this point in the counseling, Miriam sighed: "Gregory just doesn't make me happy anymore?"

"Is that his job?" I asked. "'Can you make someone happy? Don't we have to take responsibility ourselves, too?"

Caroline and David, in their late thirties, had been together for over fifteen years. They lived and worked in a very small apartment and David was helping Caroline launch a business. Whenever Caroline got stressed and upset, she would unburden herself to David:

"I had a difficult childhood—my parents split up when I was a teenager and my mother married a man who I hated—so I can easily get overwhelmed and let it all out."

There's nothing wrong with sharing a problem, but for Caroline it normally came out as a torrent with one problem sparking another.

"The other day I got worried about a problem with the business and how hard it was to work together and if we can't work together could we cooperate and have children. What if our whole relationship is doomed?"

After an hour of pouring out all her fears and escalating worries to David, Caroline felt much better. Unfortunately, David, who up to that moment had been doing all right, became overwhelmed and sank into depression.

So what's the difference between outsourcing—making someone else responsible for our emotions—and asking for support from someone who loves us? It's fine to want a partner to be a companion on the journey through life and help us over the obstacles—like bereavement or illness—but not to expect them to carry us.

Downside: Waiting for someone else to sort your problems will leave you feeling helpless and hopeless. The only strategy is to exaggerate the upset and play the "poor me" card and before long your feelings have been pumped up into a genuine and overwhelming pain. Both Miriam and Gregory had played the 'poor me' card at the beginning of the week-end and stoked their dissatisfaction with the pickup into dissatisfaction with their whole relationship. It is only a short step from here to thinking your partner is being deliberately cruel—while perhaps he or she is just coping with their own issues—and beginning to feel like a victim.

If you're using someone else to boost your self-esteem, rather than feeling comfortable in your own skin, you will be particularly vulnerable to knock backs. Returning to Jackie, who acted out rather than confronting directly her loving but controlling father, her six week affairs had all been with extremely good-looking men and her husband looked like he had stepped out of a men's clothing catalog. "I would get a great boost when everybody told me my latest boyfriend was gorgeous," said Jackie. "I'd feel great but all the attention he would get from other women made me incredibly insecure. Why did he want to be with me?"

Central Task: To take responsibility for your own life rather than dumping on your partner, boss, or friends.

LOOK AT THE TRIGGERS

During the next week, be aware of how you react when faced with difficult or painful feelings. Think about the following questions:

- Which coping strategies did you use?
- What are the particular triggers?
- Why are these events particularly difficult?
- What memories from the past do they trigger?
- What times of the day are you particularly vulnerable?
- When is it best not to answer the phone, reply to emails, or bring up difficult topics with your partner?
- What would happen if, instead of slotting into your old automatic responses, you did nothing for five minutes? If you use denial, what would happen if you stayed in the difficult situation for five minutes more (for example, listening to your partner rather than walking away)? If you use acting out, what would happen if you did nothing and slowly counted to ten?
- Consult your feelings diary and overlay when you used negative ways of filling your inner void. What links can you make with the past? What changes would you like to make? (If you haven't started your feelings diary yet, think back to a difficult moment over the past few days instead.)

Self-medicating

The fifth negative way of filling your inner void is perhaps the commonest. If we're feeling down, we eat a doughnut, light up a cigarette, or have a well-earned glass of wine. We might lift our mood by buying something nice or block out our worries at home, by throwing ourselves into our work. Other examples of self-medicating include managing our frustration with an uninteresting sex life by disappearing into passionate romantic novels or switching on the computer and getting an instant fix from pornography.

All of these strategies will make us feel better, but throwing a bit of trash into our inner void is hardly going to fill us up. Of course, in small doses there is nothing wrong with taking the edge off our feelings with the comfort of a bar of chocolate or flirting with someone to get an ego boost, but it becomes self-medicating when you are blocking out the underlying pain.

Graham, forty-nine, had been unhappy at work for a long time. Although his job involved a long commute, and he found the day-to-day tasks dull, it paid spectacularly well. "I knew we'd never get the same standard of living if I did something else, so I just bit my lip and got on with it," he explained. Meanwhile, his twenty-five year marriage had deteriorated into companionship at best and the sex had almost stopped. Instead of tackling either of these problems, or even thinking about them, Graham would go out running instead.

"I was training for a double marathon and I'd be out for four plus " he explained.

His wife, Carol, would often joke: "I wonder what he's running away from!" Unfortunately, she was also medicating away the pain from her unfulfilling marriage with a bottle of wine each night:

"I thought it was my reward, something I deserved, but it stopped me looking at what was really going on and drove him further and further away."

Unfortunately, Graham started flirting with a woman he met at a conference and continued their inappropriate friendship online. The "boost" from her sexy emails made him feel special and, in effect, he was medicating himself with her attention too. Three months later, the "friendship" became a full-blown sexual affair.

Everything came to a head when, within the space of a fortnight, Graham's affair was discovered and he was made redundant. Graham and Carol's whole life could have come crashing down but, fortunately, with the main distractions removed, they could focus on their marriage and rediscover their love for each other.

Downside: The underlying problems are managed rather than solved. There are often health implications (for example, obesity from comfort eating), social fallout (for example, poor judgment, fights, or infidelity after excessive drinking) and crossing over from using to abusing (for example, prescription drugs, street drugs, multicharacter computer games, pornography).

Central Task: To assess the full implications of self-medicating and whether something that helps you cope with problems has turned into the problem itself.

ADDICTION

Whether it is a substance like alcohol or marijuana, or an activity like exercise or computer games, there are four types of users:

1. **Social User:** Most people can have, for example, a couple of drinks and stop without any ill effects.

2. **Binge User:** These people can go for weeks or months without using their particular substance (or only in moderate quantities) but then go off the rails in a spectacular way. Binge users often tell themselves that they don't have a problem because they can stop (if only for short periods).

3. **At Risk:** These users are regularly taking their preferred substance to manage their moods and cope with problems. However, there is a fine line between a "crutch" and a "handicap"—and this makes it harder to spot when you're about to cross the line. Often, a particular trigger—like a job loss, serious accident, or marital breakdown—can make someone move from using to abusing.

4. Addicted: The behavior is compulsive. It interferes with normal living and causes severe stress on family, friends, and work colleagues. The particular substance or activity is regularly used to
block out feelings or as a "reward" for getting through something stressful or painful—even though afterward the "addict"
feels guilt and disgust. Unfortunately, shame just triggers
another round of abuse. There is also denial about the full
extent of usage and dependency. So when an addict is faced
with how many hours are consumed by his addiction or the size
of the bill, he or she finds it hard to believe.

How can you tell if you've crossed the line from "at risk" to
"addicted"?

- Do you spend longer in your chosen activity or consume more of
  your chosen substance than planned? (Shows compulsion.)

- If you can't get access to your chosen form of stimulation, does
  your mood change? (Indicates self-medication.)

- Do you become irritable, moody, or feel unwell? (Suggests withdrawal symptoms.)

- Do you still consume your chosen substance or participate in
  your chosen activity—to regulate your mood or cope with stress
  —even though your usage causes even more stress in the long
  run. (Confirms addiction.)

Combination ways of filling an inner void

Although perfectionism, denial, acting out, outsourcing, and self-medication
can ease shame and help us cope with painful situations, they can never fill
our inner void. That's why many people resort to a second, and sometimes
a third, negative strategy. However, there are several classic combinations.

For example, Rob used perfection and outsourcing: praise for his cake
decorating and culinary skills became external proof that he was "perfect"

and therefore acceptable. However, the praise was for what he did, not who he was (and he still carried the childhood shame of being gay); therefore, none of the compliments would feel truly authentic. "I always fear that if people could see behind the drape—the messy complicated person—that they couldn't love me," explained Rob. "So I put on a show and keep people at arm's length."

Jane, however, used another common pairing: perfectionism and self-medication. When her "perfect" Christmas didn't work out, she self-medicated by getting drunk (and thereby ruined the Christmas for everybody else, creating the shame that she sought to avoid).

Meanwhile, Jackie used acting out and outsourcing. Despite rebelling against her father's desire for her to have a high-paying profession, she was desperate for his approval (and that of others).

Finally, there is denial and self-medication. Graham denied his problems at work for many years and propped up his refusal to face his deep-seated unhappiness by first long-distance running and, then, affairs. In many ways, Graham illustrates how dangerous these negative ways of filling our inner void can be. Rather than stopping and dealing with underlying problems, the temptation is to add another negative strategy and when that doesn't work look for a stronger fix (like an affair). The result is that we feel even more shame and create ever bigger problems (like marital breakdown).

Instead of digging ever deeper holes by perfectionism, denial, outsourcing, acting out and self-medicating, there is another solution. However, it is so radical, and goes against almost everything that we instinctively feel, that it takes my clients a while to get their heads around it:

PAIN MIGHT BE TELLING US SOMETHING IMPORTANT

We make hundreds of decisions every day. Should I send that email or not? Shall I have a piece of cake with my coffee? We do them on autopilot without really thinking why we decided to take the car, delete the email, or eat the cake. Perhaps with bigger decisions, like should we have children or move house, we might look deeper and question our motivations, but generally we never stop and question the underlying philosophies that drive our choices.

If we did, we would probably find that our decisions are based on the ideas of an eighteenth-century philosopher called Jeremy Bentham, who was two centuries ahead of his time in advocating equal rights for women, the right to divorce, and the abolition of laws criminalizing homosexuality. Bentham was the founder of Utilitarianism, which advocates considering the consequences of every action and weighing up the resulting pleasure or pain. If the sun is shining, I might get more pleasure walking to the station than sitting in a stuffy car in a traffic jam. If I send an angry email, the pleasure from getting my feelings off my chest will be dwarfed by the pain caused by my boss's reaction. If I eat the cake, it might ruin my appetite for our anniversary meal tonight. On a wider scale, Utilitarianism drives the philosophy of all modern political parties: "the greatest pleasure for the greatest number of people." Ultimately, pain is something to be avoided and pleasure to be maximized.

However, there is a competing philosophy that is even older than Utilitarianism. Buddhism believes that we need to embrace pain and argues that unless we acknowledge our suffering, we can never be free of it—only mask it. Worse still, if we turn our back on pain, it will chase us forever and maybe even devour us. Ultimately, pain has a lesson to teach us and our task is to stop, listen, and make the necessary changes. I know this sounds really depressing but, rest-assured, I'm not going to ask you to wallow or be a prisoner of your suffering. You can still enjoy the good things in life—like the cake and the ease of driving to the station—with a few provisos which I will outline later in the book. However, I think there is an upside to embracing pain. While Utilitarianism suggests that we cannot be happy until we have driven out all the suffering from our lives (which puts off feeling calm and contented to some unspecified time in the future when we have more money, a better car, and a more considerate boss), Buddhism suggests that we turn our suffering into something positive today.

So could your pain be trying to tell you something important? If your leg hurt, you'd sit down, rest, and attend to the problem. But if your life is giving you pain, the temptation is to look the other way, find something to distract yourself, hope for the best, and press on regardless. No wonder so many people get depressed, have a breakdown, or imagine something like an affair or running away (leaving their partner and all their responsibilities behind) is their only way of coping.

FEAR OF DEPRESSION

There is another reason why people are reluctant to listen to their feelings —beyond them being unpleasant or inconvenient—and that's fear. What would happen if they stripped away all their coping mechanisms? Carl, forty-nine, had spent much of his twenties feeling depressed and suffered another major burst in his midthirties:

"I know I'm using work and sex as a bit of a crutch, but I'm keeping my head above water and stopping myself from slipping into depression. Believe me it wasn't nice. I don't want to go back there again."

"Except your coping strategies are not helping you reach your goals?" I replied. Carl had come into counseling to find a partner—which was hampered by long hours in the office, taking home work at the weekend and occasional visits to prostitutes (when he got too lonely). "You're not going to find a wife at work. Considering the amount of time you spend there, you'd have noticed her already."

Carl laughed: "And I don't want to marry a prostitute."

Crystal, thirty-one, had similar reasons to fear depression. She had one course of psychotherapy as a teenager (when her parent's marriage broke down) and another at university (to cope with bulimia), and, although her eating was normal, she was self-medicating with glamorous and exciting men (who were unlikely husband or father of her children material) and episodes of binge drinking.

"My needs are overwhelming, I'm never going to have them met," Crystal sighed. "I feel depression is stalking me. Like some black dog in the shadows, about to pounce and go for my throat. I don't think I dare stop, turn around, and face it."

Meanwhile, Carl was suffering from a low grade form of depression which didn't stop him functioning but was more like a constant low rumble in the background—pulling him down, drowning out everyday pleasures, and poisoning his life.

If you can relate to these fears of depression, you are probably wondering if you dare to stop using negative ways to fill your inner void. But before you make your mind up, please consider these three statements about depression and how they might apply to your life:

1. Depression is about suppression.

2. Depression is about anger turned inward.

3. Depression is about having fixed outcomes.

When Crystal looked at statement one, she said, "My Dad will do upsetting things like when we're planning to meet in town for a coffee, phone and tell me, 'I've just had a cookie and a cup of coffee so I'm all sorted.' I want to scream. 'I haven't seen you for weeks, it was not about coffee but catching up.' Except, I say, 'OK, Dad. Another time.' You see, I love him desperately, so I don't want to upset him. Meanwhile, my mother is prone to dark moods and I don't want to prompt one, so I'll tiptoe around her too." It was clear that Crystal had been suppressing her feelings. However, the pain had not disappeared, it had simply re-emerged as depression.

When Carl looked at statement two, he acknowledged how angry he was with himself: "I have a lot of negative loops going around in my mind. I'll meet an attractive woman—maybe on some course—and we'll be chatting and I'll want to ask for her number but lose my nerve. And I'm telling myself, 'You coward' and 'You can't even do this one stupid thing' and 'You're hopeless' and 'No one will ever want you.'" No wonder he felt depressed!

'What about the third statement, do you pin everything on one fixed outcome and shut out everything else?' I asked him.

Carl nodded: "At that moment, only this woman will make me happy. So I start babbling about last night's TV or the latest movie and I can feel her slipping through my fingers and all my future happiness with it."

"Is she really the only woman who will make you happy?" I replied. "Maybe you're so fixed on this one outcome—getting the number—that you don't notice another woman in the room who is dying to talk to you and would love to go on a date. Perhaps you're so downcast that you don't notice the twenty dollar note on the sidewalk outside or that the market stall has sweet ripe peaches or whatever else could lift your mood."

Whether you're frightened of depression, or just wish to avoid something unpleasant, the pain that is being masked by negative ways of filling your inner void has an important message: you need to make changes.

For example, Crystal needed to be more honest with her parents (rather than pretend she was OK). Carl needed to rethink where and how he looked for a partner (instead of one-off events where he was under a lot of time pressure, he would try on-going courses where he had longer to get to know women and more chances to ask one out).

SECOND MAXIM IN ACTION

I know it is really hard to stop and think **What is this feeling trying to tell me?** and easier to react first and think later. Unfortunately, it's these automatic responses that are keeping you stuck, making change harder or promoting the sense of "one step forward and two back."

To give you an insight into how your mind works when you're acting on impulse rather than taking time to truly consider your feelings, I want to introduce you to the work of Nobel Prize-winning economist Daniel Kahneman. He divides our thinking into two types: *fast* (Type 1), which registers general impressions and is based on intuition, and *slow* (Type 2), which follows rules and makes deliberate choices. (There is more about Kahneman's work in the reading list at the back of the book.)

Obviously, we need to harness both types of thinking to make good choices. However, when we're under pressure, stressed, or panicking, we tend to use Type 1 which opts for the familiar (whether it's any good for us or not). A classic piece of research that illustrates this tendency was conducted at the University of Michigan where a series of Turkish or Turkish sounding words were put on the front page—in an advertisement-like box—of the student newspaper. The frequency of each word varied dramatically; some came up a lot and others were used only once or twice. After the advertisements stopped, researchers asked the students to rate the random words—like *kadirga, nanosoma* and *iktitaf*—as either good or bad. The results were spectacular. The words that featured the most were consistently rated the best and those that occurred only occasionally as the worst.

So why have I included this piece of research? I want to illustrate just how tempting it is to opt for the familiar and, when it comes to your behavior, it's familiar because it stretches right back to your childhood (and your inner void). Familiar isn't always best for you and might be one of the reasons you have reached this crossroads or keep going back down the road from whence you've come. Consulting your feelings—your inner compass —allows you to begin to slow down your reactions and use all your brain power.

Returning to Rebecca and Jerome from the beginning of this chapter, who were still trying to recover from his infidelity three years after the discovery, they had a terrible row over a bottle of orange juice which had been replaced back in the refrigerator without properly fastening the top. Rebecca went to pour herself a glass of juice and the contents of the bottle went all over the kitchen floor. As it turned out, it had been her son not her husband who hadn't put the top on properly, but it caused several days of grief between Rebecca and Jerome. In our next counseling session, they were reluctant to discuss it—because it seemed so trivial—but I was interested in understanding their automatic reaction and applying the second maxim:

What is this feeling trying to tell me?

"I just sighed because I was upset, annoyed and fed up," said Rebecca.

"I was just trying to explain that I hadn't touched the orange juice," replied Jerome.

"And I can't get upset about anything?" Rebecca snapped back. "But what really got me going was your tone and your thoughtlessness and, before I knew it, we weren't arguing about orange juice but how you could have betrayed me with that woman."

"While I was trying to explain that they were quite separate issues and I didn't leave the top off the bottle."

I could easily understand how this trivial incident had descended into two days of misery. However, their standard default reaction—accusation on Rebecca's part and defensiveness on Jerome's part—was not only unhelpful but keeping them trapped.

"So what are your feelings trying to tell you?" I asked.

"We don't have a future?" Rebecca sighed. "It's all too painful."

"That might be the case," I replied, "but I'm more interested in your feelings at the beginning—when the orange juice spilt—than after two days of rows. What did you feel then?"

"Upset that I had to clear up after everybody—yet again."

"So what could *that* feeling be telling you?"

"Perhaps the division of labor in the house needs to be looked at again. Jerome is working from home so he could possibly be doing more than when he was doing a long commute, and my son is not a small boy anymore and perhaps he should have more responsibility, too."

I turned to Jerome and asked him to pinpoint his emotion at the beginning of the row:

"What did you feel when you heard the sigh from the kitchen?"

"Here we go again."

"That's a thought, not a feeling." I responded.

"I felt helpless and hopeless."

"Well done, so let's look at what this feeling is telling you."

"My response to Rebecca isn't working and getting angry doesn't help —in fact it makes it worse."

"So what could you do differently?"

"We could talk calmly about everything," he said after a moment's thought. "Rebecca's response is linked to mine and I can control that."

So, summing up, I know pain is horrible and I wish there was a way around this, but you can only move forward when you listen to what it is trying to tell you.

GREEN SHOOTS

- Feelings are clues about how to react. If we control or ignore them, we risk losing valuable information. If we treat them as simple directions, we might respond too quickly without truly absorbing their lessons.

- When feelings are too painful or dangerous, we use coping strategies—like perfectionism, outsourcing, denial, acting out, and self-medicating—which might make us feel temporarily better but stores up more problems for the future.

- The second maxim to change your life is: "What is this feeling trying to tell me?"

CHAPTER THREE

Making Lasting Changes

We've done all the preparation work. You've got a better idea why you've reached this crossroads and I've introduced a revolutionary idea: the protections you thought were keeping you safe are really part of the problem. With a little luck, there's a feeling bubbling up inside—one that you haven't encountered for a while. It's called hope. You really can change. Your life *can* be different. It's one of the most exciting moments of the journey so it's worth savoring. However, there are other feelings mixed in there, too.

"I had a bit of an 'a-ha' moment yesterday, realizing that the reason I've built all manner of defenses around me is because I fear that if I cannot cope with dangerous feelings, e.g. anger/vulnerability/hurt, I will get sick," wrote Angela, a forty-two year old client, after her third counseling session. "While consciously I long for closeness and intimacy, my subconscious is protecting me from vulnerability because solitude and loneliness are preferable to losing control and getting sick again." (She had conquered bulimia seven years earlier but it had affected her for over twenty years.) "If I can use tools, other than fortresses and firewalls, to manage these dangerous feelings, it will be a huge improvement for my life. I feel much like a chick that's just hatched from the shell—I've had a breakthrough, but quite a bit more development is needed before I can cope outside the peace and safety of this egg I've created to protect myself."

If Angela's story strikes a chord, or you're feeling raw at the moment, I'm about to introduce the most important of all my maxims and, in many ways, this is the most important chapter in the whole book.

THIRD MAXIM

If you are going to make only one change after reading this book, I would suggest adopting the third maxim. It is not going to come as a big surprise because I've laid the groundwork in the last chapter.

Accept the feelings, challenge the thoughts.

It is a deceptively simple idea but there's a lot to unpack. Let's start with the first half: **accept the feelings**. As I've explained, we need to listen to our feelings because they might be telling us something important—even if it is uncomfortable, unpleasant, or inconvenient. However, I'd like to go a step further and ask you to not only listen but to *accept* your feelings. It doesn't matter if your feeling is something "good" (like happiness, joy, or excitement) or something "bad" (like anger, anxiety, or even shame), it is important to accept them all. I imagine that you've got a million questions or want to say, "Yes but ..." So why am I asking for something as radical as accepting all your feelings—even the so-called bad ones? Doesn't that risk accepting the situation, becoming a victim, and letting people walk all over you? Don't worry, that's not what I'm suggesting and hopefully by the end of the chapter everything will be clear.

First of all, dividing feelings or events into good or bad is not helpful, because life is not that black and white. Although nobody likes anger, it has some excellent qualities: for example, providing energy and a sense that "something must be done." It had brought Angela into counseling because she was angry that her boyfriend could not commit. While everybody likes love, I've witnessed some terrible things done in its name. For example, I had a client (with mild learning problems) whose parents loved him so much and did so much for him that when they both died, one shortly after the other, he was left, at forty-one, unable to manage simple tasks like changing the vacuum cleaner bag, doing his own laundry, or getting to work on time.

Next, I'm going to share a personal experience of how pointless it is to divide feelings and experiences into "good" and "bad." In my mid-thirties, I was recruited to launch a new national commercial radio station. (My first career was in broadcasting.) Unfortunately, I was not aware that the shareholders couldn't agree on anything and I got caught in the middle. After about three months, I was not only fired but my humiliation was reported in the morning papers, so friends found out before I'd had a chance to put my side of the story. If you'd asked me at the time, I would have labeled this event as "bad." My reputation had been trashed and I had no regular income. I might even have labeled the feelings as bad, too—certainly I didn't want to be rejected, humiliated, or angry. However, twenty plus years later, I have a totally different viewpoint. Losing this job was an important turning point; I went back to my first love: journalism and writing. (I had been promoted into management and spent most of the time coordinating other creative people rather than creating myself.) I also had more time to concentrate on being a therapist (previously I'd worked only part time for the British couple counseling charity Relate). With the benefit of hindsight, I left commercial radio at the right time—just before the internet explosion that decimated the work force. I also prefer working for myself rather than for a large company. So, was losing my job something "good" or "bad," or a combination of both?

Let's move onto the second part of the maxim: **challenge your thoughts.** Back in the early eighties, I had a lot of thoughts about being fired. I thought I would never find another satisfying job (and probably end up being an accountant). I thought everybody would be laughing at me or secretly pleased at my downfall. I thought my home might be repossessed and I'd have to move in with my parents (which was the worst fate imaginable). I expect you can spot that these are exaggerations: I currently spend half my day writing books (which I find extremely satisfying); *some* people might have been secretly pleased about my job loss but certainly not *everybody;* and I love my parents and they love me, so I doubt living with them would have been the *worst* thing that ever happened to me. However, this is the important bit: my unchallenged thoughts were driving my feelings. No wonder I felt so angry and misunderstood. It was a vicious circle—the more upset I became, the more negative my thoughts, and vice versa, and down and down I spiraled. Fortunately, I had some good friends who helped me look at the upside of being fired, but I could have saved myself (and everybody else) a lot of grief if I hadn't branded my feelings or the event as "bad." Ultimately, it would have been much better to **accept the feelings** because it was natural to feel hurt and frightened for the future but to **challenge the thoughts** and see the opportunity as well as the danger.

When I covered this maxim with Angela, she had another realisation:

"I've been doing the opposite: challenging the feelings but accepting the thoughts."

I asked her to explain.

"If I'm down because my boyfriend doesn't want or can't be with me on the weekend, I don't accept that but tell myself to 'count my blessings' or 'it's a lovely day so cheer up and get out there' and force myself to lighten up. How else could I have stuck in this relationship for so long? Meanwhile, I've been accepting as gospel my thoughts that I'm 'not good enough' and therefore why would he want to commit?"

Before you can fully take on board the third maxim, I need to explain more and suggest making some other important changes.

FIND POSITIVE WAYS OF FILLING YOUR INNER VOID

One of my favorite pieces of wisdom comes from the French philosopher Blaise Pascal (1632–62) as he neatly sums up both the negative and positive ways of filling our inner void: "Man's unhappiness springs from one thing alone: his inability to stay quietly in one room." So how do we ombat our instincts that "something must be done right now" or "pain is horrible and best avoided" or "if I just did ... everything would be better?" There are four positive ways of filling your inner void and although each one by itself might seem difficult, they will reinforce each other, quieten your demons, and allow you to access your own common sense.

The first one will already be familiar:

Accept your feelings

Every family has rules about what is acceptable and not acceptable. Some of them are very clearly stated—"Don't get up from the table without asking permission" or "Don't put your shoes on the couch"—but most are unspoken and every family member somehow knows that, for example getting upset or talking about emotions is "not something that we do." Anybody who does break the rules is either ignored or made to feel uncomfortable, bad, or just plain wrong, and, often, without saying a word, the family norms are reinforced. Unfortunately, many "forbidden" feelings—like getting angry, feeling sad, or simply needing a hug—are part of being human, and as much as we'd like to banish them, it's simply not possible.

Rosemary, fifty-one, came into counseling because she could not accept that her husband wanted to end their marriage, split up their family and set up home with another woman. She had been trying to put off applying for the decree absolute but had reached the point where, if she did not act quickly, her husband could have forced her hand (and increased her already considerable legal fees). Rosemary arrived at the next session, after delivering the paperwork to her solicitors, looking happy, upbeat, and together, but when I asked how her week had been she reached for the tissues.

"What are those feelings?" I asked.

"I feel I don't want this divorce. It's not fair. He's ruined everything."

Those are thoughts not feelings, so I looked sympathetic but asked if she could try again. Slowly, we pieced together the emotions behind the thoughts: sadness, failure, entrapment, anger, anxiety, pushed about, shame. At first sight, it is a devastating list—and no wonder Rosemary cried—but no feeling lasts forever. Remember sitting by the river in Chapter Two, another feeling will soon float past. Buddhists call this impermanence. As we talked, I could sense another feeling in the room and asked Rosemary what it might be:

"I feel a little better; a little calmer."

"While feelings come and go—as you've just proved—thoughts stick around," I told her. "It's perfectly possible to go to your grave still thinking the divorce was not fair, something you didn't want, and which spoilt your family life, but feelings burn themselves out."

Rosemary went onto explain how she'd been so strong at the beginning of the week:

"I had a really positive attitude, sailed into my lawyer's office, and paid the bill. No problems. By coincidence, I saw an old friend on the street and she guessed where I'd been and she was really nice. I told her not to be 'too nice' or I'd crack, but I kept up the positive attitude. At yoga, my instructor and another friend wanted to be supportive, but I kept my distance. So I suppose, deep down, I knew that I was feeling sad."

The dam had finally burst when a friend phoned and confessed that she and her husband had been to dinner with Rosemary's ex-husband and his new girlfriend.

"She had every right to see him! It's been three years. I can't control her social life—or his. So I struggled to be fine on the phone and pretend I didn't feel betrayed. Except I didn't sleep that night and here I am in tears with you."

Unfortunately, Rosemary had not been able to accept her feelings during the first part of the week—and rationalized them away with a "positive attitude"—so they returned stronger and deeper at the weekend. What would happen if she allowed herself to go with the flow of the river and just feel the feelings as they arose?

At this point, I need to unpack more of the first part of the mantra because accept the feeling is just one part of a five step process:

Recognize: What is the feeling? Try and name it to yourself. Next, locate the feeling in your body: is it in your stomach, your chest, your neck, or lower jaw? Have your shoulders tightened or your fists clenched? (Don't worry if you can't pinpoint the feeling—that's quite common— just recognizing and naming it is enough.)

Accept: It is OK to be angry, sad, or impatient. Do not rationalize away the feelings. Do not push them away. Just simply accept them.

Witness: Sit with those feelings—even if they make you uncomfortable. Hold them. Nurse them like a mother holding a crying baby. After all, she gives just as much love and attention to her baby whether it's crying or gurgling.

Look deeply: What has truly bought about your anger, sadness, or impatience?

Take the insight: It might be about yourself or somebody else or both of you. For example, you might need to grieve—especially after you've been through a terrible loss. Moving onto an insight about somebody else, maybe your friend spoke harshly because his father has died and his reaction was not about you at all. Perhaps you're not only sad because your friend is having trouble with her husband but because it reminds you that you're alone and wish you had a partner.

COUNTING MEDITATION

If you have been keeping your feelings diary, you will know that no feeling lasts forever—because you have the solid proof that each one is replaced by another and then another and another. Returning to the imaginary river, it's possible for some emotions—like fear, anxiety, or pain—to be overwhelming as they float past. For this reason, you need an emergency first-aid kit to enable you to feel calmer and able to *accept* a difficult emotion (rather than resort to a negative coping strategy):

- Take some deep breaths through your nostrils.

- Be aware of the air passing in and out of your nasal passage.

- Take another deep breath and hold it for a second. Say the number "ten" to yourself and let out the breath.

- Repeat, but this time say the number "nine" and let go of your breath.

- Continue breathing in, counting down, and exhaling until you reach zero.

- On the next breath, count "one" again, let your breath out, and repeat, but this time counting back up to ten.

This counting meditation can be done somewhere quiet with your eyes closed, sitting down, and your hands on your lap. If it's not possible to close your eyes, focus on one point—like the back of the person in front of you on the bus or the hood of a parked car —as this will help to filter out distractions. Generally, it's hard to count and think at the same time but if you are still obsessing about something—tell yourself "I'll address that later" and push it out of your mind—and return to the counting. This meditation can be done once—and takes about two minutes—or repeated as many time as you wish.

SELF-SOOTHING

Self-soothing is a concept that I will be returning to over and over again. The idea is that on a day-to-day basis we are responsible for dealing with our own problems (rather than expecting our parents, partner, or supervisor to automatically pick us up and soothe us). This does not mean keeping your feelings to yourself—it is fine to *report* them: for example, "I'm feeling low and stressed"—but avoid dumping them on to your partner or friends: "Nothing ever goes my way," "I can't cope," "I'm never going to finish." While reporting keeps your partner or friends informed, dumping risks "infecting" them with your anxieties and stress. Let me explain what I mean by infecting.

Returning to Caroline—from Chapter Two, who lived and worked in a small apartment—when she was unable to soothe her own anxieties and center herself, her partner David felt obliged not just to listen but to take on all her problems and solve them. "When Caroline is upset, I get upset and it starts a vicious circle because I get more and more stressed," says David. "Perhaps she's right. If we can't sort out an accounting system for her business, perhaps we are doomed. I'm trying to solve the accounts problem and our whole relationship at the same time. So I'll get snappy or more likely switch off and walk away—as it is the only way to process everything." In fact, David found it just as hard to self-soothe as Caroline. Instead of being able to tell himself: "I love Caroline but I'm not responsible for sorting out every detail of her life," he started to panic, become infected by her anxiety, and resort to another unhelpful alternative to self-soothing: blanking out.

When someone has been told by their partner, "I love you but I'm not in love with you" or that the relationship is over, it is easy to panic and reach out to their partner for reassurance and soothing—"You do think this relationship can be saved," "At least give it a try," "It wasn't all bad"—but this can be fatal for the relationship's chance of recovering. Richard, a thirty-six year old man with two sons, came into counseling to save his marriage but his wife would only discuss separating.

"I alternated between pleading for another try and looking for some reassurance that there is hope. If she says there 'might' be a little chink of light, I'll be up for at least twenty-four hours but ultimately I'm living on my nerves," he explained.

Unfortunately, he was coming across as extremely needy, and his wife, Julia, found this a complete turnoff.

"I've got enough to cope with. Two small children. A job. My own guilt about falling out of love. It's hard enough making it through the day without being ambushed by a grown man in tears," she explained. In effect, she had hardened her heart as a form of self-protection and to stop herself being "infected" by Richard's growing panic.

When Richard failed to get any reassurance from Julia (and get her to soothe him) he resorted to drinking whisky and blocking out his feeling (self-medicating rather than self-soothing).

Teaching Richard to be responsible for his own feelings provided a breakthrough in counseling and helped him to listen to Julia (and finally begin to address her needs), and self-soothing allowed both Caroline and David to have constructive conversations and address fundamental issues—like shall we have children—that had previously been impossible to discuss.

So how can you begin to soothe yourself? The good news is that you have already begun to incorporate the first elements of self-soothing into your coping mechanism:

Acknowledging: Sit quietly and accept your feeling and what they are trying to tell you.

Processing: When the feeling is strong—or induces panic—concentrate on your breathing or try the counting meditation outlined earlier in this chapter. When you are calmer, start to assess the problem and what can be done about it. Taking an exercise class, having a shower, or walking the dog can similarly help process and understand the feelings; they are also soothing in their own right. Once you have isolated the relevant issue, your partner is more likely to listen rather than be overwhelmed by a pile of problems and switch off.

Engaging: If you cannot find an immediate solution, where could you get information or advice? Think about your specific needs. For example, if the car has been broken into you might need to contact the police, your insurers, and a glass repair company—rather than dumping the problem on your partner.

Reporting: Keep your partner and loved-ones informed about your feelings—"I'm tired" or "My boss is a nightmare and I'm at my wits end" —so they don't feel excluded or imagine they've done something wrong. It also invites your partner to offer help, advice, or support (rather than expecting them to know what the matter is and come riding to your rescue like a knight in shining armor).

Choosing: Ultimately, reaching out to your partner or friends becomes a choice not a necessity. When it is a large problem—like bereavement, redundancy, or serious illness—it may well be sensible to ask for help to soothe.

Doing nice things for yourself: It could be picking up a ready-made meal after a tough day at the office rather than cooking from scratch, having a long soak in the bath, a weekend away in the countryside, an early night with a good book, or relaxing in the garden for half an hour with a cup of coffee and the crossword. These activities all come under the heading of looking after yourself, or finding ways to unwind or destress, but don't block-out feelings or risk tipping over from self-soothing into self-medicating behavior.

Humor: Laughter is an important positive coping mechanism because it provides a different lens to look at the world, stops us from being overwhelmed, and cuts problems down to size. It also allows us to poke fun at our own inconsistencies, smooth them over, and ultimately embrace them. This is especially important because, unfortunately, we are seldom consistent. For example, we will criticize our mother for running us down and then go and do the same thing to her. In addition, a shared sense of humor helps to define communities. When outsiders look on perplexed, the joke just gets funnier, and those who understand feel closer still. No wonder, "good sense of humor" is one of the most prized assets on a date. (However, humor is a double-edged sword. It can also be used to avoid looking at what is really going on and can easily cross the line into cruelty. So use this coping mechanism sparingly—probably after acknowledging the full scale of what has just happened.)

HOW TO STOP A BAD HABIT FROM GETTING OUT OF CONTROL

If you're concerned by your level of usage of substances (like alcohol, street drugs, and comfort foods) or the amount of time consumed by potentially addictive behaviors (like shopping, exercise, and gambling) and the effect on your own self-esteem and on your relationships, take control with the following exercise.

(To give you an idea what to expect, I've illustrated each point with Shane, forty-five, whose use of internet pornography was becoming a problem and stopping him from forming a lasting relationship.)

1. **Don't go cold turkey.** You have probably vowed never to use your particular substance or behavior, and maybe even stopped for a while, but slowly slipped back into your old habits. This is because stopping alone is not enough, you need to understand what unpins your behavior.

   (In the past, preinternet, Shane had thrown away his collection of magazines and videos, only to start collecting again.)

2. **Monitor your consumption.** These are the key things to note:

   What are the triggers?

How do you feel when using your particular substance?

How much time has passed?

How do you feel afterward?

(When I did this exercise with Shane, he found his triggers were: "feeling sorry for myself," "I deserve this for working hard," "an aching feeling inside," and "celebration after hearing some good news." The feelings while consuming were "trance" and "out of body" and "paralysis"—all signs that he was using pornography to self-medicate. Shane reported that he was using for about five or six hours a week and afterward felt "resignation," "shame," and "pathetic.")

3. **Tackle the triggers.** Think about other alternatives for dealing with triggers. If you are feeling stressed and need to unwind—what about phoning a friend or talking to your partner about what happened? If there are particular danger points—like Friday night—plan ahead and find other ways of occupying yourself. What other diversion tactics could you use?

(Shane discovered that one of his triggers was feeling lonely, so he joined an organization which arranged dinner parties in different member's houses, and planned to see his friends more often.)

4. **Live the feelings.** When it comes to difficult feelings—like sadness, feeling sorry for yourself and loneliness—there are three ways to cope. The first is blocking them out (which you have been doing with a particular substance or behavior of choice). The second is diverting your feelings (for example, switching on the TV and distracting yourself). The third is to look the feelings directly in the eye. By this I mean acknowledging them (I'm feeling ...), accepting them (Everybody feels ... from time to time) rather than trying to rationalize them away or ignore them. Next, allow yourself to experience the feeling (just sit quietly and see if you can bear that feeling). Normally, the feelings are magnified by blocking

them out. When they are "lived" they are normally unpleasant but not as scary as you might imagine.

(Shane was amazed to discover that rather than plunging into depression, as he feared, the down feelings quickly passed. There was another bonus, no more morning-after regrets from a night of internet pornography.)

5. **Listen to the feelings and make the changes.** Our feelings normally have something important to tell us. (For example, Shane's were telling him that he needed to spend less time at work and more socializing so he could find a partner.) Unfortunately, we don't always like the message and rationalize it away (Shane would tell himself: "I've got to work hard or my business will suffer"). Sometimes the message is inconvenient, frightening, or threatens to turn our life upside down. (Shane admitted: "I'm bored and unfulfilled by my sex life with my girlfriends but perhaps that's because I don't let them get close."). Perhaps you are a square-shaped peg trying to fit into a round-shaped hole (and self-medicating to cope with the pain). What would be better: face the problem head-on and change or keep blanking out the feelings and maintain the status quo?

6. **Be realistic.** If the problems are deep-rooted—for example, abuse when you were a child—it might be too painful to listen to your feelings without professional support. If you have been using substances in a compulsive manner for a long time or your life has become chaotic and your behavior destructive, you should consider entering a twelve-step program or joining a support group.

SELF-VALIDATION

The best way to understand self-validation is to compare it with out-sourcing self-esteem. While out-sourcing rests on the idea that if everybody thinks we're great then we must be, self-validation puts the emphasis on our own opinion of ourselves. While out-sourcing makes us hypersensitive to criticism and sometimes so primed to expect it that we can hear an attack when none is meant, self-validation allows us to have a good enough opinion of ourselves so that we can weigh up both the compliments and complaints—without getting defensive—and decide for ourselves which are valid. With out-sourcing, the validation is often about surface characteristics or particular behaviors rather than the real us (and therefore does not warm us very long), self-validation is about valuing who we really are (and therefore feels authentic).

Mark, forty-eight, came into counseling after his wife, Zoe, discovered his affair with a colleague: "It had been very flattering that someone saw me as attractive and desirable." Although he was profoundly sorry, Zoe worried that he would succumb to flattery again: "I can't be a one woman confidence booster twenty-four seven and I don't want to be forever flattering him." The importance of self-validating came to the fore when Martin arrived downcast for their next counseling session.

"I've decided to follow my dream and try my hand as a stand-up comic. I took some classes, did a couple of open mic nights, and entered a talent competition," said Martin. "I was really thrilled when I was short-listed but the boost didn't last long. Not only did I not win the prize but I wasn't even runner-up or specially commended. You see, I never win anything. The following night, I tossed and turned: I just don't have what it takes to succeed."

"But everybody laughed when you did your set," said Zoe. "Lots of people came up to me afterward and were very complimentary."

Martin nodded glumly.

"What about your career?" I asked. Martin managed the emergency department of a local hospital. "It seems to me that you've had lots of success if you have been promoted so often."

Once again Martin nodded, but I sensed he was going to say "Yes but ...."

It was clear that our attempts to validate Martin did not feel authentic to him and that he needed to validate himself. But how do you learn to self-validate?

Once again, you have already begun to achieve this goal. If you have allowed yourself to have a feeling and accept it as valid, you are a step closer to accepting yourself. Once you have learned to soothe yourself, you will become less dependent on others and less likely to need outside validation. However, for self-validation to feel authentic—rather than just self-flattery—you need to put the following in place:

Aim for good enough: To explain this concept, I need to bring together the thoughts of two very different men. The first is the pediatrician and psychologist Donald Winnicott (1896–1971) who coined the term "good-enough mother." He believed that if a mother could be "perfect"—and fulfill every need of her baby—this would not be in the child's best interest as it would never have the chance to struggle, overcome obstacles, and grow into a self-sufficient adult. The second man is author and poet Rudyard Kipling (1865–1936) whose poem *If* contains the line: "If you can meet with Triumph and Disaster, and treat those two imposters just the same." What he meant is that success is not as straightforward as it seems (as we can get pigeon-holed or other people become jealous and try to pull us down) and failure is a great learning opportunity (and can contain the seeds of a future success). So, summing up, we should aim for "good enough" because success and failure are "imposters."

Value your accomplishments: Mankind's ceaseless struggle for better is probably what has brought us from caves to cities but it does make us overlook what we've already achieved and take it for granted. Martin, for example, could not value his ability to manage a large team full of strong personalities because he was too focused on becoming a stand-up comedian.

Integrate all the parts of yourself: Many people present different sides of their personality to different people. For example, Martin saw himself as serious and responsible at work but creative and funny in his stand-up work (and longed to be able to give up the former for the latter). So, during his counseling, I encouraged him to experiment with integrating his creativity into his work life and his clear-thinking business-like approach to his comedy career.

Meanwhile, Naomi, who grew up with evangelical Christian parents but became an atheist, had two distinct personalities: the staid responsible mother who lived close to her parents and relied on them for childcare and the rebel who partied with her friends at weekends in a nearby city. In the first life, she seemed older than her thirty-five years (possibly in her fifties) as her social life revolved around dinner parties with couples who had had their children much later. In the second life, she went drinking into the early hours of the morning with other singles and seemed much younger (possibly in her late teens and early twenties). To make matters more complicated, she saw the authentic version of herself as the one that she presented to her friends in the city, but spent most of her time with her parents in a small community. No wonder she felt rootless and unhappy. During her counseling, Naomi began to recognize that she was a combination of both personalities and began to integrate the two.

Other common examples of leading a double life include being ruthless in business and considerate at home, having several different circles of friends but keeping them apart and believing one thing but doing another.

Aim for truthfulness: Instead of editing your emotions or locking them away, for fear that other people might find them "unacceptable" or "unreasonable," be truthful and show this side of yourself to the world. Contrastingly, rather than pumping up every passing feeling or forever flying off the handle, stop and think which emotions are true and enduring (as if carved on tablets of stone) and need to be communicated, and which are fleeting and momentary (as if written on scraps of paper blowing in the wind) and, although true for a second, have no enduring truthfulness.

Do things for joy not validation: Ultimately, there cannot be prizes for everyone and, if it was somehow possible, the prizes would lose their value. However, if you take up a hobby or play a sport for the pure joy of taking part, you will always feel good about yourself (and therefore be a winner).

CHANGE THE FRAME

Sometimes it is hard to validate ourselves because the pain seems so overwhelming. If this is the case, this exercise will help:

- Look at the time frame. Instead of concentrating on the traumatic events and the hours, days, weeks, or months that followed, look at the experience through the bigger window of the rest of your life. How does this affect the picture? What did you learn from this traumatic period that is still of benefit today? (For example, when I did this exercise with one client, he looked back to his first divorce and how he'd met someone else within six months and made a whole new circle of friends. So he had solid proof that he could start again.)

- Look at your frame of references. We all compare ourselves and our situation to other people—as this gives us a way of measuring how lucky or unlucky we have been. Often we feel hard done by because we compare ourselves to people who are more successful or famous. But what if you compared yourself to someone less fortunate? (For example, I did this exercise with someone whose partner had died aged forty-five and couldn't get over how "unfair" it felt. However, when we changed her frame of reference away from her contemporaries, she began to think of the parts of the world where forty-five was not so young, or, historically, when life expectancy was significantly shorter.)

- Look at how your memory is stored. When we remember painful experiences, we nearly always reexperience them as snapshots or moving pictures. Step back and think: How do I see these images. Are they in front of me? Are they all around me? Are they in the corner of my eye? Once you have a clear idea, change the frame by changing how the memories are played back. (For example, when I did this with one client who had snapshots, I asked him to play what happened next: walking away from the car crash. In this way, the images of his buckled-in car were softened by viewing them as a survivor. In another case, with someone who saw her memories of the end of her marriage as a movie, I asked her to project them onto a wall rather than experiencing them up close, to speed it up and then slow it down. Not only did she distance herself from the pain, but she learned to sometimes stop the movie and think about something else.)

WORK ON YOURSELF

One of the most constructive ways of filling your inner void is to look a problem squarely in the eyes and start to sort it out. For example: What's wrong with our marriage? Why am I single? Why has my partner left? However, these questions can make us feel very uncomfortable. Many people find it easier to look at other people's behavior rather than keep their gaze inward.

"I put all the blame on my ex for the problems when we were together," said Maria, twenty-five, when she first arrived in counseling. However, over a couple of sessions, she began to reflect on her contribution to their problems. "I was partly to blame. I've started to realize that I am a very insecure person. I did not trust him. I would get extreme anxiety when I saw him add a girl on Facebook or talk to a girl at work. It made me feel so uncomfortable and upset. It was not that I was worried he would cheat but that he would like them better, then break up and leave me for them. Finally, I had a bad day and let out a bunch of insecurities, neediness, and pushiness and he broke it off." Ultimately, Maria needed to work on herself, understand why she had such low self-esteem, and tackle her own insecurities (rather than expecting her boyfriend to see inside her head, understand how her mind worked, and organize his life so as not to spark her fears).

There is a second way of diverting attention from yourself and, although at first sight it seems better than blaming, it causes just as much heartache in the long run. I call this tactic "Rescuing." These people are so busy trying to sort someone else's life out, that they are distracted from what's wrong with their own. In effect, instead of filling their own inner void, they are trying to fill someone else's.

Gus, thirty-one, divorced his wife after her affair turned serious; but as infidelity is a negative way of trying to fill an inner void, her new relationship did not make her feel better for long. "We fell back into being together when I 'rescued her' and helped get her back on her feet," explained Gus. "She claimed to have learned a valuable lesson and we were working on a future together, but not in enough depth as I was just so thrilled to have her back." After six months of living together, his ex-wife began acting strangely. "She had secretly taken up with a different married man—initially flirting, but now a full affair. This guy is also everything I'm not, a happy-go-lucky macho builder (as was the first)."

Despite being rejected for a second time, Gus was still trying to hang onto the relationship: "I've confronted her calmly, after all we are no longer married, and said I will be the best father I can to our daughter and do my best to help her personally, but that I can't keep getting my heart broken. We have short honeymoon bursts, and when it's good it's great, but I am struggling to walk away permanently as she's so confused and damaged from formative experiences with her parents."

Instead of trying to fix his ex-wife, I asked Gus to change *his* behavior. First, to step back so his ex could begin to work on herself (rather than running to him like a little girl to her father) and, second, to look at himself and understand why he preferred to be a rescuer rather than to have an equal relationship. Slowly, I helped Gus rebalance himself and become more inward looking (what was best for him) rather than outward looking (what was best for everybody else). There is more about rebalancing yourself in my book *Learn to Love Yourself Enough*.

So how can you work on yourself rather than blaming someone else or using their problems to distract yourself from your own?

Banish blame: After almost thirty years of counseling, I've yet to meet a couple where the problems were not six of one and half a dozen of the other. So, although there is something about human nature that makes us long to blame someone else, I find it particularly unhelpful. For example, Gus blamed his wife for their divorce (she had an affair) but when he looked deeper he blamed her parents (her father had affairs and left her mother). However, her parents were the product of their parents and so on, back through history. In addition, blaming someone never solves anything. It just makes the other person defensive, angry, and likely to fight back.

Take your share of the responsibility: Relationship problems don't happen because one person is wicked, irresponsible, or sick, but are part of a complex cycle where both partners contribute something unhelpful. I call this idea *Circularity*. Of course, there might be an initiator (who kick starts an argument) but there is also a responder (who reacts in an unhelpful way), and each partner's behavior is both reinforced and constrained by the others.

In the case of Deborah and Julian, in their late forties, she might have been the initiator for one particular row about what time their daughter should come back from a party (as she lost her temper and started shouting) but Julian responded in an equally destructive manner (by storming out and refusing to discuss the matter). When we took the focus away from this particular argument, Julian admitted that he would appease (and then go his own sweet way) because he feared Deborah's temper. Meanwhile, Deborah would have a store of resentments because nothing got solved and because Julian would agree to her face about their daughter's bedtime but do something contrary when she was away on business. "He is forever undermining me," she complained. Fortunately, the concept of circularity allowed them to see their arguments had no beginning and no end point, but just went around in one continuous circle. Ultimately, nobody was to "blame" and the argument was not one person's responsibility but part of a destructive pattern where each of them played an equal role.

So think about your contribution to a recent row. What did you do that reinforced the circle? What would you like to change? Remember you only have to take your share of the responsibility, not all of it.

Empower yourself: Some clients think blaming their partner or taking all the blame themselves will make them feel better, but actually it leaves them trapped or overwhelmed. By contrast, taking your share of the responsibility for a problem is empowering.

"I'm a reasonable man," said Julian. "At work, I listen to every side of a case but Deborah won't listen, she just shouts me down."

"Except we're not talking about work, we're talking about the pattern at home," I explained. "And waiting for Deborah to change has you stuck in the same old circular arguments. So think about what *you* could do differently? What would happen if someone shouted at work? Would you walk away?"

"No I wouldn't. I'd suggest that they sat down, calmed down, and we'd talk about it," he said. I could see the beginning of a different way of tackling disputes with Deborah, and Julian feeling empowered.

Meanwhile, Deborah often tool *all* the blame for their rows: "I have a foul temper, just like my mother, and I can say some nasty things. Not that I mean them, but at the time they sound horrible. I don't know why he puts up with me sometimes."

"Except that, by taking all the responsibility, you are likely to feel stuck, depressed, overwhelmed, and demotivated," I explained. "What I'm looking at is changing your behavior—not your whole personality. You can still care passionately and wear your heart on your sleeve. So what would you like to change about how you tackle disputes with Julian?"

"Perhaps if I didn't tiptoe around him—biting my tongue—perhaps I wouldn't build up so much resentment and be so ready to ignite at any moment. Instead, I could talk about the problem while I'm still reasonably calm."

Although change is always easier when both parties decide to behave differently, you don't have to wait for your partner. Even if only Julian or only Deborah had put their individual resolutions into action in isolation, it would still have created an opportunity to break circularity. As I told them:

"You've tested 'shout and retreat' to destruction and we've learned that it doesn't work. So what are you going to do differently?"

I get lots of letters to my website asking, "How can I recruit my partner to try your program?" I always respond that working on the relationship might take two people—and can leave you feeling trapped if your partner is unwilling or unable to commit—but working on yourself is empowering because you can start today. There is also a side benefit, by changing *your* behavior you will also change the ingrained patterns in your relationship.

Break problems down into smaller chunks: When you finally face the task of working on yourself, it can seem a huge and daunting task. Where do I start? How do I begin? The best place to start is the next argument or the next time you catch yourself doing something unhelpful. In many ways, it doesn't matter what you do different. Anything is better than the same old unhelpful reactions.

In addition, by keeping the focus on changing over the next seven days, every new behavior is an experiment (which might or might not be adopted) and not a "success" or a "failure" (and the stakes are kept lower). Finally, small changes can be built up into good habits which help fill up your inner void and change your life.

DEMONS OR ANGELS?

Many people who have trouble valuing themselves have an inner-voice which starts up whenever they are feeling low, stressed or in crisis. Unfortunately, it comes up with lots of black and white terms like "worthless" or "stupid" or "ugly," and because those terms are largely exorcised from daily life—for very good reason—we think our inner-voice is being "honest." No wonder, on one hand, we seek out other people to drown out these demons with sweet compliments but, on the other hand, find it hard to truly believe them. So how can you challenge the thoughts whispered into your ear by your demons?

- Don't block out your demon's voice—as this will give it more power.

- Instead, listen to what it has got to say. I find writing everything down is helpful too as it stops everything from going around and around in your head. It's also easier to challenge the thoughts when it's all down in front of you.

- Imagine that you've got an angel voice too. This voice is calm, rational and questioning.

- Using this voice, go back over the arguments of your demon and question if its assertions are true or just exaggerations. If they are simply ludicrous, just cross them out or delete them. If they hold some truth, correct them. So, for example, "I've got no friends" becomes "I'm making new friends" and "one of my old friends came to stay last weekend."

- Using your angel voice to double-check: What is the evidence for each statement? Has the demon voice taken something from one part of your life to make an assertion in another? (For example, taking a problem with your sister and using it to illustrate why you won't get a promotion at work.)

- Look out for black and white terms like "never" and "always" and find examples which contradict these statements. (Even minor changes can help lift your mood. So, "I always upset my friends with my thoughtlessness" could become "I sometimes upset my friends.")

- Finally, turn statements into questions and empower yourself. (For example, "I often upset my friends with my thoughtlessness" would become "How can I stop upsetting my friends with my thoughtlessness?")

THIRD MAXIM IN ACTION

It is easy to live life on autopilot without really noticing your feelings or being truly aware of the negative voice that pulls you down and limits your choices. That's why the third maxim is: **Accept the feelings, challenge the thoughts.**

To illustrate how this idea can transform your reactions to challenging events and change your life, I'm going to use an example from Jon Kabat-Zinn, Professor of Medicine Emeritus at the University of Massachusetts, where he developed a groundbreaking stress-reduction program that used meditation to help patients manage chronic pain. He is considered the founding father of mindfulness, which is a philosophy and a therapy based on Buddhist meditation and involves being present in the moment and being nonjudgmental about your feelings. In his book, *Wherever You Go, There You Are* (Piatkus, 2004), he describes an ordinary domestic incident just like the ones that my clients report and you've probably experienced yourself: a dirty cat bowl left in the sink. The distinguished professor admits that the dish, caked with bits of dried food, pushes his buttons—especially when it is mixed in with the family's dirty plates. He writes that his reaction could be because he wasn't brought up around pets, or perhaps he believes it's a health hazard because his children will eventually eat off the plates lying in the sink with the cat's bowl. However, he decides to recognize the feelings and name them: anger, disgust, and hurt (he's told his wife on countless occasions). At this point, it would have been tempting to do something about these unpleasant feelings and shout up the stairs to his wife. Rather than trying to discharge the emotion by losing his temper or passing the bad mood onto his wife by shaming her, he accepts his feelings, and witnesses them. By looking a little deeper, he recognizes another emotion: justified (he is "right" because "cat food bowls shouldn't be in the sink") and there's also betrayal (his wife has not listened to his polite requests). However, if he accepts his feelings and witnesses them (rather than acting out), he notices that the disgust and revulsion isn't that strong. In fact, he can live with it but what's really making him angry is not being listened to or respected. Actually, it's not really about cat food at all!

At this point, he begins to challenge his thoughts. He knows his wife and children see the dirty cat food bowl differently and think he's making "a big deal out of nothing." They try to bow to his wishes, but his wife, if she's in a hurry, can sometimes forget or run out of time. So, perhaps, he decides, at that moment, she's not thinking about him but most probably fixed on getting out of the house, remembering to put on the washing machine before she leaves or a million other possible distractions. In which case, she was not deliberately thwarting his wishes.

As you can imagine, his feelings have dropped down to a more manageable level and Kabat-Zinn and his wife no longer have nasty fights about this topic. With years and years of practice, and study with Zen Buddhist masters, Kabat-Zinn not only doesn't take the cat food bowl in the sink personally but even smiles when he sees it there because it has taught him so much! I have to admit, I wish that I could reach the same evolved place but it's something to which to aspire.

For the rest of us, it is important to realize the difficulty of embracing "**accept the feelings, challenge the thoughts**" and incorporating the maxim into our everyday life. Unfortunately our parents and teachers were not always interested in our feelings, or actively discouraged us from listening to the ones they considered unacceptable. We live in a world with hundreds of distractions and constant time pressures that make us react without always understanding why. Therefore, if you find yourself falling short, I'd like you to **accept your feelings** (because it is annoying to keep making the same mistakes, or frustrating or whatever) but I'd also like you to **challenge your thoughts** (perhaps "I'll never learn" or "I'm stupid" or other negative messages) because you have years of conditioning to overcome. So, it will take time to make this change, but, over the following weeks and months, it will get easier and easier.

GREEN SHOOTS

- Accepting your feelings and accepting the situation are not the same thing. Once you have challenged your thoughts, you can respond with the right degree of force—neither overstating nor minimizing your upset.

- Constructive ways to fill your inner void—and dealing with this crisis—include accepting your feelings, self-soothing, self-validating, and working on yourself (rather than expecting other people to change).

- The third maxim to change your life is: "Accept the feelings, challenge the thoughts."

CHAPTER FOUR

Learning Your Limits

So far my maxims have looked at the importance of exploring and understanding before moving onto action, how your feelings can be a guide and the impact of your thoughts on your feelings (and why sometimes you need to challenge them). In the last chapter, I discussed positive ways of filling your inner void—in particular, working on yourself. At this point, I want to delve deeper into this concept and find a deeper understanding of what you can change and what is beyond your powers— however determined or skilled you might be.

FOURTH MAXIM

One of the greatest sources of misery, on the couch in my counseling room, is a misunderstanding about what we can control and what we might be able to influence but can't actually control. The problem comes in two forms. Many of my clients feel powerless because other people— normally their partner—have taken control. Others are frustrated and angry because they want to take control but other people—normally their partner—refuse to cooperate.

In my opinion, the first set of clients have severely underestimated their agency (by which I mean their choices and capacity to act), while the second set have grossly overestimated their agency. So my next maxim is about finding the balance. The key is to understand our zone of control (areas of our life where even a brutal dictator or a totalitarian government cannot reach) and our zone of concern (areas of life that matter a lot to us

91

but over which we might some have influence but ultimately no control).

Whenever you're about to set off on some course of action, I'd like you to ask yourself:

What can I control?

At first sight, this seems reasonably straightforward, like a lot of my maxims, but actually it is really complex. I have an exercise—which I will cover in more detail at the end of the chapter—where I draw a large circle and inside it a smaller one. The outer circle is the zone of concern and the inner one is the zone of control.

I explain the difference to my clients in this way: "The state of your marriage and how well you're communicating is definitely in my zone of concern. But can I *control* how well you do? Of course not. Can I make you come here? Of course not. All I can control is that I am sitting here each week at the same time, ready to engage with whatever you bring."

Here's another example that I often use. If you're planning a picnic at the weekend, the weather is definitely in your zone of concern, but obviously you can't control the weather. So what can you control? At first sight, the answer is nothing; but you do have control over something important: your reaction to the weather. If you tell yourself the day will be "ruined" if it rains, then you're setting yourself up for disappointment. However, if you tell yourself the weather cannot spoil my enjoyment because being with friends is what really counts (and have a backup plan just in case it rains) then you can still have a great weekend.

When I set the exercise for my clients, they always ask if they can have something in both their zone of concern *and* control but I insist they make a choice—one way or the other. You can either control something or you can't—and if not, it goes into your zone of concern. Unfortunately, when it comes to our relationship, we really want to put it in our zone of control (because it is of so much concern to us), and tell our partner, "If you love me, you would ..." or "Why can't you do this one little thing for me?" We try and get support from the wider culture: "Wives should ..." or "Husbands need to understand that ..." And when our partners do not play the game, we start to despair: "If you can't do this or that for me, it means you can't love me."

ATTACHMENT THEORY

Your relationship is really important to you. When it's going well, you feel loved and cherished but when it's going badly, you feel sad, lost, and even alienated. Even if you accept that you can't control your partner, because it holds the promise of both happiness and fulfillment, you still want to control your relationship. So what I see, time and again, is the push and pull of love. You need intimacy, so you try and get closer to your partner, but he or she distances him or herself. Alternatively, you need some time or space for yourself (to follow activities that are important to you or to unwind and relax after a stressful day), but your partner always wants something. It's almost like a dance, a dance of intimacy where you seem to take one step forward and then two back but neither you nor your partner feel completely happy (beyond for brief moments). Certainly, neither of you feel "in control" or, worse still, you or your partner might feel "controlled." This dance of intimacy causes endless unhappiness. Some people think their relationship is fundamentally flawed and start looking for someone else with whom they think they will be more compatible (but normally end up repeating the same dance or a variation on it).

Fortunately, three of the greatest minds in psychology have developed a theory to explain the dance, and understanding it will not only lessen the distress but prepare you to be more in synch with each other. Attachment theory was first outlined by John Bowlby (1907–90) who was one of the founding fathers of British psychology. He worked with "maladapted and delinquent" children in the UK's first children's psychiatry unit—in the late 1920s in Islington, London—and studied the impact of separation from their mothers caused by the First World War.

Bowlby backed up his theories by drawing on the experiments of Harry Harlow (1905–81), an American psychologist who studied rhesus monkeys. Some of the baby monkeys were raised by their mother, some were given just food and water, and a third group had a cloth figure to attach themselves to. Not surprisingly, the baby monkeys with mothers were most likely to grow up to be well-adjusted adults, but the ones with a cloth figure did significantly better than those with just food and water. As you can imagine, Harlow's experiments into maternal deprivation were controversial—even in the 1930s—but if you search for "Harlow Monkey Experiment" on YouTube, you can see how the baby monkey clings to the cloth figure (rather than the wire figure which feeds it). Harlow also did experiments to test what would happen when the young rhesus monkeys were frightened by a machine. He found the baby monkeys would run to the cloth mother for comfort (thereby demonstrating attachment) and not only calm themselves down but be secure enough to display aggression toward the source of their fear.

The third figure in the development of attachment theory is Canadian/American psychologist Mary Ainsworth (1913–99)—who was a pupil of Bowlby. While Bowlby believed that you were either attached to your mother (or primary caregiver) or not, Ainsworth concentrated on the quality of that attachment. From the late 1960s through to the 1970s, Ainsworth conducted a test called "Strange Situation." A mother and child (between twelve and eighteen months) would be brought into a strange but interesting situation—in effect, a laboratory set up to look like a living room with lots of toys for the child to play with (plus a two-way mirror behind which the team would monitor and film the results). Ainsworth was interested in how the child reacted to the mild stress of being in a new environment. (Once again, there are videos of the experiment on YouTube.) Did the child cling to the mother or use her as a safe base from which to explore the unknown space and play with the toys? Or maybe ignore the mother altogether and just play with the toys? Once the pattern had been established, a stranger would arrive in the room and read a magazine. How would the child react at this point? Next, the mother would leave the room. How would the child react and would the stranger be able to comfort him or her? The final part of the research was key for Ainsworth—what happened during the reunion when the mother returned.

Ainsworth noted three distinct responses. First, the child would be quickly and easily calmed by the mother—which she considered secure attachment. Second, the child would approach the mother but resist attempts to be calmed and maybe even push the mother away—this she considered ambivalent attachment (or more commonly called anxious attachment). Third, the child would show little interest when the mother returned—this she considered avoidant attachment (or sometimes called fearful). In Ainsworth's findings, seventy percent of infants were securely attached, fifteen percent ambivalently attached and a further fifteen per cent avoidantly attached.

HOW DOES THIS IMPACT ON
YOUR RELATIONSHIP?

Your childhood and your subsequent experiences with key figures (like friends, teachers, first boyfriends and girlfriends, etc.) will have a profound impact on the dance of intimacy between you and your partner (or, if you're single, prospective partners). As I discussed in Chapter One, whether your parents picked you up when you fell over and kissed it better, told you not to be stupid, or never seemed to be around will impact on the size of your inner void and how you feel about yourself. What Bowlby and attachment theory tell us is that it will also influence your expectations of your partners and whether your dance is secure (two people in step with each other), pushing for more closeness (anxiously attached), or pulling away for more space (avoidantly attached).

To get an idea of your attachment style, I've reproduced the basic assessment questionnaire used in standard psychological tests (as the ideas of Bowlby and Ainsworth have been developed, tested in different cultures, and refined over time). I expect you will approach this test with trepidation because the terms "anxious" and "avoidant" carry a lot of negative connotations and only tell part of the story. In previous books, I've tried to avoid these labels—and instead concentrated on the types of dances that spring from the different attachment styles—but the terms have started to enter popular culture and dating self-help books, and clients often arrive full of panic and worried about the prognosis for their relationship or their chance of ever finding lasting love. So let me offer a little reassurance; the situation is not as black and white as the terms suggest and attachment styles are not fixed. With those caveats out of the way, let's look at the following questionnaire.

WHAT'S YOUR ATTACHMENT STYLE?

Thinking about your relationship patterns before your current crisis —not just with your partner or lover but also friends—which of the following statements is most applicable:

a) It is easy for me to become emotionally close to others. I am comfortable depending on them and having them depend on me. I don't worry about being alone or having other people accept me.

b) I want to be completely emotionally intimate with others, but I often find that others are reluctant to get as close as I would like. I am uncomfortable being without a close relationship, but I sometimes worry that others don't value me as much as I value them.

c) I am sometimes uncomfortable getting close to others. I want emotionally close relationships, but I find it difficult to trust others completely or to depend on them. I worry that I will be hurt or swallowed up if I allow myself to become too close to other people.

d) I am comfortable without close emotional relationships. It is very important to me to feel independent and self-sufficient, and I prefer not to depend on others or have others depend on me.

If you answered **a)** see Secure Attachment, if **b)** Anxious Attachment, if **c)** Fearful Attachment and if **d)** Dismissive Attachment, and if you found it hard to pick just one please read Combination Attachment. (However, I would recommend reading all the sections to help interpret how other people might react to you. Understanding the other attachment styles will throw light on yours.)

Figures on how common each style might be vary dramatically depending on how the characteristics are measured, but, to give you some general idea, I've included figures from a study at Texas A+M University that reviewed all the scientific papers on this subject and combined the data.

Secure Attachment

You generally feel good about yourself, your partner and your relationships. You find it reasonably easy to empathize with other people and listen to what they have to say. Your thinking is flexible and you're open to a range of ways to resolve any difficulties in your relationship (rather than fixed on one favored solution). However, a recent crisis has made you doubt your judgment, wonder what sort of person your partner really is and, in the worst cases, whether he or she *ever* really loved you. (Researchers feel that forty-six percent of the population have secure attachment.)

Impact on your relationship: On a daily basis, you have a positive relationship and probably take many aspects of it for granted (rather like we expect electricity in our homes and don't really notice how important it is until there is a power cut). However, your confidence has recently been knocked. Perhaps your partner has been unfaithful—or betrayed you in some other way—and despite his or her protestations, best behavior, or hard work, you find it hard to trust again. Although you might long for reassurance or a hug, you can't stop yourself from pushing him or her away because you're frightened of getting hurt again. Alternatively, your partner has announced that he or she doesn't love you anymore, or distanced him or herself so much that you have become anxious and need more support but get angry with yourself or are criticized by your partner for being "clingy."

Anxious Attachment

Nobody likes to criticize their parents but one of your parents was emotionally unavailable (sometimes through divorce, illness, or something else beyond their control); maybe you watched your mother and father fight a lot or do the "pursue and distance" dance of intimacy themselves. Alternatively, one or both of your parents would get anxious or frightened if you expressed certain emotions. Therefore, it's not surprising that you often feel anxious and worried about relationships, work too hard to please, and become increasingly resentful if your caring actions are not properly appreciated. Although you try to boost yourself up, deep down you don't have a particularly positive self-image. Perhaps you've been rejected by previous lovers or you've been married for years but still feel alone—because your partner is always preoccupied with their job, sport or the children and never wants to open up, have truly loving sex, or talk about your relationship. No wonder you think there is something "wrong" with you. Meanwhile, you can put your beloved on a pedestal and worry whether he or she loves you. (It's thought that about sixteen percent of us have anxious attachment.)

Impact on your relationship: You can be so keen to make a new relationship succeed that you come on too strong and frighten off a potential partner or have a "where do I stand" conversation too soon. Maybe you've even broken up with someone—despite not really wanting to—because you're frightened that he or she might get there first and you couldn't stand the rejection. When your relationship goes through a bad patch, you tend to become preoccupied with your partner's movements and look for evidence of his or her "true" feelings. After infidelity or an "I love you but I'm not in love with you" confession, you can be so worried about the future that you will push for clarity (which your partner can't give) and make a difficult situation even worse.

Fearful Attachment

Ainsworth would have called this type of attachment avoidant, and the children in her experiment exhibited little or no distress when their mothers left the room, could be soothed by the stranger, and showed little interest when reunited with their mother. She believed that in adulthood they would not necessarily reject their partner's attention but neither would they seek comfort or contact from them because they had become adept at taking care of their own needs.

Rather than using Ainsworth's term avoidant, I find the description "fearful" more helpful for two reasons. First, it begins to engage with the reasons why these children did not look to their mothers for soothing in the strange situation. Returning to the image of the child running down the street and falling over: these are the children who were smacked or punished for running off, criticized for not listening, and for making such a fuss about falling over. It's not that these children don't want to be picked up and nurtured but that they have learned not to show their feelings (to grit their teeth and grin and bear it). In other words, if they show any vulnerability or ask for closeness, they are frightened of being rejected (or worse still, *know* they will be rejected). Perhaps the fear of rejection goes so deep that they don't even admit these needs for care and attention, even to themselves, because that would open them up to despair. Second, I prefer the term fearful rather than avoidant because lots of people who show this attachment pattern desperately want a relationship or are in a long-term relationship but frightened that they've chosen the wrong person and worry that somewhere out there is the right one.

If you answered c) to the questionnaire, you could be in a long-term relationship but hold back something (for fear of being hurt) or value your independence so highly that you put up artificial barriers (like some all-consuming hobby) to stop your partner getting too close or expecting too much. Alternatively, you might distance yourself by still holding a flashlight for an ex or having intense "friendships" with members of the opposite sex.

If you're single, you have either lusted after unavailable people or don't seem to find the right person. Perhaps you blow hot and besiege the object of your affections with calls, sexy texts, and wild promises about your future together. However, once you've worn down his or her defenses and feel sure of their love, you begin to question whether he or she *is* "The One." Suddenly, you notice faults that you've previously overlooked, there's a couple of arguments, and your beloved begins to make demands (after all, you have made promises). Therefore, you begin to blow cold and become less available. Things go from bad to worse and you decide to end the relationship or find someone else who, at the time, seems to offer everything you dream about. (Don't worry if you've fallen into this category because you're not alone. Twenty-three percent of the population are also described as fearful.)

Impact on your relationship: You feel relatively negative about both yourself and your partner or potential lover. No wonder you feel vulnerable and unsure as to whether it is truly safe to rely on someone—especially when the fantasy of them being "perfect" is stripped away. So you pick a fight to give you an excuse to go off in a huff or simply switch off your phone. These tactics might provide a breathing space to get your head together but stop your partner from getting close and, ultimately, from you having the type of relationship for which you long.

Dismissive Attachment

Since Ainsworth did her work in the 1960s and 1970s, as is often the case with psychological theories, other people have come along and developed her ideas and added a fourth pattern of attachment. In some ways, dismissive attachment is what happens when you are both ambivalent (anxious) and avoidant (fearful).

If you answered d) to the questionnaire, I want to acknowledge just what a dark place you are probably in at the moment. You don't want or need close relationships and can't imagine that changing for a while. It sounds like you have been so hurt by betrayal or by life in general that you need to retreat into your cave and lick your wounds. I hope that my book will help you recover, and, when you're stronger and ready to emerge back into the light, to consider having a relationship sometime in the future.

The good news is that you have a positive image of yourself but a poor one of everyone else. (Perhaps the simplest way to express this is "I'm OK, You're not OK.") In many ways, it is a great step forward from fearful attachment (I'm not OK and You're not OK) and a more comfortable place than anxious attachment (I'm not OK and You're OK) but still a long way off secure attachment (I'm OK and You're OK). If you are interested in reading more about this idea, it comes from Transactional Analysis, which I cover in my book *Help Your Partner Say 'Yes': Seven Steps to Achieving Better Cooperation and Communication* (Bloomsbury), or get the classic book by Thomas A. Harris, *I'm OK, You're OK* (Arrow).

So why did you answer d) to the questionnaire. It could be that you have always valued self-sufficiency but allowed yourself to be persuaded into starting a relationship. Perhaps you're focused on your career or you're an artist and your creativity comes first, and your partner is making you feel guilty. More likely, your partner has done something terrible and you've decided that you'd be better off alone, or the drip, drip, drip of everyday unhappiness has destroyed your love.

However, before you split up, I want you to take a long hard look at yourself. I meet people who proclaim, "I can stand on my own two feet" and "I don't need anybody else"—almost to the point of being aggressively defensive. They are often extremely denigrating about their partner too. As Shakespeare puts it in *Hamlet:* "The lady doth protest too much, me thinks." In most cases, they are getting angry or running down their partner to avoid looking at how bad they feel about themselves (which is Fearful Attachment) or trying to persuade themselves that they really will be OK on their own (and therefore might have Anxious Attachment).

In my experience, true Dismissive Attachment is more in sorrow than anger. (Psychologists at Texas A+M University reckon that fourteen percent of the population fit into this profile.)

Impact on your relationship: No matter how much your partner or ex begs for a second chance, you remain impervious. Of course, you may be right that the relationship is over, but what would happen if he or she genuinely did deliver on his or her promises to change? And have you ever let down your defenses and given him or her a chance to get close? After all, the less you put into a relationship, the less you will get out.

Combination Attachment

Although psychologists talk about four categories of attachment, I think it is better to imagine a scale rather than distinct categories where you have one type of attachment or another. In the middle of the scale would be 'secure' and on either side "anxious" and "fearful," and because "dismissive" has elements of both anxious and fearful I would curve both ends round until it becomes a circle—like the diagram on the following page:

I am not surprised that you did not fit neatly into one of the four categories or have one type of attachment with your friends or at work and another at home. It's also common to exhibit one style in one

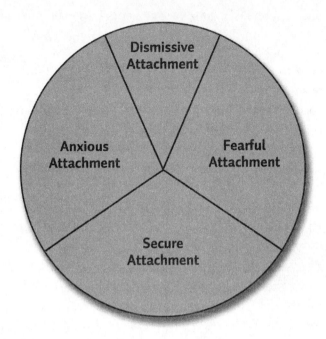

relationship and another in the next. I often counsel single people who become obsessed and empty their diaries to be with their beloved, even if he or she seems to be pulling away, but in the next one hold the prospective partner at arm's length (perhaps they do not fancy him or her, he or she was unsuitable, or they are still carrying a torch for an ex). However, I would argue that they probably have a core attachment style.

I've also met plenty of people whose attachment style is secure but who fell in love with someone insecure and were destabilized by a passionate but destructive relationship. Finally, it is possible that a recent crisis has made you bounce around the scale, responding one way to your partner today and another tomorrow.

Impact on your relationship: If you're in a crisis, it is like the ground is forever shifting under your feet. You don't know who you are and, therefore, what you want. It is highly likely that you are sending mixed messages to your partner and that he or she, in turn, doesn't know how to respond, or they alternate between being angry and welcoming (further confusing you).

THE DANCE OF INTIMACY

With a greater understanding of how our childhood and subsequent experiences with intimacy shape how we attach to significant figures when we're adults, I'm ready to explain one of the most common problems that people arrive in counseling seeking to change. The dance of pursue and distance.

In established couples

Returning to Simon and Alina, the couple in their midfifties from Chapter One (see page 34) who argued over watching TV together, they were unclear about whether they were both anxious or fearful.

At first sight, Alina could relate to the idea of anxious attachment because in her previous marriage—to a functioning alcoholic—she had wanted more intimacy but he had been unavailable.

"However, I think I've changed because in this relationship I'm worried about maintaining my private space. I love Simon and I want to be with him but sometimes I fear he wants first one thing, and then another and another. I want to give them, but can I?" she explained.

"That sounds remarkably like fearful attachment," I replied. "But what I want to stress is that there is no right or wrong style of attachment because they were part of your survival tactics as child—what I would question is whether they are still necessary today." (There will be more about this idea in the next section.) "Why do you think your core response is to pull away and exhibit fearful attachment?"

"My father left when I was ten and my mother blamed me because I'd been badly behaved. So I would go around to his house and beg him to come back," she explained. "When something goes wrong, I always think it's going to be my fault."

"So your fear is that you're going to let people down or you're going to be blamed and have a barrel-load of pain tipped over your head."

'I know I can survive on my own and, when I'm in a dark place, I think "If people would just leave me alone".'

"And when we did your family history, you told me that you come from several generations of immigrants from Eastern Europe who had to flee from one country to another with jewelry sown into the seams of their clothes."

"Nowhere is safe and you have to know where the exit might be," Alina agreed. "It must be Fearful Attachment."

Moving onto Simon, I asked him if he had any ideas about why he always wanted more closeness.

"That's easy, when I was a child, my mother never seemed interested. It was always 'Run along and play.' I yearned for acceptance but all the physical affection went to my younger brother. In my first marriage, I chose a woman who turned out to be just like my mother and if I disagreed with her I'd get the silent treatment for two or three weeks."

It was clear that Simon was exhibiting Anxious Attachment and would do almost anything to avoid being unloved:

"My blood runs cold. It's like my world is ending. Death ..." His voice trailed away.

When they had first started talking on Facebook, a year after their previous marriages had ended, the attraction was immense and they were firmly under the influence of what psychologists call limerence. Neuroscientists have scanned the brain and discovered the feel-good hormones of oxytocin and dopamine are at their height when in this state. It's what all the pop songs are written about where you're happy just to be "On the street where you live" and "I only have eyes for you" and "With you, I'm born again." Under the influence of limerence, even someone's faults become attractive or an asset to the relationship. For example, for Simon it didn't matter that Alina wasn't interested in rally-cross because he could introduce her to the joys of revving engines and the adrenalin rush of watching cars speed by. No wonder his anxieties of being told to "run away and play" were soothed—because new lovers want nothing more than to be together. No wonder her fears of being blamed for things going wrong were washed away—because under the influence of limerence all differences melt away and therefore any problems. Although we'd like to believe that limerence lasts forever, its peak is reached somewhere between six and eighteen months—and then the impact slowly subsides. There's more about limerence in my book *I Love You But I'm Not In Love With You* (HCI).

Even during Simon and Alina's courting and honeymoon phase there had been some nasty rows, but they were buoyed up by the "feel-good" chemicals. Once limerence had subsided, the couple found themselves stuck in the dance of pursue and distance. Simon would want to "make-up" almost before the argument had finished and Alina would feel coerced into agreeing and stressing the need for space. They would eventually make-up again—because Alina also wanted togetherness—but they were doing a lot of damage to their loving bond and their individual sense of self-worth.

When I explain about pursue and distance, some couples worry that they have chosen the wrong partner. Wouldn't it be better if two anxious people got together? On the face of it, this should be a great combination as they could be joined at the hip, fulfilling each other's need for complete fusion and togetherness. However, each partner would lose their individual identity and have to put aside their personal needs.

I remember working with a woman in her early forties who admitted: "When we first got married, over fifteen years ago, we agreed never to spend a night apart. It seemed terribly romantic, but I'm really beginning to wonder if we made a mistake because my husband has turned down jobs—which involved traveling away from home—and I've not gone on training weekends or had time away with girlfriends."

Similarly, two fearful (or avoidant) individuals would have all the space they needed but, because we need both closeness as well as separation for a relationship to thrive, they would be unlikely to get together in the first place.

At this point, Simon and Alina asked the most important question of all: "How do we become more secure?"

This is the key because it helps you *both* be responsible for both "closeness" *and* "separation"—rather than expecting your partner to change.

When dating

It's when you're dating that the dance of pursue and distance is particularly stark because both the anxiously and fearfully attached get their world views reinforced. For the fearful (or avoidant) person, he or she has confirmation of being strong and independent (which of course are great qualities, but not to the point that it is difficult to make lasting relationships). For the anxious person, he or she has confirmation of wanting more intimacy than their partner and of being able to open themselves up to a deeper and more fulfilling relationship (which of course is great, but not if you are only attracted to people who are unable to offer what you want).

The dance of intimacy also stops both partners from looking deeper and recognizing their underlying similarities. Both the anxiously and fearful attached felt hurt, rejected, or not good enough as children but dealt with it in opposite ways. In the dance, the fearful person does not need to address their underlying anxiety about letting others get close (and thereby risk being hurt) and further distances him or herself by criticizing and policing the forbidden behavior in their prospective partner. The technical term for this in psychology is *projection*.

When we cannot face something, we suppress it and do everything in our power to distance ourselves. However, those emotions or parts of our personality have not disappeared—they are only lying dormant—but we can give ourselves the illusion, or further distance ourselves, by attacking someone else for exhibiting these forbidden qualities. It's why men who are not secure in their sexuality go to gay cruising areas and beat up gay men. It's also the reason why we can get irritated by work colleagues—out of all proportion to the offense—because we recognize forbidden parts of ourselves mirrored back to us in their behavior.

In the dance, the anxiously attached does not need to look at any fears about getting close because he or she really *wants* the relationship (but the other person is holding back). With their conscious mind, these people are desperate for a relationship but, unconsciously, they choose people who put obstacles in the way. In effect, they are projecting too, but in this case it is commitment. Their prospective partner becomes a commitment phobe or has "issues"—and the anxiously attached comes up smelling of roses (after all, he or she really wants the relationship). In the meantime, they don't need to think about their own fears of getting hurt and rejected on any more of a profound level than not getting their phone calls returned.

The beginning of the dance—when an anxiously and fearfully attached person starts dating—is often explosive.

"If such a thing as love at first sight exists, then this was it. Elliot and I first saw each other at Coachella Festival, two strangers in a field. He held my gaze and before we'd even swapped names, I took his hand and he led me into the night. Without a second thought, I abandoned my friends and my sensibilities to fall in love," says Olivia, who interviewed me for a newspaper article about her disastrous dating history.

All the bells and whistles need to go off in order for each partner to overcome their respective fears and anxieties about love. In this phase, where both parties are certain that they've found "the one," and limerence is at its height, the chemistry is almost overwhelming. It's only when Olivia looked back that it seemed almost too good to be true—almost as if they were trying to sell their "perfect" union to themselves and everybody else.

"Our relationship escalated at speed, and from the outset I was adored. Elliot thought I was magnificent and made no attempt to restrain his affection. That summer I was love-bombed with flowers and heart-melting emails at work. Suffocating in our adoration of each other, we were 'that couple'."

However, Elliot had go away on business a lot and there would times when he simply wasn't available. At the time, Olivia put it down to pressures of work—until she found an email from another woman who was desperately trying to contact him. Olivia met the girl, who had come to London to surprise Elliot, and her darkest fears came true. She was also Elliot's girlfriend (and had no idea that he was living with someone else or anything about Olivia's existence). Later, Olivia found that there was a third girl too.

This is classic fearful attachment. Elliot had distanced himself by becoming less available, and frightened that Olivia might not be THE ONE had dated first one and then two other women (but unable to let go of Olivia—just in case she might be—had kept everything secret and, even after being discovered, tried to persuade Olivia that the other women were "mad" and "deluded").

Meanwhile Olivia had been mistaking the heady brew of anxiety, preoccupation, and obsession—mixed in with short bursts of joy when Elliot did come through—for love, and was not listening to her internal alarm systems. While a securely attached woman would have said, "I can't be doing with all this" and put up barriers to protect herself, Olivia dismantled them and became more and more available rather than less (which is classic anxiously attached behavior).

"I am now able to admit that there was a darker side. Elliot's wild tendencies grew more frenetic; he became possessive, paranoid, and accusatory. Prone to exhibiting a bizarre spectrum of emotion, he oscillated me between pedestal and perjury and I began to manage my life in such a way as to not offend him. I told myself this was the price you paid for passion."

That's the danger of the pursue and flee dance. You can get addicted to the highs and lows and feel bored by a straightforward relationship with no tension and suspense, or so busy playing hard to get, making each other jealous, and kissing and making up, that consistent, calm, and honest communication seems dull (and therefore that you have no connection).

HOW TO MAKE SECURE ATTACHMENTS

Whatever your core attachment style or combination, I want to stress that these are *not* fixed. In fact, I know from personal experience that it is possible to change, as I shifted from fearful in my twenties to secure in my thirties. As I have previously explained—see Combination Attachment—it is more helpful to think of attachment as a spectrum and aim to move toward the center.

My aim is to help you be securely attached on a day-to-day basis and even if you might lean toward your old attachment style in a crisis, you will have the skills and knowledge to avoid the pursue and flee or flee and pursue dance of intimacy. So what are these skills and what knowledge will help?

From anxious to secure attachment

When you were a child, it often seemed that one of your parents or both were not truly available, busy doing something else, or preferred one of your siblings. Therefore, the only way to get the attention that you needed, and craved, was to shout louder, become more upset or in some way "up your game." So what's the alternative now you're an adult?

Be aware of your feelings. When you begin to get upset or fear your partner is pulling away, notice the feeling and name it to yourself: "I'm feeling anxious" or "I'm feeling panicky" or "I'm feeling angry," etc. Just naming the feeling will help, as it is will start to ground you, and knowing where on the scale from mild to strong it is can provide guidance on how to act. Remember my maxims: Accept the feeling (but challenge the thought) and What is this feeling trying to tell me? Be aware that you could be going on high alert (and into panic mode) when the threat is only mild—which brings me back to the first maxim: I need to explore and understand, before I can act.

Be aware of the dance. What happens when you pursue your partner? How does he or she react? If he or she distances him or herself, what do you do in response? What is the long-term impact on your relationship – even if you do finally get some reassurance? If you're dating, what happens when you make excessive attempts to reestablish contact or keep removing barriers so you are completely available?

Notice your protest behavior. At the bottom end of the scale, this is keeping score and acting hostile (by rolling eyes, looking away, or storming out). In the middle, it is being manipulative—by playing unapproachable or pretending to be busy to get revenge and show the other person how it feels, or trying to make him or her jealous. At the top end, it is threatening to leave or declaring the relationship over (when you don't really mean it).

Soothe yourself. Remember the maxim from this chapter: What can I control? However much you might beg, reason or try to influence your partner's behavior, ultimately you cannot control him or her. Thank goodness! But you can control your reaction to his or her behavior. You can say to yourself: I'm not going to participate in this dance. I can choose to soothe myself, rather than pursuing my partner to soothe me. So try the counting meditation or something else that calms you down.

Remind yourself about your other resources. If you are looking for affirmation from your partner, remember that he or she is not the only source. You have friends and family who can provide support and understanding. You could distract yourself by doing something pleasant or pressing. You are no longer a child, you have enough resources and agency in the world to resolve the issues for yourself. Please remember this important fact. Otherwise you will plunge back into the dance and, at this point, you are likely to overestimate your partner or date's qualities and abilities (by overlooking their bad points) and simultaneously underestimate your own.

Watch what happens when you don't pursue. As an experiment, try breaking the dance and don't push for closeness. My guess is that your partner will still distance him or herself. But does he or she go as far or for so long? How do you feel yourself when you don't pursue? I hope calmer and more in control of your reactions.

From fearful to secure attachment

When you were a child, one or both of your parents' love seemed conditional or they were rejecting or even dangerous. Although you craved love and attention, you trained yourself to be self-sufficient or closed down to protect yourself. So one half of you longs for connection but the other feels more comfortable when it's on *your* terms. So what's the alternative?

Be aware of your feelings. If you haven't started a feelings diary yet (see Chapter Two), please do. Instead of ignoring your feelings, rationalizing them away or swallowing them, I'd like you to name and accept them. Remember the second maxim: What is this feeling trying to tell me. You're probably feeling like this for a good reason: what is it? If you become more emotionally aware, you will notice when the pressure builds up so much that you need to escape in order to decompress and feel normal again. Instead of running away, if you catch the sensation soon enough, you will have more choices than just fleeing and the opportunity to try some new skills.

Be aware of the dance. What happens if you do shut down or walk away—without any explanation? How does your partner react? What is the impact on you? Do you feel powerful and independent but only by making your partner feel incapable and needy? Although, there might be relief in the short term from achieving some space, what other feelings follow? Are you angry, resentful, full of self-justification, and guilt? Notice the feelings and the longer-term impact on your relationship.

Notice your distancing techniques. By this point, you will have discovered something really interesting. You don't just walk away but prepare the ground in advance. So what's going on? You start to notice small problems or imperfections—perhaps the way that your partner interrupts when you're with company—and in your mind, they become BIG obstacles. Each example on its own isn't that problematic, but as you focus on them they grow and grow until they become intolerable (and you're justified in turning cold or distancing yourself). In the worst case scenario, you decide that the two of you are wrong for each other (so you're justified in chatting to someone else, developing feelings for them, and considering the relationship over—although that would be news to your partner). If you're dating, look out for intimacy deactivating strategies. Do you choose someone who's not your equal and thereby permanently feel something is missing or that there's someone better out there? Do you pull away when things are going particularly well—for example, not calling after a good date? Rather than saying "I love you," do you imply it instead? Do you flirt with other people or keep in contact with an ex—even though you're interested in the person you're dating? Although, you think you're keeping your autonomy, actually you're trying to manage your fears.

Ask for what you need. Instead of letting the small problems build and thereby needing to distance yourself, what would happen if you addressed the issue? For example, tell your partner that he or she kept interrupting you. He or she might not be aware of being rude, concede the point, and change the behavior. There might, alternatively, be a row, but there's a possibility of resolving this one issue. In contrast, by the time you're overwhelmed and walk away, there is probably a dozen or more problems—plus the upset and fallout from the dance of intimacy. No wonder nothing gets solved and you go around and around the same issues.

Watch what happens when you stand your ground. It's fine to need "me" time. Your partner is much more likely to agree (and not be anxious), if you tell him or her when you need space and negotiate when and for how long—rather than just unilaterally switching off or fleeing. What you read as anger in your partner might be just distress and, if you listen and acknowledge his or her feelings, they will diminish down to manageable proportions. At this point, you'll probably find that you're better at negotiating and have more communication skills than you realize.

THE **ABC** OF CHALLENGING YOUR REACTION

We think there is a straightforward link between something upsetting (Adversity) and how we react (Consequences). So, of course, you will be anxious if your partner is distant. Equally, if your partner is clinging, you will need space. This simple relationship between adversity and consequence means we long to change our partner—if he or she would stop pursuing or fleeing then everything will be fine. Case closed!

However, you are overlooking a vital stage in your reactions. As between A for adversity and C for consequences, there is B for beliefs:

- **A**dversity: dance of intimacy
- **B**eliefs: this is my only chance for love
- **C**onsequences: upset, anger, despair.

But what if you challenged your beliefs and thoughts about the situation? Remembering this chapter's maxim: What can I control?

OK, if you can't change your partner's behavior, what can you control? I would say, your reaction to that behavior:

- **A**dversity: my partner walks away

- **B**elief: she needs time alone to destress and she'll be back soon

- **C**onsequences: sympathy, understanding, patience.

Let's take another example:

- **A**dversity: my partner is clinging

- **B**elief: my partner needs some reassurance. I don't have to agree to everything he wants but I can listen and negotiate

- **C**onsequence: being engaging and open.

My final example of ABC comes from my infidelity support group. One wife, dealing with a husband going through a midlife crisis, made everybody think when she said: "I know my husband wouldn't do anything deliberately to hurt me, so when he does something horrible or rejecting I think 'What was his good intent?' It might take a while to come up with it, but I always do." Instead of adversity (his bad behavior) leading to anger or revenge, she had a central belief that was incredibly generous, and the consequence was that she listened first and reacted second. I doubt many people would have the same response to infidelity—and that's fine—but it does underline how your beliefs shape your reactions.

Summing up: Next time you're facing adversity and feel overwhelmed by the feelings—in other words have gone straight from A to C—slow down your reaction and look at the beliefs. Are they true? Are they an exaggeration—full of black and white thinking? Might they have been true when you were a kid but are out of date now you're an adult?

FOR BOTH ANXIOUS AND FEARFUL
TO SECURE ATTACHMENT

The dance of pursue and distance points up the differences between anxious and fearful attachment but, as I've already explained, there are a lot of similarities. Anxiously attached people are fearful of never getting their needs met and fearfully attached people have an underlying anxiety about being vulnerable and letting others get close. Therefore, I have come up with five tips which simultaneously addresses both attachment types.

Challenge the myths about love

We have been fed a series of myths by Hollywood romantic comedies which give us unreasonable expectations about love. For example, "Love is a magic bullet." It doesn't matter how much your life is messed up because love will save the day. However, this encourages us to believe that either we can "fix" our partner or he or she will "fix" us. Remember, life is a journey and your partner is a companion—rather than someone to carry you or you them. Of course, you're going to help each other ford a stream or climb a stile but, as I've said before, you can't expect your partner to carry you. The love is a magic bullet myth is reinforced by two more that I hear all the time: "If you loved me, you would ..." and "If we're having problems then we're not meant to be together." While the first is manipulative, the second is catastrophizing.

However, the most damaging of all myths is: "There's one special person" or rephrased as "We should be soul partners." With this myth, you end up in one of three traps. You risk obsessing about a relationship that's going nowhere or worse still verging on the abusive. Alternatively, when your marriage doesn't live up to your expectations, you think someone else is THE ONE and risk breaking your husband or wife's—and the children's—hearts. And if you're single, you don't accept a second date unless the chemistry is so strong that you've told each other your whole life story, discovered ten million things in common and stayed out till dawn.

The truth is that love takes skills and investment as well as connection. I know it is much nicer and easier to believe in soul partners—in fact after a talk on the subject a woman came up to me and said, "I still believe in love" and I felt like I'd told a small child there was no Father Christmas or Tooth Fairy. However, there's an upside. Skills can be learned. You can decide to truly invest in your relationship and build a better connection.

So what are these skills? You need to listen to each other rather than assume you know what your partner is thinking. You need to feed your love—especially when you have children who also need your attention—and spend quality time together as a couple (rather than expecting to stay magically in love when your only meaningful communication is about kids' pick up times). If you're single, a slow burn can be just as good a foundation as instant attraction and often longer lasting.

There's more about how the myths about love set us up for disappointment and intimacy issues in my book *What Is Love? 50 Questions About How to Find, Keep, and Rediscover It.*

How it works in practice: Brian and Carol were in their late and mid-fifties and had got married relatively late after an off-on courtship. They had one son who was ten. They were a typical pursue and distance couple. Carol's parents had followed a similar pattern (her father had severe depression that included manic phases and others just staring at the wall) and she had grown up to be anxiously attached. Meanwhile, Brian's father was an alcoholic and his mother exhausted from bringing up four other kids. Brian was withdrawn and self-sufficient as a child and grew up to be fearfully attached. He'd often question if he and Carol were "right" for each other and his work brought him into contact with lots of interesting women—with whom he had close friendships—and Carol often felt jealous.

Brian was particularly concerned about whether they were similar enough. He thought they shouldn't argue so much and admitted: 'If we didn't have a child, I don't know if we would still be together.' He was also concerned about the way they had split up and got back together several times before getting married and about his doubts on their wedding day. "Shouldn't you be more certain? Aren't you just supposed to know when you should be together, rather than having all these comings and goings."

However, two things changed their dynamic (as they had been on the verge of splitting up before they came to see me). First, understanding that someone who is fearfully attached will use distancing tactics.

"I suppose you'd say, 'That goes with the territory,'" he told me.

I nodded and replied: "I wish that life was more like in the movies. That love was a magic bullet and you did just 'know' you should be together. But then I also wish that the polar ice caps weren't melting and that chocolate didn't make you fat."

After a moment of reflecting on the disappointment, he said:

"But we do have a child together and we get on pretty well, so perhaps we should concentrate on how to sort out differences rather than worry about how life might have been."

Wise words indeed.

Give up on perfection

When you've seen your parent's destroy each other or the struggle of bringing up a child on your own, you will have told yourself—with all the confidence of youth—I won't make the same mistakes. Perhaps the best defense against all this pain and heartache is to have the "perfect" relationship, or to be "perfect" yourself because if you're "perfect" your partner won't leave you, or hope that your partner is "perfect" and can lift you up to the heights of perfection. (I know you won't have put it quite like this in your mind but in essence that's the belief.)

However, I've spent thirty years studying relationships—not just couples in counseling but observing friends, acquaintances, work colleagues, and family—and I've never met someone with a perfect relationship. I certainly haven't got one myself and that's fine, because it's the problems that challenge us and help us grow.

With the weight of being perfect off your shoulders, and more realistic expectations, you can begin to engage in the messy complexities of making things work in the real world and creating something wonderful together. Trust me, reality is always more interesting, surprising, and satisfying than any fantasy.

How it works in practice: Gail, thirty-five, contacted me because a close friend had suggested there could be something more between them.

"After several negative experiences with men, the thought of a relationship with a loving, caring person seems wonderful, but I don't think

I'm in love with him. Can you learn to love someone? Or is it just enough to be content—can you have a marriage without passion?"

"Let's rephrase the questions," I replied. "Starting with 'Can you learn to love someone?' Instead, let's put that as: Can you fall in love with someone that you already know?"

"Of course," she replied.

"Let's rephrase the other question from 'Can you have a marriage without passion?' Well, if you mean can you have a marriage without love —probably not. However, if you're asking do you need to feel passion all the time—so you're always ready to rip each other's clothes off—I don't think any marriage would pass this test."

It was clear that Gail was flipping from feeling passionately connected (but with men whose behavior was neither loving nor caring) and feeling just content (with a kind and caring man).

"You seem to think you have to decide immediately. I believe it takes three dates to decide if you're interested in seeing someone and then three months to decide if you're boyfriend and girlfriend (and no longer see other people), and then up to eighteen months to decide if you want to spend the rest of your life together."

"But wouldn't that be misleading him?" she asked.

"No, you're just agreeing to go on a few dates and see what happens," I replied. "It doesn't have to be perfect at the start, that's what dating is all about: getting to properly know each other."

Once the pressure of perfection had been removed, Gail went out with her "friend" and reported back after a couple of months.

"We're taking it really slowly and I'm really enjoying seeing another side of him and, as for passion, well, he's great in bed!"

Be aware of your script

Our first relationship with our mother, father, and other caregivers taught us a lot about ourselves, how acceptable we were to others, and how love works. Meanwhile, watching our parents interact tells us a lot about relationships (even if they were not together). These complex messages can normally be boiled down into one sentence. I call this your script. Sometimes, it will be something your mother or father might say: "Don't make a scene" or "You can't trust anybody but family" or "Nobody will love you like we do." However, more often that not, the messages are so strong and so frequently reinforced that they don't need to be said—which makes them even more powerful and harder to challenge.

So, stop and think about the messages that you were given—both verbally and through your parents' actions. To help the process, try completing the following sentences. Don't spend too long thinking, just take what comes from the top of your mind:

Love is ...

Life is ...

Men should ...

Women should ...

Don't get ...

Look back at what you've written down and find what really speaks to you. Can you put it down into a sentence or two?

How it works in practice: Returning to Simon and Alina, they both had powerful scripts from their childhood which had been reinforced by subsequent relationships.

"You're unacceptable and nothing you do will be good enough," said Simon.

"There's another bit to it ..." I prompted.

"So I'm going to reject you."

I nodded.

"And it's not just my relationships but at work too," he continued. "I set up this firm and it does really well but my business partner doesn't want to listen to me."

"Run along and play?" I remembered.

"And not listening or taking my well-thought-out proposals seriously, that's rejecting too."

I turned to Alina

"I know my script: 'You're to blame,'" she replied.

I nodded.

"And because that's so overwhelming, I need to flee."

So let's look at how the two scripts mesh and reinforce each other. If Alina is upset, Simon's script says, "See, you are unacceptable, you've done all these wonderful things and she's going to reject you and you're going to have to get a dark and dingy apartment on your own," and Alina believes it's all her fault and needs to flee—which feels like rejection to Simon. Alternatively, Simon is upset and Alina believes it must be her fault; her script kicks in and we're back in the same cycle again. And, indeed, before they started counseling, they would have a huge argument about once a month to six weeks with one or both of them declaring the relationship over. Understanding the script helped to break the pattern because being aware stops a small issue being magnified into a big one.

The eighty percent to twenty percent rule

This point follows on neatly from the last one. In my experience, over thirty years of couples' work, when a problem is particularly intractable—like the anxious and fearful dance of intimacy—it is always eighty percent about the past and only twenty per cent about the subject in hand. So the argument is never just about whether you should clean your children's shoes (or let them clean them themselves), the best place to keep the garbage bags or who should have the TV remote.

So ask yourself, what is this argument really about? Why do I feel so strongly about my partner's behavior? Am I angry not just about his or her behavior but because he or she is the latest in a long line to act this way?

How it works in practice: Once you have separated off the eighty per cent from the past, you can begin to negotiate over the twenty percent that is about today.

"When I'm getting really upset and thinking the whole world is against me," Simon said, "before I become completely devastated, believing that I don't count and I'm invisible—I tell myself that the pain is eighty percent about my childhood and my first marriage and only twenty percent about Alina and I. With the problem down to something more rational, I can employ the skills that we're learning."

"When I feel myself getting agitated and finding reasons why I'm to blame for something, I tell myself that's just the script speaking and that calms me down," added Alina. "In our most recent argument—over my son—I was aware of my script saying 'flee, flee, flee' but I didn't have to follow it through to the logical conclusion and declare the relationship over. Instead, I told Simon, 'I can't cope with this at the moment, so I'm going out.'"

"That was much easier for me and I don't panic," Simon added.

"When I returned, we talked about the twenty percent: my son cooking a pizza for himself and not considering anybody else. It wasn't about whether I was a good mother or a good daughter or a good person after all, just my son being a typical teenager."

Appreciate the your partner's viewpoint

When you're locked in the dance of flee and pursue, there is a danger of being so busy trying to defend your position that you can be blind to the virtues of your partner's position.

If you're fearfully attached, focus on the value of being part of something bigger than yourself (i.e. a loving and supportive relationship). If you're anxiously attached, focus on the value of being independent and responsible for sorting out your own problems (rather than being reliant on someone else to lift your mood and getting angry or upset when they don't come through).

In this way, you will share the responsibility for the "I" and the "we" in the relationship, the separation and the closeness, and finally dance in sync with each other.

How it works in practice: Returning to Brian and Carol, I found the best way to appreciate their partner's viewpoint and to work as a team was to change the metaphor. Instead of a dance, I asked them to imagine being on different ends of a seesaw. When Carol pushed down on her end (let's do lots of things together), Brian would rise up in the air (close down or walk away). When Brian pushed down on his end (I need time to myself), Carol would rise up in the air (panic, send long emails, or two or three texts before Brian had replied to the first one). Being flung up and down on a seesaw is not only a bumpy ride, it can also make you feel sick. So what makes for a smoother ride? Moving closer to the middle by appreciating each other's viewpoint. In this way, neither person goes so high in the air or drops so low.

When Carol realized that she couldn't change Brian but she could change the dynamic by learning to appreciate his viewpoint, she got creative: "I'm fine with him having time to himself, as I've got plenty to be getting on with. It's not knowing when he'll be back and then starting to worry what he's thinking about and whether he's angry. So I'm going to make up a set of cards and get them laminated with everything from 'off for five minutes' to 'need the rest of the day to myself.'"

CONCERN VERSUS CONTROL

At the beginning of this chapter, I introduced the ideas behind this exercise and now you get the chance to work out the line between control and concern for yourself.

- Look at the two circles on the following page: your zone of control in the middle and your zone of concern on the outside.

- You will see your zone of concern is larger than your zone of control.

- Think about what areas of your life—from the trivial (what I wear) to the important (work, family, children)—belong in which zone.

- You might like to copy the diagram onto a piece of paper so you have plenty of space.

- Double-check everything in your zone of control: can you really control everything (or think you *should* be able to)?

- I sometimes get my clients to undertake this exercise twice. The first time, where they would put the different areas of their life before starting counseling (or in your case reading the book) and the second time using their knowledge today. What difference would that make?

• Finally, think about what is it like trying to control something over which you have no control?

When you've finished, read the next section. In it I will go through some client examples and this will help you check if there's something in your zone of control that really belongs in your zone of concern.

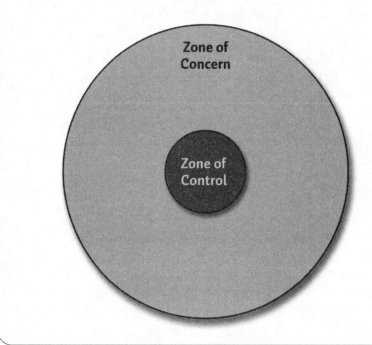

FOURTH MAXIM IN ACTION

A lot of people feel helpless and their situation is hopeless because they are trying to control an area of their life which belongs in their zone of concern. That's why the fourth maxim is **What can I control?**

Brenda, forty-six, started counseling after her husband left home, declared he was miserable, and wanted a divorce. She later found out that there was another woman in the background—although her husband Christopher claimed this was not his reason for leaving.

In her zone of concern, she put "Christopher returning home as a husband," "Christopher's depression," "the future." I agreed that these were things that concerned her but which she could not control.

In her zone of control, she wrote "Christopher being a good Dad to Zina" (their six-year-old daughter), "my financial future," "Zina," "my career," and "my social life." However, I wanted to challenge some of these.

"Can you control how often Christopher has Zina? Last weekend was his birthday and he decided he'd rather be with friends than see her," I reminded her. "You can facilitate their relationship by being flexible and accommodating to his schedule, but that's where your influence ends."

Brenda sighed.

"Can you control your daughter? Maybe when she's young, but how much really?"

"I have terrible trouble getting her to sleep. I can control what time she goes to bed and has her light out but nothing more."

"So even at six, she has begun to have a mind of her own. Let's move onto your career; you can certainly control the quality of your work, but what if the company relocates to the other side of the world or there's a global recession?"

"So my career is more in my zone of concern and therefore my financial future too belongs there. When it comes to my social life, I can phone a friend and suggest going to the movie theater but not whether they accept."

So we went back to the exercise and looked at what she could control:

- Her reactions to Christopher's behavior

- Her actions

- Her thoughts (that she believed he was wrong to leave without giving her a proper chance to resolve their problems)

- What she offered Christopher (access to daughter, how much cooperation for the divorce proceeding, etc.)

- Her ability to ask for what she needed

- Her daily timetable

There is no right or wrong answer to this exercise but most people come up with some variation on being able to control their reactions (to other people's disagreeable behavior), their thoughts, their beliefs, their standards, their own behavior, and we have a debate on whether they can or cannot control their emotions (and whether this is helpful or not).

However, whichever way you answer the question **What's in my control?** having a more realistic list helps make you feel more empowered.

GREEN SHOOTS

- Childhood experiences will have an impact on the nature of your relationships today.

- Psychologists have identified three key types of attachment: secure, anxious, and fearful.

- When an anxiously and fearfully attached person falls in love, they often get trapped into a pattern of pursue and flee. If this dance of intimacy is familiar, don't despair because it is possible to break the pattern and become more securely attached.

- The fourth maxim to change your life is: "What can I control?"

CHAPTER FIVE

Dealing with Other People

Life is difficult. Just getting through the day, fulfilling our obligations, and sorting out our own personal stuff can often take all our energy. That's why many clients complain about being overwhelmed by demands from other people or feel that they could manage their life if only they weren't constantly being blown off course by someone else.

FIFTH MAXIM

When your partner is upset, it's likely that your first reaction will be: What have I done now? This is especially the case if you're going through a crisis. However, more times than not, your partner's upset might not be about you. It could be the pressure from a tough day ahead at work, a poor night's sleep, annoyance with your son or daughter, or maybe his or her baseball team are selling their star player. So why is our first reaction about us?

You won't be surprised to know, this goes right back to your childhood again. When you were small, you were the center of the world. Babies' brains are not developed enough for empathy and the imagination to step into other people's shoes. If they are going to make sense of their surroundings, starting with themselves makes a lot of sense. So when you were a child, if someone didn't pick you up when you cried, you didn't think what's wrong with my mother or father but what have I done wrong? At school, you met other children and slowly but surely you realized that you were not the center of the world. However, if a teacher or a classmate didn't like you, or you didn't fit in, you would have concluded there was something unacceptable about you or your behavior—not that the teacher had just qualified and was finding her feet, not that the boy at the next desk was being beaten up by his older brother and taking it out on you, not that the school's ethos didn't match your needs.

Fortunately, you are no longer a small child. You have the knowledge and experience in the world to realize that there are plenty of reasons for your partner—or family member, colleague, etc.—to be upset. However, when stressed or distressed it's easy to revert back to the standard default or, even worse, to misread your partner's simple distress as something more dangerous—like anger or blame or punishment (which sets up an unpleasant row). That's why my fifth maxim is:

It's not all about me.

Of course, it's possible that *part* of your partner's upset is about you. For example, you're not carrying your share of running the household, so the work pressure is greater, perhaps you snored and kept your partner awake, or didn't back him or her up in the argument with the kids, or laughed when the star player was sold. That's why my maxim is: **It's not ALL about me.** The "all" is incredibly important because it stops you focusing in on your small part of the upset and forgetting you are not responsible for allocating work at your partner's place of employment, or managing his or her relationship with the children, or the financial decisions of a baseball club.

If you're dealing with a crisis at the moment, I'd like you to imagine three boxes. One is labeled "my problems." One is labeled "your problems." The last is labeled "our relationship's problems." Next, think of all the current issues: how many belong in your box, how many in your partner's box, and how many are about the relationship (how the two of you interact with each other). I doubt they are ALL in your box, because: it's not all about you. And if your partner is not responsible for sorting out the contents of your box, you are not responsible for his or her box (and the material in the relationship box is a shared responsibility and not ALL down to you).

The concept of boxes is important—couples dealing with infidelity find it particularly helpful—because it brings us to another important ingredient for coming out of this crisis stronger, wiser, and happier.

GOOD BOUNDARIES

Many people find relationship boundaries hard to grasp—partly because the ideal of romantic love is about surrendering and two people blending into one, but mainly because it is all a question of degree. On the one hand, we should support our partner, but, on the other, we are not responsible for them. We need to be connected but not enmeshed in every corner of each other's lives. No matter how much we love our partner, we still need our personal space: to be separate without disengaging all together.

Perhaps the best way to understand boundaries is to look at how they operate in a work environment. Each person has a job description: explaining the full extent of their responsibilities. For example, if you are the receptionist, your employers will not expect you to drive a delivery truck. Meanwhile, if you work as part of a team, you can reasonably be expected to take a message or cover for one of your colleagues.

There are also boundaries between work and your private life. Although modern work practices are chipping away at these boundaries, we know when it is acceptable for our employers to contact us and when it is not. With company secrets—for example, turnover or a new product line—there are rules about what is acceptable to discuss with people outside the firm.

Work places are also hierarchical—rather like a family—where the management plays a similar role to parents. So, there are boundaries between what the bosses should and should not discuss with the workers (for example, tensions between different personalities in the boardroom are nothing to do with the staff).

Turning to marriage, what makes for good relationship boundaries? First, they need to be flexible and able to respond to different circumstances. For example, if your partner's father is dying, he or she will need more support and help. (Although you still can't do the grieving for your partner—that's his or her responsibility.) In effect, you might take something out of his or her inbox and put it into yours—on a temporary basis.

If the first aspect of good boundaries is where they are drawn, the second is how protective they are. If they are too low, they can easily be knocked down and you can be drawn into your partner's problems (for example, his relationship with his mother or her issues with her boss) even when they have nothing to do with you. Conversely, if the boundaries are too high, you will find it hard to spot if your partner really does need your help.

As well as personal boundaries, there are boundaries round an adult couple relationship (what should and should not be discussed with other people), between parents and children (so children are not drawn into adult problems and parents are not overinvolved in their children's lives), and around the family as a whole.

When boundaries are too low: Esmé, thirty-five, had been single for a long time. After several months of counseling, her confidence grew and she entered into a serious relationship for the first time in almost five years. Unfortunately, they hit difficulties and her boyfriend panicked and ended it. The pain for Esmé was so overwhelming that she spent the first couple of weeks almost permanently on the phone to her friends getting them to talk down her anxiety and soothe her fears. There is nothing wrong with getting help, but Esmé needed round-the-clock support.

"If I get on a train to go somewhere, I literally can't sit there with my own thoughts because they will be too horrible, so I will work my way through my closest friends—who have been wonderful—until I find someone who's in," she explained.

She had lowered her boundaries completely—so her friends were responsible for regulating her emotions—and lost sight of her own resources. However, I knew she had turned a corner when she told me: "I've been feeling really horrible but I sort of think that's normal. I've been through a horrible rejection. I'm still crying, and feeling down, but it's not as overwhelming as before. I'm still phoning friends but not so often and sometimes have a little weep instead. It's all so unfamiliar because I've never allowed myself to have these sorts of feelings before. But I'm right, aren't I: This is OK?"

I was happy to explain that Esmé was grieving—a healthy part of recovery from a relationship.

Meanwhile, Louise, fifty-one, was facing multiple problems. Her husband of over twenty-five years had left home and started a new relationship; he was angry and uncommunicative and their daughter was traumatized by the fallout. Her counseling sessions were filled with what her friends thought, her parents believed, her acupuncturist had said and even the opinions of her hairdresser.

"But what do you think and feel?" I asked.

"Sometimes I don't know which way to turn," Louise sighed.

"So you pick up the phone?"

"It gets me through the long dark nights, when I'm down and alone, and I get a fresh perspective—which must be good."

"How do you separate the helpful from the not so helpful?"

Louise looked at me blankly.

Unfortunately, it was also making her focus on what her husband might be thinking and stopping her from developing her own sense of what was right for her. Over the next few weeks, Louise started to cut down on the phone calls, not fill her free time to bursting point, and leave enough time for personal reflection.

"It had almost been like I was asking my friends to vote on what I should do or I kept asking for advice until it matched with what I thought," she explained a couple of weeks later. At this point, she could begin to think for herself because, ultimately, she was the world's expert on herself.

When boundaries are unbalanced: Amanda, fifty-two, wanted to understand why she couldn't form lasting relationships with men—despite having lots of lifelong intense friendships. It quickly became obvious that Amanda had sky-high boundaries with men—she would not sleep with someone unless they had been going out for at least three months – but once she had let a woman into "best friend" category she became completely available to her.

"I switch my phone on around 6 a.m. when I get up for work. I'll tell friends that I'm in a hurry, about to go out the door, but they'll have to 'just tell me something,'" Amanda explained, "and this will continue until 10 p.m. when I switch my phone off and go to bed."

She had about fourteen close friends who she spoke to, texted, or emailed every day, and would see each about once a week. ("Not much free time to see any potential partners," I wrote in my notes.)

"It's like I'm their permanently on-call agony aunt and if I left my phone on, I'd do a night shift too."

This role had not struck Amanda as a problem—"It's what friends do for each other"—until she had had a life-threatening illness and discovered that she could count on only one or two of these women in whom she had invested so much time.

"I've been there for them through their divorces, new men, and getting married. After that, they'll disappear for a while—until they are over the honeymoon phase and back on the phone again."

Her illness, and time off work, gave Amanda time to reflect and take stock. She had also shredded the numbers of friends who were "too busy" to visit her in hospital and put a timer on calls from friends.

"There will be a couple of minutes about my treatment and then it's onto all of their problems. I clocked an hour and a half on the ins and outs of one friend's legal problems. I can't cope. I've got to concentrate on my health, so now I've set an alarm that goes off after ten minutes and I tell them I've got to go."

I was relieved that Amanda had put in some appropriate boundaries (high enough to protect her but not so high people couldn't offer help). In addition, she had enough time to take stock. "It's like these girlfriends have been my surrogate partner, taking up my time and energy, but giving back nothing in return. I need to invest in myself. I want a relationship myself, not just listening to the problems of other people's relationships."

When there are no boundaries: When I explain boundaries, sometimes I watch the person on my couch getting lower and lower or becoming angry and resentful. They might intellectually accept the idea that ultimately they are responsible for their own life and their own problems —but not emotionally.

"So I might as well give up now, if no relationship is going to make me feel better," said Carrie-Ann. "What's the point?" Although she was thirty-one, I felt she was six years old. When I get these strong feelings, it is important to listen to them. So I asked about her childhood. It turned out that her father was remote and her mother was unhappy and wrapped up in her own problems. My guess was that nobody was around when she was small to pick her up when she fell. No wonder the romantic myth of the knight in shining armor (who would sweep us off our feet, put us onto the back of his horse, and take us off to his magic castle) or the passionate woman (whose love will redeem us and prove our masculinity) is so compelling. However, it can also leave us trapped (looking for someone to save us) rather than taking charge of our own life.

It's not that I don't believe in the transforming power of love. Of course relationships are a source of strength in difficult times. Helping our partner navigate his or her problems can make us feel strong and boost our self-esteem. However, our partner is our companion—an equal.

"But when my ex and I first met, the connection was incredible and I felt together we could do anything," Carrie-Ann explained. "And he told me he'd always be there to look out for me—no matter what, no matter when, I just needed to call and he'd be there."

When we looked more deeply at Carrie-Ann's ex, he had more than his fair share of problems himself: "He'd just come out of a very bitter divorce. His kids were angry and weren't talking to him and his business was struggling in the downturn." Their relationship had been off and on for three years and, although it had now officially ended, Carrie-Ann still found it hard to let go. "I know he needs some support because he doesn't talk to anybody about his feelings. How can I be close to him without putting on pressure? And be his woman without him realizing? He is tired from working all day and emotionally more down than he wants to admit," she explained.

In the same way that Carrie-Ann's ex could not "save" her, she couldn't "rescue" him. However much we love or are loved, ultimately we cannot live our beloved's life for him or her and neither can he or she do that for us in return. With appropriate boundaries, we are responsible for our own lives but willing to ask for help when we need it or offer it when our partner needs our help.

BOUNDARIES IN ACTION

The importance of good boundaries for the health of an organization is best illustrated by looking at what happens when they break down. So, think about what is currently making you or your colleagues unhappy at work: What boundaries have been crossed? Personal, team, or organization? (If you don't have a job at the moment, think of an organization that you know well; it might be a club, charity, or somewhere you volunteer.)

Below are a series of questions about boundaries. Can you find an example from your current or previous workplaces?

• What happens when job descriptions are ignored?

• What happens when the boundary between work and home breaks down and personal issues are brought into the office?

• What happens when management has low boundaries and discusses issues with one particular employee but not others at a similar level?

• What happens if the management has very high boundaries and keeps a lot of information back?

• What happens when two work colleagues have a relationship outside the office—perhaps they are lovers, partners, or father and son? In what way are the boundaries confused and how does this impact on everybody else?

• What happens when boundaries are erected within a team, so there are people who are "in" and those who are "out"?

• What happens when someone is too rigid with their boundaries and refuses to be flexible under any circumstances?

WHEN BOUNDARIES BREAK DOWN

When someone feels helpless or hopeless and at the mercy of other people's actions, it is nearly always due to poor boundaries. Maybe they have let down their own personal boundaries or tried to knock down their partner's boundaries (without success), or maybe the boundary between the couple and everyone else has collapsed. Here are four common examples of compromised boundaries: infidelity, relationship breakdown, children in crisis, and mixed signals from a potential partner.

Infidelity

When Nick, forty-three, had an affair, his wife, Rebecca, forty, was angry about him being sexually unfaithful, but she found other aspects of his betrayal harder to get over: "I hate the idea that he discussed me, asked her for advice on how to 'handle' me. As if I'm a horse that's going to bolt at any second. He told her about our sex life and how it left him unsatisfied. Did he tell me? No! And that's not all; they discussed a life together and he kept a note of the date of her son's birthday—because she couldn't leave until he was older."

"I don't remember writing down his birthday. I must have done because it's in my handwriting but I didn't dwell on it or tick off the days," Nick replied. "I've apologized for betraying Rebecca, I accept it was a massive abuse of trust. What more can I do?"

"But you had plans. That's what I can't understand. Solid plans. Where you were going to live and you were going to buy a boat."

"It was just silly fantasy," Nick said glumly.

It had been six months since Nick's affair was discovered but I sensed they'd had this argument many times.

"He'll be sitting at the computer staring out of the window and I know he's thinking about her, missing her and wishing he could speak to her," said Rebecca.

"You know I want to be with you," Nick replied.

"Sometimes, I think they're still in contact and I'll go through his inbox. I found a couple of emails from her."

"I didn't reply to them."

"But you didn't delete them either."

How boundaries have been compromised: At the most basic level, an affair breaks the sexually exclusive boundary around a relationship. However, once that barrier has been crossed, there are a series of other secrets and confidential material that is shared with the affair partner. Sometimes, a line is crossed when the partner who has been unfaithful brings their lover to the house or has sex in the family car. On a more complex level, the discoverer of the affair will also cross the normal boundaries of confidentiality (when searching for evidence) and read private mail. Although it is understandable (and helpful for recovery) in the short term, to be continually checking on a partner six months after the affair ended can become an invasion of privacy. However, the most destructive element of Rebecca and Nick's situation was the way she tried to read Nick's mind (as if she could enter into his thoughts, divine what they meant, and hold the results against him).

"How do you know that Nick is thinking about the other woman?" I asked. "He could be wondering who will win the 3.47 race at the Kentucky Derby or where he left his wallet."

"I haven't lived with him for nearly twenty years without learning something," Rebecca replied.

"Why don't you ask him instead?" I suggested.

"Last Sunday, when I caught you crying in the backyard, were you missing her?"

"No. I was thinking about us. I can't go on like this anymore."

In many ways, mind reading is crossing your partner's personal boundary and imagining that you can understand everything about him or her.

When Rebecca stopped making assumptions about Nick's behavior and started asking instead, she had a very different take on his affair: "Because I wouldn't have had an affair unless I really was planning to leave, I sort of assumed that Nick would be the same."

By reasserting the boundary between Rebecca and Nick, that they were not two peas in a pod but different people with different understandings of what the affair meant, we were able to change the focus from the affair to improving their relationship (thereby reinforcing the boundary around their relationship and placing the affair partner firmly on the outside).

STOPPING MIND READING

Whether your partner has had an affair or not, mind reading is one of the most unhelpful relationship habits. It assumes that you can speak for your partner and know his or her opinions, feelings ,or reasons for doing something. It is particularly dangerous for long-term couples—who think they know each other very well—as the "evidence" for these interpretations are often based on some random statement from years ago, stripped of its original context, and overlooks how people change over time. Worse still, "knowing what your partner is thinking" robs them of the ability to surprise you and makes for a dull relationship. So what is the alternative?

1. **Use "I" statements instead of "we" statements.** Don't talk for your partner and say "We enjoy vacations in Mexico" but "I enjoy vacations in Mexico." This gives your partner the chance to consider his or her opinion: "I've really enjoyed our Mexican vacations but I would quite fancy a change."

2. **Check it out.** Instead of assuming your partner's reaction (for example, angry), ask what he or she is feeling. It might be only annoyance.

3. **Look for jumps in your logic.** When we spend too long analyzing something, it is easy to take a few random pieces of information and blow them up into something hurtful. For example, "My partner is not interested in sex ... and therefore she finds me repulsive." (It could be that she was tired or maybe found the way you approached her a turn off.)

4. **Try asking.** Instead of making an assumption, ask a question: "Why did you say no to having sex last night?" or even better: "What would have made you more likely to say yes?"

Relationship breakdown

When we're in love, we interpret everything that our beloved does in the best possible light and, even if he or she does something hurtful, we put the slight down as a misunderstanding or something temporary: tiredness, stress or being in a bad mood. Meanwhile, our beloved gives us the same benefit of the doubt and we have a virtuous circle where one good deed sparks another. Unfortunately, when a relationship is in crisis or breaking down, we interpret everything that our beloved does in the worst possible light and, instead of their failings being down to something temporary, it shows their character in a new, unflattering light. He or she is selfish, out to get us or downright cruel. With this viewpoint, we have a downward spiral where one "so-called" bad deed sparks another—which justifies something equally unpleasant and so on.

After Tim, thirty-two, told his wife Sandra, also thirty-two, that he didn't know if he loved her anymore, she was heartbroken. When he couldn't explain why and, worse still, in Sandra's eyes, showed no desire to try and fix the problem, she asked him to move out. At the next session, Tim arrived full of anger and it did not take him long to launch an attack on Sandra.

"She's been going through money like its water, buying all sorts of things to do up the children's bedrooms and they were only done last year," he complained.

"Why do you think she's done that?" I asked.

"Isn't it obvious?" he replied. "She wants to punish me by running up bills and making me pay them."

Tim might have been right, but this was just one possible interpretation. So, instead of making an accusation, I suggested that he asked a question. It took a while for him to calm down enough but finally he said: "Why did you decorate the children's bedrooms?"

"Because it was the only thing that stopped me thinking about you and crying. I'd also sleep better because I was exhausted from stripping wallpaper."

Unfortunately, Tim's anger had made Sandra uncooperative, too. Instead of chivying their boys along after swimming, she had allowed them to mess around in the changing rooms and they were late for his pickup.

When this downward spiral of misinterpretation, retaliation, and revenge goes on for a long time, it is easy to consider your partner or ex-lover as evil. However, Simon Baron-Cohen, Professor of Psychology and Psychiatry at Cambridge University, UK, thinks it is deeply unhelpful to think of people as evil and brand their behavior as incomprehensible. He believes that what we consider evil is better understood as "empathy erosion"—where someone has no space in their mind to consider the impact on other people. In his book *Zero Degrees of Empathy: A New Theory of Human Cruelty* (Allen Lane, 2011), Baron-Cohen interviewed a man who smashed a bottle into a man's face and killed him for staring at him in a bar. When Baron-Cohen asked if he was sorry, the man told him, "Were the kids at school sorry when they bullied me? Was my boss sorry when he fired me? Was my neighbor sorry when he deliberately hit my car? And you ask me if I'm sorry that that piece of shit died? Of course I'm not sorry. He had it coming to him. No one's ever been sorry for how they've treated me."

So what causes empathy erosion? In a few cases, like the prisoner interviewed by Baron-Cohen, it is the result of sustained emotional damage as a child. Scientists have scanned the brains of women who were sexually abused and found abnormalities in their empathy circuit (for example, a smaller than usual amygdala). However, in the majority of cases—and in particular the relationship problems that I see—the empathy erosion is caused by something so commonplace that we almost don't see it: alcohol, fatigue, depression, or stress. No wonder once-loving couples can slip so easily into angry sniping or all-out warfare. Just like Baron-Cohen's prisoner, these clients are so wrapped up in their own misery it is impossible to empathize and understand the impact of their actions on those around them.

Time and again, I help individuals who are overwhelmed by the pain of a nasty divorce. They will often be having a good week until their soon to be ex-partner does something horrible and knocks them off course. Although I sympathize with their upset, I find it much better to help them step back and wonder why their partner behaved in an unhelpful manner—rather than branding him or her "evil" or "mad" or "ill." Normally, it's because they are hurt or frightened and, like an animal trapped in a corner, bite or kick when approached.

How boundaries have been compromised: In some ways, this is the opposite of infidelity (where the boundaries have been removed). When a relationship is breaking down—or at risk—one or both partners will raise their barriers and make it hard for the other person to penetrate (to try and protect themselves from further hurt). Meanwhile, the situation is often made worse because some people will try and batter down their partner's high boundaries by trying to shock them into behaving differently or to deliberately hurt them. "I thought, if only he could hurt like I'm hurting, then he'd finally register how I'm feeling and maybe think again," Sandra explained. However, it had just made Tim retreat further behind his defensive barrier and empathize even less.

MEASURE YOUR EMPATHY LEVELS

If your relationship is currently in crisis, go through the list of questions twice. On the first time, answer as if you are imagining dealing with a friend (or your partner when the relationship was happy) and the second time imagining current or recent interactions with your partner. Choose one of the following answers for each statement:

STRONGLY AGREE	SLIGHTLY AGREE	SLIGHTLY DISAGREE	STRONGLY DISAGREE

1. I find it hard to know what to do in a social situation. _____

2. I get upset if I see people suffering on news programs. _____

3. Even when I'm pretty sure I'm right, I'm patient enough to listen to other people's arguments. _____

4. I feel uneasy when someone I know casually tells me a personal problem. _____

5. I'm not particularly bothered if I'm late for a social occasion or a business appointment. _____

6. I can spot if someone says one thing but means another. _____

7. In a conversation, I tend to focus on my thoughts rather than what the other person might be saying. _____

8. It is hard sometimes to see why things upset people so much. _____

9. I am quick to notice if someone is feeling awkward or uncomfortable. _____

10. When someone is upset about something, I find a way to distract them or change the subject. _____

11. I can be blunt, which some people take as rudeness, when I'm just speaking my mind. _____

12. Other people tell me I'm good at understanding their thoughts and feelings. _____

13. I usually stay emotionally detached when watching a movie. _____

14. I am good at predicting what people will do. _____

15. I can normally appreciate the other person's point of view, even if I don't agree with it. _____

16. I tend to get emotionally involved in other people's problems. _____

17. If someone asked for my opinion on something they had bought, I would answer truthfully, even if I didn't think much of it. _____

18. If I don't know enough to properly understand, I'll ask more questions. _____

19. I am able to make decisions without being unduly influenced by other people's feelings. _____

20. I can sense if someone thinks I'm intruding, even if he or she doesn't say anything. _____

Scoring

Score two points if you "strongly agree" or one point if you "slightly agree" with the following questions: 2, 3, 6, 9, 12, 14, 15, 16, 18, 20. Score nothing for "slightly disagree" or "strongly disagree."

Score two points if you "strongly disagree" or one point if you "slightly disagree" with the following questions: 1, 4, 5, 7, 8, 10, 11, 13, 17, 19. Score nothing if you "slightly agree" or "strongly agree."

Results

0–16   **Low empathy:** You find it hard to step into other people's shoes.

17–26   **Average:** You are aware of other people's feelings and act on them.

27–32   **Good empathy:** Friends will consider you a good listener and bring you their problems.

33–40   **Very high empathy:** Sometimes you are so concerned about other people that it is hard to know your own mind or you often downplay your own needs.

Children in crisis

Once I have helped my clients to stop using negative ways of filling their inner void and begin to stabilize, they often tell me: "I've had a really good week but my daughter has been impossible" or "I'm fine but I'm worried about my son because I had to go into school after he attacked another boy." Sometimes the child's behavior has been a problem for a while—but the parent has had more pressing issues to bring to therapy. Sometimes the parent beginning to recover allows the child to release all their pent up worry and frustration. Whatever the reasons, when children start acting out (throwing tantrums, being rude, disruptive, or aggressive), it is nearly always a sign that boundaries have been compromised.

Alison, forty-seven, and Miles, forty-five, were going through a diffi-cult divorce and their two daughters and one son were caught in the middle. Alison blamed their problems on Miles leaving (and quickly establishing a new relationship) and Miles blamed Alison for turning the children against him. (There was probably some truth in both these allegations.) However, to break the blame cycle, I put a pile of coins on the table in front of Alison and Miles and asked them to choose a coin to represent themselves, their partner and each of their children. Next I asked them to show the family dynamics five years ago—when they were happy—by arranging the coins to demonstrate who was close to whom. Next, I asked them to pick another set of coins and sculpt their family today.

In the first sculpture, they both had their eldest daughter closest to Miles and the younger daughter closest to Alison—with the son (who was the youngest and only eight) shuffling backward and forward. Although mother and father were close to each other, I was interested that the eldest daughter—who played a lot of sport like her father—had been placed even nearer Miles than Alison.

In the second sculpture, there was a divide between Miles and Alison (not surprisingly) but the eldest daughter and the younger daughter had switched places. The elder daughter had been sending angry texts to her father and the younger daughter (who had probably been jealous of her sister's special relationship) had leaped into the gap and become her father's confident. There had also been several nasty scraps between these two children.

How boundaries have been compromised: When parents are coop-erating and have a healthy boundary around their relationship, they are responsible for adult decisions: general disciplining of the children, management of the family budget, resolving work issues, choices about schooling, etc. Unfortunately, when the parental boundaries are weak or shifting, one or more children can get drawn into suballiances with their mother or father. Not only does this flood a child with adult issues—I have many clients who were asked as a child "Is it OK if I divorce your mother" or told by their mother about the sexually transmitted diseases that she had caught from their father—but it further weakens the adult boundaries. Before too long, children are taking sides and acting out their anger to the other parent or withdrawing into themselves and turning the anger inward.

When Miles and Alison understood the concept of boundaries, they made a conscious decision to try and resolve parenting issues between themselves and stop the suballiances. Alison rearranged the coins so that she and Miles were closer and the children were at a greater distance but each equally close to their parents: "I'm not suggesting that we should get back together," she explained, "but we can start to discuss issues civilly together without involving the children."

A few weeks later, when I was seeing just Alison, she reported that their eldest daughter, who had just turned fourteen, had been very difficult. "It's like I'm treading on egg shells. If I flout one of her demands she just explodes and gets really abusive. Fortunately, we were at the home of an old family friend who calmed her down and listened to her. Later, my friend told me, 'She just wants to be a little girl again.'"

So we looked at this event through the lens of boundaries. Alison's daughter was crossing the threshold between being a girl and a woman. Furthermore, Alison had weakened the boundaries between what she would and would not allow (clothes, bedtimes, etc.) as she hoped to "appease" or "compensate" her daughter for the pain she'd been going through.

"Boundaries make children feel safe and contained," I explained. "Think of 'emotionally holding' her so that she doesn't spin out of control, if that doesn't sound too abstract. Decide on your new rules for a fourteen-year-old and stick to them. You also need to give her the message: 'I know things have been tough but Daddy and I are going to sort things out, so you don't have to worry.'"

Divorce is not the only situation where boundaries are compromised; step-parenting is fraught with boundary issues, and in any family there are times when one parent will be closer to a child—for example, during a serious illness (where one parent is the principal carer) or after the birth of a baby (because of dependence on the mother).

SCULPTING YOUR BOUNDARIES

To get a better picture of the boundaries in your family and discover what needs to change, try this exercise that I often do with clients:

- Take a pile of change, buttons, or other tokens and spread them out on the table.

- Choose a token to represent yourself, your partner, your children, and anybody else who is significant—for example, your parents, in-laws, or au pair. If you are single, you might want to put your friends and your ex into the sculpture.

- Start with you and your partner (or ex). How far apart should your tokens be to represent the state of your relationship.

- Next, place each of your children into the sculpture. Is your daughter closer to you than your partner? What about your son? Does either child act as a go-between? How could you show that? Does one of your children act as protector for you or your partner? What is the best way to show that?

- If you have more than one child, make certain the sculpture represents the closeness, rivalries, and alliances between the siblings, too.

- Finally, add a token for your parents and any other significant people in your life and find the right place to represent degrees of separation and closeness.

- Mentally step back and have a look at your sculpture. What are the patterns? What strikes you as significant? Are all the tokens so close together that it feels a bit claustrophobic? Are they so far apart that you feel lonely or disconnected? If you are married, is there anybody who is coming between you and your partner? If you are single, is there enough room in the sculpture for a new partner or are your children, friends, and ex crowding them out?

- The final part of this exercise is perhaps the most important. If you could make any changes to the sculpture, what would they be?

- Move the tokens and reflect on how the different boundaries might feel.

- How could you turn this arrangement into a reality?

Mixed signals from a potential partner

Many of my single clients feel out of control in the first tentative steps of a relationship. "I'm fine if I'm not particularly interested in someone," explained Cicely, thirty-two. "I'm cool, it's a case of 'If he wants to phone fine and if he doesn't, well, that's fine too.' But if I cross over into caring, I spin out of control. 'What's he thinking?' and 'If he really cared, he'd want to see me next weekend.'" Cicely could keep her anxiety in check while she was at work, but the moment she left work it was like she became controlled by all her worst instincts. "I'll phone one of my friends who will tell me to leave it, but another will tell me to call him and I'm even more confused." She would then start plotting to achieve her goal. Her most recent relationship—about three months' duration—had broken down over just such a campaign.

"It was Easter and I thought, 'Wouldn't it be nice to see each other over the extended weekend'—especially as he'd been really busy and it hadn't been possible to meet up. So I started by dropping a hint: how we'd both be up North over the holiday. However, he told me, 'But we live just a few streets away in London.' So I didn't know what to think; he was sending such mixed messages. One moment, he's texting several times a day and then he can't fit me into his 'busy schedule.' So in the end, I forced the issue and we talked about 'us' and he decided the relationship was not for him."

How boundaries have been compromised: Even though Cicely and her ex had been on fewer than ten dates and were not officially "girlfriend" and "boyfriend," she had let down all her boundaries. First, she had made herself completely available. "If a girlfriend phoned with possible plans for Sunday and I'd known his baseball was canceled, I'd be holding open that slot as it would be nice for us to do something together. So I'd take a rain check on seeing my girlfriend," she explained. Second, she was already outsourcing her self-esteem to this man: "If he texted or phoned, I'd feel on top of the world, but if he didn't, then I'd feel undesirable and, at my worst moments, completely worthless." Worse still, she was trying to knock down his boundaries—discover his plans, check his movements through Facebook and Twitter, and work out what he was thinking.

Chelsea, who had an overly intrusive mother, came into counseling after her three-month relationship had swung from hot (spending almost every free moment together) to cold (where he had unilaterally declared the relationship over and disappeared). In effect, they had both let down their boundaries and become entirely enmeshed in each other's lives. Chelsea's ex had even started discussing the possibility of marriage but, almost the next week, he had panicked. On one hand, being really close to someone is wonderful, but on the other, it is frightening—especially if like Chelsea your parents fought all the time; at eighteen, she had described marriage in a college project as: "being trapped in a perpetual battle of unhappiness." Chelsea's ex had had a difficult childhood, too (his father had been an alcoholic), so he had put up the highest and most unhelpful barrier of them all: he'd run away (just like his father had done when he was a teenager).

During counseling, Chelsea's ex contacted her and they started texting again. Fortunately, we had covered boundaries and, instead of dropping them, Chelsea kept them at a reasonable height (as opposed to an unreasonable one and refusing to talk to him). A few weeks later, she arranged to meet him in a bar with a group of friends (which provided a boundary against their conversation getting too intimate too quickly). The next time, she asked if he would help run a stall at a county fair (so there would be no alcohol and the associated risk of lowering boundaries) and she had a social event in the evening (so the encounter had time boundaries too). Finally, she initiated a discussion: "How could things be different this time?"—rather than just jumping into bed with him.

WRITING YOUR RULES OF ENGAGEMENT

Whether you are starting on a new relationship or your long-term relationship is in crisis (and your partner has left), the best way of keeping appropriate boundaries (not too high or too low) is to draw up a contract with yourself. In this way, the sane side of yourself can set the rules, rather than the anxious or needy side making them up as you go along. Here are some questions to ask yourself:

- *When is the latest that I can phone?*

- *How long should I be on the phone?* (If calls last too long they can spin out of control or compromise boundaries.)

- *What is the latest that I should send a message?* (Texting under the influence of alcohol or when tired is best avoided.)

- *How late should I check messages?* (Too late can make for a bad night's sleep or encourage web-stalking.)

- *How long should I leave it before answering a text or email?* (In this way, you can reflect not only on what you want to say but how it might be received.)

- *What tone should I use?* (If you are angry, you will send angry emails and make a difficult situation worse.)

- *What are the exceptions to the rules?* (Try to make these as few as possible—real emergencies—and redraft your rules in light of your experiences.)

To give you some inspiration, here are some of the "rules" that Cicely drew up for herself:

- A first date should not last longer than an hour and a half.

- From three dates to three months together, no more than two dates a week.

- After he's asked for three dates, I can suggest further outings (e.g. "I've read good reviews about this movie, do you fancy seeing it?").

- Don't sleep with anyone until the fourth date.

- When the trail goes cold—i.e. no communication from him—I will wait four days from his last message before contacting him. (In the meantime, she could get on with her life and if tempted to obsess, she would remind herself she was not permitted to do anything until four days were up.)

- No asking for advice from friends—i.e. should I call him—during the first three months.

- If I find myself trying to mind read or second-guess him, I will tell myself "It's pointless, so stop it" and do something more productive.

- Don't hold potential windows for dates and, instead, accept a firm offer from a friend.

- If I want to do something on a certain date, I should ask rather than drop hints.

- When I've been going out for less than three months with a man, I should not plan in my head further than two weekends ahead.

WHAT CREATES GOOD BOUNDARIES

Once you have become aware of the central importance of boundaries for feeling good about yourself and maintaining a happy and healthy relationship, it becomes easy to spot when someone else has compromised boundaries (and lets other people take advantage) or too high boundaries (and does not let people help, switches off, or runs away). So how do you avoid falling into those traps yourself?

Awareness: Think about your own boundaries. If you had to draw them, what would they be made of? Plexiglass (like a police riot shield), concrete (like a castle), fabric (like drapes)? How high would they be? Around your ankles, above your head, across your chest? Over the next few days, monitor what happens to your boundaries. What makes you raise and lower them and how do those changes feel?

Saying no: In many ways, this is the key to good boundaries. Unfortunately, many people think being in love means doing anything your beloved asks, but this risks turning yourself into a doormat or become increasingly resentful. So let me be clear: It's OK to say no. Sometimes, we simply don't have the time, energy or ability—or perhaps the request is unreasonable. However, saying "no" doesn't mean being unhelpful or rejecting—especially if you use the ABC approach. A is for address: "I would like to help." B is for bridge: "but" or "however" or "unfortunately," and C is for communicate or compromise: "I have to finish this report for a meeting at 5 p.m." or "I could look at it tomorrow" or "I know someone who could help instead."

Stop outsourcing your self-esteem: Clients who find saying "no" difficult are normally worried about how the other person will react. "She will get angry if ... I don't drop everything and come around immediately?" or "He might not like me if ... I don't agree to sleep with him?" So I always ask: Why does your ex-wife or some random stranger's opinion matter so much? Wanting to be liked by everybody is often a sign that you need everybody's approval.

Withdrawing: If you are about to lose your temper or someone else has crossed the line into rage, it is likely that boundaries—particularly between acceptable and unacceptable behavior—will be crossed. It is better to make a strategic withdrawal, and talk about the problem when everybody is calmer, than to stay and make a difficult situation worse.

Respect other people's boundaries: It is fine to sympathize and offer support but not to take over or control—however much we love someone. The two jobs of a parent are to nurture and empower (so children have enough confidence to leave home one day) and these are the same attributes that we should bring to our relationship with our partner.

FIFTH MAXIM IN ACTION

A greater understanding of what belongs in your box and what belongs in your partner's box makes for a better relationship. Without good enough boundaries, you risk becoming overwhelmed by your partner's material or imagining that your behavior has triggered his or her upset. At this point, telling yourself **It's not all about me** will calm you down and provide enough time to explore and understand the issue rather than losing your temper and acting out.

When you look deeper, even a personal attack might not be ALL about you. Take Oscar, sixty-one, and Lily, fifty-two, who had been married for ten years and together for thirteen. Oscar had seen an inspiring quote on his gym wall about how regular exercise helped mental as well as physical health.

"He came home and criticized me for not going to the gym enough, and considering I'd spent the previous day in casualty because my doctor had been concerned about a bad migraine ..." said Lily as the temperature in the room rose five notches.

"I've admitted that my timing was off."

"It was so mean because I'm in the best shape of my life. I might not go to the gym but I play tennis twice a week and I do an intense yoga class."

Before I could begin to explore the first issue, Oscar had lobbed another one into the room.

"It's the same with your drinking, too."

"I love a glass when I'm cooking and yes I drink most nights but I never get drunk."

"You don't listen to me," Oscar retorted.

"Because you make me mad with your hurtful comments."

I stopped the escalating anger by reminding them of my fifth maxim: **It's not all about me.**

"It seems like it is to me," said Lily. "He's saying I'm lazy and drink too much. That sounds pretty personal."

So I explained about projection and how issues that make us uncomfortable are not just suppressed but further distanced from ourselves by pushing the problem area on to someone else. (For a recap on projection, see page 106 in the previous chapter.)

"Tell me about your health Oscar," I asked.

"I've had a bypass operation and recently had a stent added," he replied. (A small mesh tube that is used to treat threatened arteries.)

"You've also had prostrate cancer," said Lily.

I mentally did the arithmetic, Oscar was also nine years older than her.

"Nobody likes to think about their own mortality, so it's easier to worry about someone else's health instead." The temperature in the room was dropping. "And why might Oscar be worried about the amount people drink?"

"My father was an alcoholic and he used to regularly hit my mother," he confessed.

"So alcohol consumption is going to be a sensitive subject."

He nodded.

"And the timing of this when I'd been to the hospital, you don't like me getting sick," said Lily.

"Why might that be?" I asked.

"Oscar only said this to me once but I'll always remember it. Right at the beginning of our relationship, I was really sick—head in a bucket—and he was not at all sympathetic, maybe even angry. He told me it reminded him of how helpless he felt when his mother was ill."

"So let's go back to my original question, Lily. Was this ALL about you?"

"No, it was also about Oscar."

And this is an important lesson that goes along with **It's not all about me** because criticism (and what people get upset about) often says more about the accuser than the accused.

However, it was important to understand why this criticism had struck home so strongly that Lily had immediately taken it to heart and made it ALL about her.

"Why were you upset about being thought not to do enough exercise—when clearly you do far more than most women of your age?"

"It was so critical."

"So why might criticism be such a sore spot. Tell me about criticism when you were growing up?"

"My father was very critical and dubbed me the 'big brat' and he would really verbally abuse my mother. Once it got so bad at the dinner table, when I was about eight, I threw my plate against the wall to divert his anger from my mother. It worked because he was angry with me instead."

At this point, I need to introduce one my mother's favorite sayings: "The fish are rising well." What it means is that we're all fish swimming along at the bottom of the river. Up on the surface is a juicy worm wriggling away; instead of getting on with our own fishy business, we're tempted by the bait and get hooked. If that image doesn't work for you, try one from my friend Kate. When she's tempted to intervene in something that's not her business (or outside her zone of control), she tells herself, "Not my monkeys, not my circus."

However, if you can remember the fifth maxim—**It's not all about me**—it is easier to recognize what belongs to you and what belongs to your partner. And however much the worm wriggles, not to swallow it, and however badly the monkeys behave, not to try to train them.

GREEN SHOOTS

- Boundaries come in all sorts of shapes and sizes: personal, relationship, between adults and children, and around families.

- If you are having problems with your partner, a potential lover, or your children are being disruptive, it is likely that the boundaries are unclear, shifting, or too high.

- The fifth maxim to change your life is: "It's not all about me."

CHAPTER SIX

The Art
of the Possible

Although you are responsible for your own material (your box) and your partner or prospective partners for theirs (his or her box), what happens when he or she is doing something annoying or even damaging to your equilibrium? Of course, you can understand why it upsets you so much—and lower the temperature—but you're still left with the undesirable behavior.

Returning to the mindfulness guru Jon Kabat-Zinn, you could see the dirty cat bowl in the sink and either smile because it has taught you so much (which needs a level of enlightenment most of us struggle to reach) or wash it up yourself (which risks us becoming a doormat). However, it's equally OK to want to resolve the problem and stop the cat dish being left in the sink in the first place. In other words, how do you deal with the material in the relationship box—where your issues and your partner's collide?

SIXTH MAXIM

With each of my books and all my counseling, there is one *central task:* improving communication. I believe that love needs skills as well as connection and that puts the next maxim at the heart of everything:

I can ask, you can say no, and we can negotiate.

It sounds relatively straightforward but actually it's packed with danger. What if you ask and your partner ignores, refuses, or even belittles your request? Sometimes it's easier to drop hints (because that feels less rejecting than asking outright and being turned down) or to manipulate (so your partner has no choice) or to bank on love (because you'll be so connected that your partner will know without having to be asked).

Sometimes, it is hard to say no because you're frightened your partner won't love you anymore and therefore agree with a heavy heart (and become resentful) or say nothing in order to avoid the immediate conflict (and go your own sweet way later). The other alternative is to rationalizes away any disagreement and pretend it doesn't matter (and slowly but surely end up switching off all your feelings and risk being brother and sister rather than lovers).

Finally, if you never saw your parents disagree, discuss their differences and make up afterward, you will have no role model for negotiation —because you were more used to tantrums, emotional blackmail, and riding rough shod over each other. Unfortunately, they don't teach negotiation at school either, so how are you going to know how to do it?

That's why this chapter is dedicated to a skill called assertiveness. It takes time to make this approach second nature, but please persevere. I can always tell when a couple has turned a corner, or an individual is making progress in their counseling when I begin to see them becoming assertive. So what does it look like and how will you know when you've achieved it? I like this test:

Assertiveness is your ability to act in harmony with your self-esteem without hurting others.

BEING ASSERTIVE

Assertiveness training has got a bad name—because some people confuse it with being aggressive. So, to be clear, what I'm talking about is being open and honest about your feelings and needs—rather than manipulating or demanding—but being equally respectful of your partner's feelings and needs, too. In effect, assertiveness boils down to three interlocking rights:

My Rights	My Partner's Rights
To ask for what I need	To refuse your request
To be listened to and taken seriously	To be listened to and taken seriously
To be myself and have time/space to develop as an individual	To rely on you for love, consideration, and support

As it is much easier to take the speck out of someone else's eye than the plank out of your own, I'd like you to watch other people communicate—for example, at work, among your friendship circle, and at any club or group to which you belong.

- What builds agreement?

- What goes wrong between people?

- How good are people at asking and how do they respond if the request is refused?

- What happens when people don't listen?

- How does each person's "rights" balance out?

When you've had enough time to notice the patterns of good and bad communication, what ONE thing would you like to change in your own behavior?

OPTIONS FOR ASKING

I'm going to break down the three component parts of "I can ask, you can say no and we can negotiate" and look at them one by one. Starting with "I can ask," let's look at the different ways that people attempt to get their needs met:

1. Don't even hint but hope your partner will somehow know what you want. (With this option, love is a guarantee for getting your needs met because the myth claims you will be so tuned into each other, all difference and misunderstandings are magically overcome.) When your partner fails to respond positively, you either become resentful or fear that he or she no longer loves you.

2. Hint indirectly but accept no and end up resentful if your partner doesn't hear the hint, misunderstands, or simply doesn't realize the importance of the request (perhaps in his or her world if someone truly wants something they ask directly).

3. Hint openly but accept no and end up resentful. Unfortunately, it is still easy for your partner to minimize the importance of the request, especially if he or she is busy and dealing with other people—such as children or an employer—who are clearer about their needs or simply demand something. Under these circumstances, your hint may be recognized but drops down the list of his or her priorities.

4. Ask tentatively but accept no. Often the way you ask, "I don't suppose you'll want to ..." or "I know you're busy but ..." gives your partner permission to turn down the request. Once again, the result is resentment.

5. Ask clearly and firmly, accept no and back down. This is a great step forward but if your partner says no, instead of finding out why or changing your request and beginning to negotiate, you end the process too early and still end up resentful.

6. Ask clearly and firmly, accept no and negotiate. Hopefully, you will recognize this option as being assertive.

7. Insist, don't accept no, and put your partner's back up. In this version, it is your partner who is resentful.

8. Demand and back it up with tears, threats, criticism, manipulation, or simply wearing your partner down (until he or she will agree to anything for a quiet life). In the short term, there will only be resentment —maybe from both of you—and before long the relationship is under serious threat.

UNDERSTAND THE DIFFERENCE BETWEEN WANTS AND NEEDS

Before looking at changing the way that you ask, it is important to think about what you're going to be asking for. There will be some items that you'd like (that if you didn't get you'd only be disappointed) and those which are of supreme importance (for your peace of mind or they are part of what makes you tick). The first category are WANTS and the second are NEEDS. It is important to distinguish where a request fits because it is OK not to have all of your WANTS met—because nobody gets their own way all of the time (and if they do it wouldn't be healthy for them). However, if not enough of your NEEDS are being met, this could have serious long-term implications.

Look at the following table and put in examples of your own:

Wants	Needs

- It is fine to have abstract topics in your "needs" category—for example, "respect" or "love"—but try and be more specific in the "wants" category as these will provide you with something to ask for over the next few weeks as you learn about assertiveness.

- If you have a large "need" (for example, "going sailing"—because it relaxes you or feeds your soul), try finding some allied smaller items for the "want" category that speak to that "need". For example, crossing the Atlantic or your partner accompanying you on an expedition to Jamaica.

- Be wary of linking something in your "want" list too closely with your "need" list and tipping over from a minor to a major reaction to NO. For example, if your partner does not want to come to Jamaica on the boat, it does not necessarily mean that she or he is against sailing altogether (and might be perfectly happy to accompany you on more short-distance trips).

- Find a small low-risk item for the "want" category, maybe a "would quite like" item and use that to practice asking in an assertive manner.

- When you think about asking, what are your fears? How could you alleviate them—without moving down to hinting or moving up to insisting? When you do ask, was the reality like you imagined? What could you learn from this experience?

- If you find it hard to be assertive at home, start with being assertive at work or with a friend instead.

OPTIONS FOR RESPONDING

Let's move onto the second part of the maxim: You can say "no." Once again, there are a range of ways to respond, some more helpful than others:

1. Do what you imagine other people want without being asked (but risk wearing yourself out because you don't know the differences between their likes, wants, and needs).

2. Express hesitancy but say yes (and risk taking on too much and becoming resentful).

3. Express unwillingness but still say yes (and risk annoying your partner and getting angry with yourself for agreeing).

4. Refuse but reconsider and say yes. It's fine if events change—for example, your boss doesn't call and you have more free time—however, I would be concerned if you were changing your mind because of guilt or simply as a result of your partner's upset.

5. Refuse and negotiate. Once again, this is being assertive.

6. Ask for more information, for time to consider the request (or check your diary) or say "maybe" and then negotiate. This is also being assertive and fits with the first maxim: I need to explore and understand, before I act.

7. Refuse firmly and don't give in. If you're not prepared to listen to your partner, refuse to negotiate or close down the topic altogether, you risk resentment and maybe even anger from your partner.

8. Put your foot down and use guilt, threats, tears, insults, or criticism to ensure the topic does not come up again. It goes without saying that you risk serious damage to your relationship.

VISITING A FOREIGN LAND

When we go abroad, we expect strange customs and new ways of understanding the world and conducting business. Hopefully, we travel with an open mind, ready to learn and accept the differences. With any luck, we return enriched by the experiences and with a greater understanding of ourselves and our own culture.

In many ways, our partners are a foreign land. The culture of their family (what is acceptable and what is not) and the customs (when, how and why they perform certain tasks) are different – even if they come from the same race, class, and creed as us. However, we like to think our partners are just like us because it provides the illusion that we can completely understand them and therefore predict their actions or have some means to control them (and thereby reduce our fears, our anxiety, and our essential loneliness).

However, we can visit our partner's world but we can't live there, we can't see through their eyes, feel with their heart or stand in their shoes. With this analogy in mind, what are the similarities between a good traveler and a good partner?

- An acceptance that there is no right or wrong way.

- A readiness to look and listen and try out new ideas (that at first will seem completely foreign).

- Knowing that it is easy to jump to the wrong conclusion (about both a foreign land's customs and our partner's behavior) and therefore asking for clarification rather than assuming our assumption is correct.

- Not trying to impose our way of doing business but being respectful of other cultures.

- Willingness to respond to what the situation needs rather than willfulness in responding in the way that we need.

Think about the differences between your family and your partner's family. How has your partner's education, socialization, and experiences of the world made for further differences? What are the differences between what is expected of a girl and a boy? How could you take a nonjudgmental stance to his or her land? How would that impact on how you both ask for something, respond to his or her requests, and ultimately how you negotiate?

WHAT GOES WRONG IN NEGOTIATION

Over thirty years and 2,000 clients, I have heard every possible permutation of what happens when two people's needs, wants, and beliefs collide. Unfortunately, I have heard many more negotiations fail than succeed. So what goes wrong?

Cross-complaining: Jill, fifty-two, had been away with the girls for the weekend and, while she was away, Petroc, fifty-three, had downloaded porn and had a long session enjoying watching couples copulate and masturbating himself. "I know that women aren't supposed to take porn personally but I can't get over the thought that he's comparing me with these young women with their pert breasts and perfect vaginas and feeling disgusting with my saggy boobs and, after two children ... well I can't compete," she said, pouring out all her distress. Petroc did momentarily address her point of view: "If every man says we don't compare our wives with the actresses, couldn't there be some truth in it?" However, before she had a chance to respond, he'd lobbed a totally different topic into the mix: "At least I told you about my porn use, but you didn't tell me that you'd contacted your ex and arranged to go for coffee with him—even though you know it upsets me."

Cross-complaining attempts to distract from one person's shame by trying to shame the other but ends up making a difficult negotiation into an almost impossible one.

Going to the extreme belief: In many ways, Jill had good self-esteem. She had a job that validated her. She had enough self-awareness to know this was partially about her father who had been repeatedly unfaithful to her mother and left home when she was a little girl. However, her language was full of self-loathing—that she could recognize as an exaggeration—and catastrophizing ("I can never get these women out of my head" and "What's the point in going on"). Meanwhile Petroc had branded Jill as a "liar"—he had conflated her behavior on one occasion (not telling him about making an appointment) with her whole personality (and made it about every corner of her life).

Going to the extreme of your beliefs will make you feel more right in your opinion and your partner more wrong. However, black and white thinking makes it harder to find common ground to negotiate.

Pushing the exit button: In the middle of the row, Jill could stand it no more and she left the house and booked into a hotel. On previous occasions, Petroc had backed down and agreed to not use porn and Jill had pretended that he was keeping his vow. Agreeing or pretending to agree also pushes the exit button because there is an illusion that the row is over or settled—at least for the time being.

By pushing the exit button, going off to the hotel, or burying the problem, it is possible to feel safe again and manage your emotions; however, negotiations have been suspended—possibly indefinitely.

Getting your goals out of balance: If I had been able to stop Jill and Petroc in the middle of their argument about pornography, I could have teased out two competing sets of goals. I call the first their long-term or prime goal: a happy marriage, to live in harmony, provide a safe haven for their daughters and enjoy a fulfilling life together. I call the second their short-term goal: to feel OK right now—most probably by winning the argument or keeping the peace.

Once your goals are out of balance, the short-term goals will undermine the long-term ones and make it harder to reach a long-term solution that is acceptable to both parties (and therefore has a chance of sticking).

Using the wrong mindset: In most arguments that go around in circles, one person is using the reasonable mind (stressing empirical facts, taking a rational approach and, at least in the beginning stages, trying to be cool and dispassionate) and the other is using the emotional mind (stressing the importance of emotions and the passions the topic brings up, and in the process facts are distorted, amplified, and logical thinking abandoned). With Jill and Petroc, they started with Jill articulating the feelings: "I feel fat and unlovable" and Petroc articulating the facts: "My use of porn is not at a volume which is considered a problem" and "One in four porn addicts are women, so some women must enjoy it."

With each partner using a different mindset, there was no common language for negotiation. They needed to move to the *wise* mind, which combines both the reasonable and the emotional mind and therefore can draw on information from feelings, intuition, and logical analysis.

Alternating between passive and domineering behavior: Piers, forty-three, had a passive approach to life. He saw other people's wants, needs, and beliefs as being of supreme importance—particularly his wife and two children—and his own of lesser importance. Therefore, he worked away from home Monday to Friday in the city, in a job he hated, so he could pay for their education and a beautiful house with extensive gardens in the country. He would intellectualize that "life is like this" or "my father did it too" to cope with his disappointment. He would use wishful thinking: "One day it will be sunny, my sacrifices will be appreciated, and I'll be happy," but he didn't consider how this might happen.

By the time he started counseling, he had swapped over and become domineering. He'd had enough, he found someone he believed appreciated him and wanted out of the marriage. In other words, he saw his wants, needs, and beliefs of supreme importance and his wife's (who still loved him, wanted to remain married and another chance to show their relationship could be different) and his son and daughters' (who felt betrayed and abandoned) of lesser importance. Obviously, he didn't put it that starkly in my counseling room, but this was what he effectively meant when he said, "After all I've done for them, I deserve this" and "I have to take control of my life" and "Time is running out."

Although this is a stark example, many of my clients are alternating between passive (your needs count and mine don't) and domineering (my needs trump yours), sometimes in the same day over different areas of their joint life. However, both Piers' needs and his wife's needs are of equal importance; this is the basis of assertiveness and the beginning point for successful negotiation.

The three horsemen of the relationship apocalypse: When there is a disagreement, we are terrified of losing, so we throw in any weapon to attack (the most common being criticism) and any to defend ourselves (the most common being shutting off and not listening). When neither of these make us feel safe or win the argument, we bring out the heavy guns (the most common being threats). I call attack, defend, and making threats the three horsemen of the relationship apocalypse. For example, Piers claimed that he had "never" loved his wife, Jill, and that their relationship had "been wrong from the start," and Jill refused to entertain or discuss divorce until he agreed to try working on their marriage: "We've had some really good times together and we could have more." Both used threats: Piers to quit his job so the children would be forced to leave their expensive private schools and Jill to never speak to him again and not attend their children's future weddings or grand-children's baptisms if he was there too.

Once a couple see a dilemma as win or lose, rather than finding a formula where both gain, it is almost impossible to negotiate.

REFLECTIVE LISTENING

At the heart of assertiveness is good listening. It sound ridiculously easy. Of course, we know how to listen but what I'm talking about is *truly* listening—without interrupting. Even if we do wait until our partner (or friend, work colleague, or child) stops talking, we are often working out our response or only half listening because we've heard it all before or are busy mentally downgrading what they're saying because it is "wrong" or "painful" or "shocking." To be fair, our partners might not make it easy for us either. All too often, they will off-load so much material—maybe even spewing it out—that it's hard to digest and therefore truly listen. For these reasons, reflective listening is a good way to tackle a contentious subject.

Flip a coin to decide who goes first (when there's been a row), or if one of you has a topic to raise, he or she goes first and becomes the "giver" and the other person becomes the "receiver."

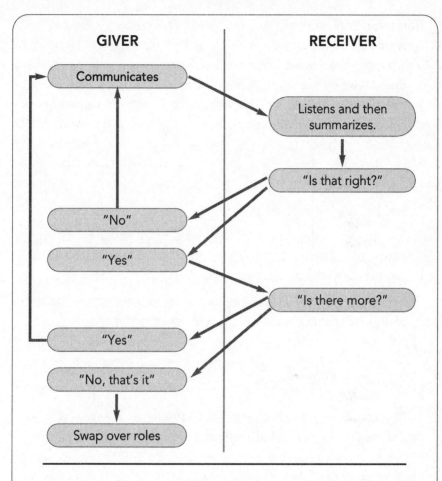

Here are a few tips to ensure that you get the most out of the exercise.

- If you are the giver try and break your message into bite-size chunks. Don't worry about getting it all out in one go because the receiver's role includes asking, "Is there more?"

- In my experience, it is hard to summarize more than three points at a time. So please bear this in mind or you will keep going around the first part of the loop.

- If the situation is tense or emotions are running high, just give one point at a time for your partner to summarize.

- It is fine to ask questions when you are in the role of the giver, but be aware that you won't get an answer when your partner is the receiver. (However, you will be certain that he or she has heard the question correctly, because he or she will summarize and repeat back what was said.)

- When you are receiving, please be careful to only summarize and not be tempted to respond to the points made. (You will get your chance when your partner has finished communicating and you are the receiver.)

- It is equally important not to editorialize when you are receiving, either. (For example, "You claim that I'm disrespectful"—which sounds like you are disputing rather than summarizing.)

- If your partner asks a question, just summarize the question back and ask, "Is that right?" If it is, you still say, "Is there more?" Your partner might explain some of the reasons for asking but, if he or she says, "No," then you swap over and become the giver and can answer.

  If you go to my YouTube site—put Andrew G. Marshall into the search engine—you will find a video called "Reflective Listening."

GREAT NEGOTIATION

Reflective listening will really slow down your communication and that's a good thing because it ensures, returning to Maxim One, that you *explore* and *understand* before you *act*. In effect, negotiation is the final part of this process: the action. So what would a successful outcome look like? There are four options:

Compromise

This is a conclusion where neither party gets exactly what they want but both parties are satisfied with the result. The example I always use is a couple where he wants to see an action movie and she wants to watch a comedy. A classic compromise would be to see a third movie which both parties would enjoy.

Trade

On this occasion, one person will get what he or she wants but the other will be happy because, on another occasion, he or she will get his or her way. Returning to our couple deciding on which movie to see, they might decide on his choice this week and hers the week after or perhaps she will choose the movie and he will choose which restaurant to eat in afterward. (My parents did a trade when they started living together. My mother agreed not to read in bed and my father agreed not to dunk his cookies in his coffee.)

Concede

With this option, it seems like one person is successful and the other gives way but it is far more complex. Let's take a binary situation—where something either happens or doesn't—so it is impossible to find a compromise and both parties feel so strongly that neither is willing to give way and to trade for success in another field of their joint life. Returning to my fictitious couple who find it hard to agree on their movies. They also have a daughter and the mother thinks she is old enough to go off to a rock festival and the father is concerned about drink, drugs, and his daughter's safety. The mother is equally concerned about safety but thinks her daughter must start to make her own choices and that they can't always be following five paces behind. Two equally good points and two equally passionately held positions. A compromise is difficult because the daughter either goes to the festival or she doesn't. They can't trade with each other because the festival goes to the core of what each partner thinks makes for good parenting: nurturing (the father) and empowering (the mother). If they were going to reach the concede option, there would need to be plenty of time to explore the situation and to understand each other's viewpoint. In this process, the mother might be able to make some points that would reassure the father—for example, she is going with several friends that they know are trustworthy and sensible. The father might come up with some options that would make him feel better—for example, an agreed time to leave the festival, collecting her himself or maybe even going to the festival as a couple (but agreeing not to shadow their daughter).

Come back to it

This option recognizes that it takes time to reach a compromise, or that one party needs to consider an offer from the other for a trade or think through the reassurances that have been given which might allow him or her to concede. While my fictitious couple could reach a compromise or a trade in the queue to buy their movie tickets, it is unlikely that one or the other would concede over their daughter's visit to the rock festival without several discussions—which they might wish to postpone so it did not spoil their night out together or alternatively choose another time when they were not tired or had not drunk a second bottle of wine with their meal.

FIVE TIPS FOR SUCCESSFUL ARGUING

Negotiating is a skill and one that doesn't come naturally to us—mainly because when we were small children our parents would lay down the law or get the behavior they wanted by making us feel guilty. When we become teenagers, we tend to rebel, but that's not negotiating either—more like demanding. Some couples naturally know how to negotiate and when Dr. John Gottman, Professor Emeritus of Psychology at the University of Washington in Seattle, studied 2,000 married couples over twenty years, he found couples that stayed together argued in a different way. They used five techniques:

1. **Build agreement.** Instead of focusing on what divides you, state what unites you. For example, "We both want the best for the kids" or "We both want to balance the budget."

---

2. **Support your partner's viewpoint.** We are often so busy trying to win over our partner to our side of the argument that we don't acknowledge the good point that he or she has made. For example, "You were right about ..." or "I'd never thought about ..." Praise also helps build teamwork. For example, "You're always very thoughtful ..." or "I admire how thorough you are."

3. **Ask questions.** We have a tendency to mind read or assume that we know what our partner means. Instead, try asking. For example, "How would that work?" or "Why is this so difficult?" A good prompt to get more information is "Tell me more." In this way, you are using your enquiring mind rather than your combative one.

4. **No is the beginning of a discussion, not the end.** It's fine to say NO to your partner but try and offer some alternatives that could also be acceptable. For example, "I can't get to the post office but I could pick up our son." If your partner says NO, thank him or her for the honesty (because it's best to know where you stand rather than reaching a superficial agreement that falls apart later) but keep the conversation going. For example, you could ask a question: "Why?" or "Is there anything that would make you change your mind?"

5. **Apologize**. When things go wrong during an argument, look at what you regret. For example, "I'm sorry I lost my temper" or "I'm sorry that I became sarcastic." You're not taking responsibility for everything, just your part in the deadlock. Over and over again, being generous will change the mood and allow you both to focus back on having a positive discussion.

Next time you're in dispute or trying to sort out a niggle, experiment by adding one of these techniques into your usual style. How does it change the outcome? On a future occasion, add another—and then another. How does this change the outcome? Keep working on each idea until it becomes second nature.

SIXTH MAXIM IN ACTION

Good communication is important because it stops resentment (which destroys love) and helps you and your partner feel connected (which builds love). My favorite definition for connection comes from Brené Brown, Research Professor at the University of Houston Graduate College of Social Work and author of *Daring Greatly* (Portfolio Penguin): "Connection is the energy that is created between people when they feel seen, heard and valued; when they can give and receive without judgement." You can achieve this goal with assertiveness, which I explain in my sixth maxim as **I can ask, you can say no, and we can negotiate.**

Returning to Jill and Petroc and their argument about pornography, they concentrated on the first maxim: I need to explore and understand, before I can act. Jill decided to find out more about why and how men used pornography, so I suggested reading *The Men On My Couch* by Dr. Brandy Engler (Berkley Publishing Group). The next week, she came back with a different take on pornography: "I thought it was all about sex. After all, the men were all waving their penises in the air when they were watching it, so it's a fair assumption. However, in most cases, they were using it to block out difficult feelings or deal with other problems in their life."

"So why did Petroc use pornography while you were away?"

"He felt abandoned," she explained, and Petroc nodded. (His mother had died when he was young.)

So I asked her to put her original beliefs into the ABC of challenging your reactions. (A for Adversity, B for Belief, and C for Consequence, see Chapter Four for a recap.)

"The Adversity was hearing Petroc had been using porn, my Belief was 'He's comparing me to other women,' and the Consequence was I flipped."

"What happens if you put your new belief into the equation?"

"If the belief is 'He's using it to comfort himself,' then the consequence is I feel sad. But I still don't like porn."

"That's were negotiating comes in. Can you use the formula: **I can ask, you can say no, and we can negotiate?**"

"I'd like you not to use porn," Jill asked.

"I don't think I can manage that entirely," Petroc said, effectively, no.

"When would you like to use it?" Jill replied.

"Although I enjoy porn, I don't feel particularly good about myself afterward and I know it upsets you and I don't want to do that. Actually, I'd been feeling quite good that I only used porn for three hours out of the three days you were away—until our fight."

"So you want to have it in your armory of coping strategies?" Jill confirmed.

They went onto discuss what would help Petroc to use porn less and what would make Jill feel less anxious and they came to an understanding where both parties felt they had been heard and their feelings taken seriously.

Like many negotiations, it was partly a compromise (because Petroc was going to use less porn), partly a trade (he would find other ways to soothe himself and she would give more notice of away trips so he could arrange diverting activities with friends), and partly a concede (because Petroc was still going to use porn). They had also learned to be honest about their needs and what didn't work for them, and kept their nerve long enough to reach an acceptable solution without trying to impose their will or appease.

GREEN SHOOTS

- Assertiveness is when your and the other person's needs are both equally important.

- When there are differences, which is inevitable when two people's lives are interwoven, it is necessary to negotiate a solution rather than expecting love alone to bridge the divide.

- The sixth maxim to change your life is: "I can ask, you can say no, and we can negotiate."

CHAPTER SEVEN

Develop Everyday Calmness

When a quote comes from the sixth century BC but is just as applicable today then it must be really powerful. Lao Tzu, an ancient Chinese philosopher, wrote: "If you're depressed, you are living in the past. If you are anxious, you are living in the future. If you are at peace, you're living in the present." The final three chapters will unpick this idea and focus on the three different time perspectives.

SEVENTH MAXIM

When you're in a crisis, it seems there's nowhere that feels safe. One moment, you're raking up old hurts (to understand how you reached this point), the next you're worried about the future (because you can't imagine how everything will come right), and you're desperate to escape today (because it is full of pain and heartache). However, when you're feeling overwhelmed, you need to break everything down into manageable pieces. That's why my seventh maxim is:

Can I cope with now?

Instead of getting depressed about the past or anxious about the future, focus down on "now" and the next few days. The furthest ahead that I ask my clients to consider is the weekend—so they are not left with empty hours and no support. Whenever the anxiety starts to rise again about further into the future—"How can I cope without him?" or "She's my whole world"—I focus back in and ask: Can you cope with today, tomorrow and the day after? The answer is nearly always yes and if they're not sure, we can discuss what would help, what coping strategies they could use and identify their inner resources or support network. In this way, if they do wobble there's always a solution to hand.

It's only when you start worrying about the unknowable future or kicking yourself about the past that the panic sets in and you risk making bad choices (that might help you feel better in the short term but undermine your long-term goals). So if you're tempted to push ahead regardless, stop and ask yourself: **Can I cope with now?** Even if you're past the initial crisis—and feeling more together—there will still be aftershocks (where you discover something new) or another dimension of the problem will hit you. When this happens, once again, ask yourself: **Can I cope with now?** And follow it up with: What would help?

FINDING THE RIGHT TIME PERSPECTIVE

Our lives are shaped by what happened to us in the past, what is happening now, and what might happen in the future. At any one moment, we can choose to interpret our lives through any one of those times. For example, if I ask you to describe how you feel about life. You could reply through the lens of the past: "I've had a lot of hard knocks," or through the lens of today: "The sun is streaming through the window and I'm sitting in my favorite chair," or through the lens of the future: "I'm learning new concepts that are really going to turn my life around." Finding the right balance between the past, present, and future (and how you perceive each of those times) is key to becoming stronger, wiser, and happier.

Philip Zimbardo is a past president of the American Psychological Association and Professor Emeritus at Stanford University. He is best known for the 1971 Stanford Prison Study where students were randomly assigned the role of guards or prisoners. The experiment had to be stopped after only a couple of days because of the traumatic effects on the participants. The students playing guards became increasingly sadistic while those being prisoners became more and more passive and dangerously depressed. Zimbardo was fascinated by how quickly future-orientated students (education is all about deferring gratification today to gain a qualification and a better job tomorrow) became immersed in the present moment with no concern for their shared past (as friends and colleagues in the psychology department) or what the impact their behavior today might have on their relationships in the future. Zimbardo took these observations and identified five different time perspectives:

Past negative: The past is seen as traumatic, painful, and full of regrets. If this is your time perspective, you will agree with statements like: "I think about bad things that have happened to me in the past" or "I often think of what I should have done differently in my life." The disadvantage of this time perspective is that even events which seemed happy enough at the time are subsequently reinterpreted as negative because of what happened later. A classic example would be looking back over your marriage after your partner announced that he or she has fallen out of love and finding all your happy memories are devalued. However, it can be helpful to occasionally look through the past negative time perspective to learn from mistakes and grow.

Past positive: The past is seen as a warm and sentimental place filled with good memories. If this is your time perspective you will agree with statements like: "I like family rituals that are regularly repeated" and "Happy memories of good times spring readily to mind." The advantage of a past positive mindset is low levels of anxiety and depression. The disadvantage is that sometimes it can be hard to try new things or be open to new ideas (especially as you grow older and become tempted to look though the past positive lens more frequently).

Present fatalistic: Everything feels hopeless and out of control and, by extension, there is little expectation of anything improving in the future. If this is your time perspective, you will agree with statements like: "My life path is controlled by forces I cannot influence" or "You can't really plan for the future because things change so much" or "Often luck pays off better than hard work." Unfortunately there are few advantages in being present fatalistic as it leads to hot tempers, a pessimistic outlook, and being less conscientious (because nothing really matters). Zimbardo, however, believes a present fatalistic time perspective can lead to self-reliance, and I suppose pessimists are seldom deeply disappointed and sometimes pleasantly surprised when things turn out right.

Present hedonistic: The emphasis is on living in the moment and enjoying today. These people are sensual and spontaneous. If this is your time perspective, you will agree with statements like: "I take risks to keep my life from becoming boring," or "I often follow my heart and not my head" or "When listening to my favorite music, I often lose all track of time." The upside is having fun and lots of friends. The downside is potentially excessive risk taking, credit card debts, hangovers, and unprotected sex. Sometimes these people can be so focused on their own pleasures that they forget their responsibilities to others.

Future orientated: These are planners who focus on goals, delay gratification, and can be relied upon to keep their commitments. If this is your time perspective, you will agree with statements like: "I am able to resist temptation when I know there is work to be done," or "It upsets me to be late for an appointment" and "I complete projects by making steady progress." In Zimbardo's research, he found that women were more likely to be future orientated than men. The advantage is good health, enough money, and the respect of other people. The disadvantage can be not enjoying today enough and, at the extreme end, looking back and seeing only responsibility and drudgery.

Time perspectives and your inner void

Zimbardo gave a questionnaire to students to establish which time perspective they most identified with and followed up with standard personality tests to quantify on which emotions and character traits each group scored most highly. For our purposes, I've focused on four aspects that are important for filling an inner void: self-esteem, happiness, friendliness, and emotional stability.

For self-esteem, people who were past positive scored highest, those who were present hedonistic and future orientated had a medium score, those who were present fatalistic had low self-esteem and those who were past negative had the lowest levels of self-esteem.

When it came to happiness, people who were past positive also scored the highest, followed by present hedonistic (with a medium score) and future orientated who scored just above the neutral line. People who were present fatalistic were unhappy and past negative were again the least happy of all the time perspectives.

For friendliness, past positive people were again the highest, followed by present hedonistic but this time they were only a percentage point ahead of future orientated, next came present fatalistic, and lowest of all past negative (but by not as big a margin this time).

Even when it came to measuring emotional stability, past positive came out on top but by only two percentage points, followed by future orientated (which I might have expected to be first). Both present hedonistic and present fatalistic were mildly positive for emotional stability but lowest, by a high margin, was past negative.

Although many people in a crisis or under extreme stress (as in the Stanford Prison Study) will view their life predominantly through present fatalistic or escape into present hedonistic, most of us shift between all five time perspectives. For the optimum way to fill your inner void, Zimbardo believes that you should score highly on past positive, balance equally between present hedonistic (to enjoy today), and future orientated (to ensure a happy tomorrow) but spend only a little time looking through the present fatalistic and past negative lens.

So what should you do if you've realized that you're currently unbalanced? Over the final two chapters, I will cover past and future perspectives but first I'm going to focus on the present.

BECOMING PRESENT FOCUSED

We are seldom living in the present. Sometimes, we are too busy thinking about the future. What shall I have for supper? How long have I got before my partner comes home? What shall I get my mother for her birthday? At other times, we will be dwelling on the past: going over an old argument, thinking of the perfect response, or worrying if something we said was taken out of context and caused upset. In many ways it's madness. What's the point of spending so long going over past events or thinking about the future? Sadly, we can't change the past and, although there is some pleasure in anticipating a treat, like our summer vacation, pleasure can only really be experienced right now. If you monitor yourself, you'll quickly discover that you are seldom present focused and truly aware of the pleasures and experiences in front of you—what is called being mindful.

You will most probably have heard about mindfulness, or being mindful, as there has been a lot of coverage in the media of the benefits. I also introduced some of the concepts in Chapter Three along with the founder Jon Kabat-Zinn (and the cat food bowl left in the sink). So what is mindfulness and how does it fit in with Zimbardo and the five time perspectives?

Mindfulness is accepting and being nonjudgmental about our feelings and focusing on the sensations occurring in the present moment. It encourages daily mediation to calm our overactive mind and stop it from rushing backward and forward, and scurrying around in circles. I find mindfulness useful because it combines the strengths of both Zimbardo's present fatalistic and present hedonistic. For example, in present fatalistic, we accept that we can't control everything—which stops us from mixing up our zone of concern and our zone of control (see Chapter Four for a recap)—while in present hedonistic, we can enjoy the moment. In addition, mindfulness avoids some of the weakness of present hedonistic and present fatalistic. (Personally, I don't like the term present hedonistic, which sounds like an excuse for getting drunk, stuffing our faces, or being selfish and enjoying ourselves at the expense of others, while present fatalistic, taken to its logical conclusion, risks helplessness.)

BEING MINDFUL

Stephanie, thirty-eight, came to see me while trying to recover from a relationship that had been doomed from the start. They had met at a conference and he had made it perfectly clear that he was up for only "no-strings fun." Even though she wanted a committed relationship and some day children, Stephanie decided to fly halfway around the world to spend a week with this man. During her vacation, she had to face the fact that he was happy to go to bed with her, liked her company, but truly didn't want a relationship. Back home, Stephanie found it extremely hard to get on with her life. Whenever she wasn't working or distracting herself with exercise, she would remember every bittersweet moment of the relationship and depress herself further.

"I'll cook myself something nice but, when I sit down to eat it, my mind will wander into 'I could be eating this meal with him' or 'He used to really like fish,'" she explained.

"I bet you spend a lot of your day thinking about what's in the refrigerator and what you could cook when you get home," I replied.

Stephanie nodded.

"But when you're finally ready to enjoy it, your mind has flown off elsewhere."

Stephanie laughed.

"What would happen if you concentrated on the taste and the texture of the food? And how good it feels to be putting something wholesome and home cooked in your mouth?"

This proved to be the turning point in Stephanie's counseling. By enjoying the moment, and not thinking about the unhappy past or anticipating a small pleasure in the future, she slowly became more mindful of the present. Of course, she still thought about this man—as that's part of grieving—but she stopped herself from wallowing. Finally, she was able to get some perspective on why she had wasted so much time and emotional energy and what changes she needed to make to achieve her goals.

So how do you become more mindful? Next time you find your mind wandering off the task in hand, make a conscious decision to stop thinking about the past or planning what you're going to do next. Instead, focus on what is happening now. Ask yourself:

What can I see?

What can I touch?

What can I hear?

What can I smell?

What can I taste?

The secret is to be mindful not only when you're doing something nice—like taking the dog for a walk on a spring morning or soaking in a hot bath—but during less pleasurable or mundane tasks, too. At first glance, it might seem a good idea to anticipate some small reward. For example, while you're washing the dishes to look forward to relaxing with a cup of coffee and a magazine. Except that you're training your mind to wander when you finally do sit down; so, instead of enjoying the break, you're busy planning the next task.

Being mindful is not just about enjoying the moment—although that's important—it can also help deal with stress. If, for example, there is a queue in the bank or you're stuck in traffic on the highway, ask yourself: "Can I change anything?" You can't push everybody out of the way and go to the front of the queue. You can't make your car levitate to the next junction. Checking your watch, tapping your feet, or constantly changing lanes will make no real difference. Worrying about being late will not make you arrive any sooner. Instead, concentrate on this unexpected time out from your planned day and notice what might otherwise have passed you by. Perhaps there is a father with his young son in the bank queue who are playing I spy or lambs in the field beside the highway. Once you have relaxed and started enjoying the moment, it might even be possible to think of the delay as a gift or, at the very least, an opportunity to practice being mindful.

SIMPLE TECHNIQUES FOR MEDITATING

One of the best ways of being mindful is to learn how to meditate. But where do you start? There are dozens of different styles practiced across numerous religions and even within one tradition there are countless different meditations. Therefore, I've taken three common techniques that provide a general introduction and an opportunity to sample the benefits of peace and contemplation.

1. Focusing on your breathing. This meditation can be done anywhere, with your eyes open or closed. If you've decided to keep your eyes open, focus on something fixed—so you are not distracted by other people or movements. It helps if you can be sitting down with your hands in your lap and your feet firmly on the ground. Take a few moments to concentrate on your breathing and become aware of the air being drawn into your nose and then being released. Take a good lungful, hold for a second, and release. If your mind starts thinking about something, concentrate on the sensation of air coming in and out of your nostrils. Target time: At least five minutes

2. Purifying. This meditation builds on the previous one, close your eyes and start to focus on your breathing. Once you are feeling calmer, imagine a golden ring hovering over your head. It feels warm, welcoming, and wonderful. Slowly let it descend toward your head and as it passes over your forehead, the ring expands and helps relax all the worry lines. Imagine the tenseness dropping from your body as the ring travels further downward, especially over pressure points like your jaw, neck, and shoulders. Unclench your hands, feel your stomach muscles unknot, and become aware of your weight on your buttocks. Next, visualize the ring passing over your knees, ankles, and toes. Once you are totally relaxed, return to your breathing and the air passing in and out of your nose. Finally, imagine that the air coming into your lungs is pure white (full of love, peace, and happiness) and the air expelled from your lungs is black (full of stress and anxiety). If your mind wanders, return to your breathing and the image of your body being filled with light. Target time: At least ten minutes.

3. Walking meditation. This technique is best practiced outdoors in a park, by the sea, or in open countryside, but it can be done walking to the car or arriving at work. Start by standing on the spot. Be aware of the weight on the soles on your feet and the miracle of being able to balance upright. This meditation is all about having your eyes open; experiencing the wind, sun, or rain on your face; the smells of nature; the sounds made by other people. Once you are truly present in the moment, set off walking normally but not too fast. Revel in the rhythm of your movement: how your arms swing by your side, putting your heel to the ground, and your toes shifting in your shoes. Once you are aware of your body, lift your head and look around. What do you see? What do you hear? What do you smell? Try and balance awareness of your outer and inner worlds until the two realms become synchronized, as this will help you to become calmer and think more clearly. If your mind starts wandering, focus on the sensation of putting your heel down on first one foot and then the other. Target time: At least fifteen minutes.

STAYING MINDFUL

Once you have stopped self-medicating, perfectionism, and other destructive behaviors, you will begin to feel calmer and better able to negotiate change. The good news is that this can be the beginning of a positive new pattern. However, to make calmness your default setting, rather than something that you need to work at, it is important to lock-in the changes. So how do you achieve this goal?

- *Calm viewpoint.* The secret is to have open as opposed to fixed short- or medium-term goals. With an open viewpoint, there are many routes to happiness and therefore the stakes are low if we hit an obstacle. With a fixed viewpoint, there is *one* thing that will make us happy! Therefore, the stakes are much higher—hence the overwhelming disappointment, anger, and need for revenge, oblivion, or acting out. Ultimately, we might pin our hopes on one particular outcome but, with a calm viewpoint we can be patient (knowing another opportunity will present itself) or look for an alternative path around a blockage.

- *Calm thinking.* It helps us notice whether our train of thought is useful or not. For example, we think about our partner and decide to send him or her a text. Here, there is a clear line between stimulus and action. In contrast, with overthinking, the initial thought about our partner turns into a developing thought—turning over an argument from this morning, worrying about what will happen on our return, what he or she will say, what we will say. The line between stimulus and action, in this case, has many twists and turns and could include false assumptions, strange leaps of logic, and several exaggerations. Ultimately, calm thinking encourages a calm viewpoint.

- *Calm speech.* To qualify as calm speech, your words need to be targeted, assertive, and timely. (I give my clients the acronym: TAT.) By targeted, I mean you're talking to the right person. (For example, if you have a problem at work, you speak to the person concerned rather than moan to colleagues or vent your temper by pushing in front of someone in the bus queue.) By assertive, I mean not only asking politely for what you need—rather than dropping hints, wheedling, or demanding—but also listening and taking seriously other people's needs. Although you have the right to ask, the other person has the right to refuse your request. Remember the fifth maxim: I can ask, you can say no, and we can negotiate. By timely, I mean raising issues at the time or shortly afterward, so there is no opportunity for a whole pile of problems to accumulate and an increased risk of becoming overwhelmed so your speech comes out as cruel or unnecessarily critical.

- **Calm actions.** Before acting, check whether the proposed behavior is good for you and not merely tempting. Calm actions also takes into consideration the impact on other people.

Although it might seem like a huge leap forward, each of these elements reinforces and supports each other. In effect, a calm viewpoint promotes calm thinking, which promotes calm speech and leads to calm actions and finally a calm and mindful life.

PUTTING BEING MINDFUL INTO PRACTICE

Duncan, forty-eight, was determined to settle down and have a family. He arrived in counseling with a very fixed viewpoint: "I'm looking for a slim, attractive, really stunning woman because I know what I'm like and I don't want to be unfaithful and mess it up. I'm attracted to Asians—in their twenties—so she will be fertile and our children will be healthy." This fixed idea of what would make him happy was the opposite of a calm viewpoint. Duncan was often anxious and, on the occasions when he did date a woman who fitted this profile, he worried about her being so overwhelmingly attractive that his friends would try to steal her—which is the opposite of calm thinking. Worse still, he was so worried about being rejected that he found it difficult to ask these women out. He would think, "Why would they be interested in me, I'm almost fifty." So, instead of suggesting a date, he would help them practice their English (he'd once been a language teacher) or offer friendship (although he was interested in much, much more). In effect, he was not being assertive or practicing calm speech. Not surprisingly, his actions were not calm either —for example, he would besiege potential partners with texts or take them to overly expensive restaurants.

Over the course of our counseling sessions, I focused on helping him become calmer—starting with challenging the assumptions that stopped him from having a calm viewpoint. Slowly, he began to realize that there were lots of women whom he found attractive—not just Asians in their midtwenties. With a calm viewpoint, he began to think about other qualities—beyond attraction—that underpin a good relationship. "I want to be able to talk to my wife, share interests, and cultural references," Duncan explained in his calmer thinking, "and we can grow together rather than having to click right away."

Once he'd stopped worrying about his date being "the one," he could bring up doubts and concerns. "I had a lot in common with this woman who I'd taken out several times. She had a fascinating job and we shared an interest in history, but I was worried that she might not be interested in me romantically. I decided there was only one way to find out. So I decided to bring the topic up when we had supper together—after a debate we'd both attended: 'I think you should know that I find you very attractive.' She was flattered and suggested that she might be interested in me romantically, too. Chancing it definitely brought us closer."

In effect, calm viewpoint and calm thinking had led to calm speech and finally onto calm actions.

SWITCHING OFF A SPINNING-WHEEL MIND

Many people find it hard to disengage their brain and be mindful, or cannot relax until all the chores have been done. If this sounds familiar, what's the alternative?

- Accept that overthinking is counterproductive. There comes a point when further ruminating just confuses or promotes bad decision making.

- Unload your thoughts. When left to go around and around in your brain, thoughts and jobs-to-do get bigger and bigger. So put everything down on paper; you will find there are less items than you imagined.

- Put off coming up with a solution or doing that "must-do" job. Having accepted most pressing tasks are no such thing, put off, for example, checking emails or tidying up until later. In the same way, put off thinking about a pressing problem. In many cases, you will have forgotten the problem the next day.

- If a thought pops into your head (for example, "We're out of coffee")—especially when you're doing something nice like making love—imagine pushing it out of your brain (rather than thinking "I could pop into the grocery store on my way back from work tomorrow"). You will be surprised how easily these thoughts disappear if you don't allow them to take hold.

WHAT UNDERMINES MINDFULNESS?

Once the case for mindfulness has been made, it seems incredible that anyone would not want to live in the moment—rather than letting bad experiences from the past or fear about the future overwhelm them. However, there are powerful forces which stop our rational selves from being heard:

Exhaustion

Sometimes, when we are overwhelmed with problems, the most important thing to do is STOP. Time and again, I find that resting is a precondition for healing.

Cassie, forty-nine, was going through a divorce that she did not want. Her husband was forever sending her angry texts pushing for her to finish the financial statement and questioning how much she spent on the weekly shop. He was also anxious about how the divorce would affect his relationship with his children. Through his eyes, if one of his children did not want to spend the weekend with him, or be picked up on Saturday morning rather than Friday night, it was not down to overdue homework, an invitation from a friend, or being tired, it was because Cassie had been "poisoning the well." The result would be another flood of angry texts between the two of them.

So I encouraged Cassie to take a break, visit friends, and unwind. Once she was rested, she could properly examine how she responded to her husband's texts rather than just firing off her first thoughts. In the next session, Cassie decided to switch off her cell phone for chunks of time: "I was so conditioned to the idea that if it rings, it must be answered, that I was prioritizing answering texts and calls over quality face-to-face time with friends or my children. It's completely mad. I've also decided to take time between receiving a text and answering it. I don't have to go scurrying around like some demented hamster on a wheel, just because he commands me."

Once Cassie was no longer exhausted or worn down, she found that her judgment improved and, better still, she did not send texts that she regretted later.

Breakthrough Tip: Every problem looks more manageable after a good night's rest, but what if you can't stop tossing and turning? Here are three techniques for unwinding and sleeping better.

1. *Progressive muscle relaxation:* Lie on your back with arms and hands by your sides and think about your breathing. Make it slower, deeper, and more regular. As you breathe out, imagine saying the word RELAX. Feel how your chest muscles tense as you breathe in and relax as you breathe out. Once you're a little calmer, start to move your attention through your body, alternately tensing groups of muscles and then relaxing them. Start with your fingers and hands. Make a fist and push your fingers into the palms of your hands. Feel the tension and let your fingers flop and your arms sink into the bed. Let them be heavy and imagine saying the word RELAX. Take a tour of other tension spots in your body. Tense your shoulders by hunching them up toward your ears, hold for a couple of seconds, and let them go— again, imagine the word RELAX. Move onto your face—screw up your eyes and clench your teeth and then let the tension flow out and RELAX. Concentrate on your breathing, breathe in through your

nose and out through your mouth, and RELAX. Next, think about your legs and feet, press the back of your legs into the bed and curl your toes up as far as they will go, and RELAX. Tense your buttocks and pull your groin up from the bed, feel the tension in those muscles, and RELAX. Finally, tour your whole body, tensing your muscle groups, then let them be heavy and flop into the mattress.

2. *Going to a beautiful place:* Instead of letting your mind turn over past horrors or imagine future setbacks, the idea is to find a beautiful place where you can visit, relax, and switch off. It is easier if you're feeling calm and relaxed, so get into the mood by using the progressive muscle relaxation technique. Next, imagine a favorite place. It might be a bench in the park or a local beauty spot or a favorite vacation destination from your childhood. (If you're having problems with your partner, please don't choose somewhere that you've been together. This beautiful place belongs to you alone.) Alternatively, you can make up somewhere from scratch. Look around. What season is it: a summer's day (perhaps you're in a grassy meadow), fall (and you're in a forest carpeted with leaves), winter (and the ground is covered in crisp snow), or spring (surrounded by buds about to burst into color)? It is a beautiful morning. What colors can you see? Look at the shades and patterns. What can you feel? Imagine the sun on your back or a fresh breeze on your cheeks. What can you smell? Imagine freshly mown grass or sea breezes. What can you hear? The lapping of waves or birds singing. What can you taste? Enjoy your beautiful place and look around. A little way off, you can see a small wooden gate. Walk toward it, open it, and follow the path beyond. Enjoy a gentle stroll through your beautiful place. What do you see, smell, hear, and feel? Imagine it in as much detail as possible. After a while, you see somewhere comfortable to relax: a grassy bank, a pile of sweet-smelling leaves, or a cottage in the woods with a roaring log fire. Lie down and retrace your journey back up the path, through the wooden gate, and return to where you started—and RELAX.

3. *Letting go:* If your mind is still churning. Get up, go to another room, and write down a list of jobs for the morning. Leave your list

behind and return to your bedroom. Lie down and do the progressive muscle relaxation. If this doesn't clear your mind and allow you to sleep, imagine packaging all your problems up in a box and writing a label which sums up the issue (for example, "work," "relationship," or "the past"). Tell yourself, "I can't do anything about these problems in the middle of the night. Therefore, I'm going to box them up." Imagine the box in detail, what does it look like? How is it sealed: gaffer tape, brown paper, and string or a fancy bow? Watch yourself open it and all the problems being blown away on the wind and disappearing over the horizon. Open another box and another and imagine yourself feeling lighter and lighter—and RELAX.

Negative thoughts

How do you stop fear, despair, anger, and craving getting the better of you? It's hard because our mind is always looking for distractions and easy alternatives. To illustrate this point, I'm going to use a personal example.

On the train journey into London, to see my clients, I like to read and prepare. Sometimes the book is by another practitioner explaining how they work. Sometimes it is about a particular philosophy or research project. Sometimes it is about the writer's personal experience of overcoming adversity. I often find just the insight or technique to help a client who is blocked or an insight for the book I'm currently writing. However, it is sometimes hard to stay focused on my "improving" and "wholesome" reading. Especially when my neighbor on the train is flicking through a glossy magazine full of beautiful women and famous men on red carpets. My eyes crave novelty. My brain would much rather forget complex thoughts and skim through the latest celebrity headline in my neighbor's magazine. Does this sound familiar? If so, what is the answer?

Instead of getting angry or beating yourself up—"Why can't I concentrate" or "This book is too difficult"—try and take the learning from the experience. Ask yourself: Why am I so easily distracted today?

In my case, I realized that I was overfilling my day. Perhaps I needed time to just stare out of the window, enjoy the streaks of blue peeking through the clouds, and be in the moment (rather than wishing I was back at home working on my book or, worse still, imagining picking up the finished item in a store).

Breakthrough Tip: Our identity is shaped by two sets of values: intrinsic and extrinsic. People with a strong set of intrinsic values put most weight on relationships with friends, family, and the wider community. They have a sense of self-acceptance and concern for others. People with extrinsic values desire wealth, status, and power over other people. They are extremely image-conscious, more likely to conform to social norms, and have less concern for others.

Obviously, we are not born with values. They are embedded and normalized by the messages we receive and, over the past forty years, there has been an explosion in the amount of advertising and marketing directed at us. According to David Shenk, author of *Data Smog: Surviving The Information Glut,* the average American received 560 daily advertising messages in 1971 but by 1997 that had increased sixfold to 3,000.

Advertising is all about making us dissatisfied and selling a potential solution. So it is no surprise that the number of people who are extrinsically motivated has increased dramatically, along with higher levels of consumer debt and longer working hours to pay for everything. Worse still, as marketing has become more sophisticated, businesses have started to target our intrinsic values—associating their products with love, family life, and strong communities—but creating the impression that these values can be purchased.

So, do a media audit and look at the messages you are feeding yourself? How much TV are you watching? Which programs? What sort of newspapers and magazines? What books and websites? Do these messages encourage love, compassion, and patience or greed, suspicion, and pride? Does what you consume make you dissatisfied and therefore widen your inner void or does it provide something useful to fill it up?

Instant solutions

Sometimes a current problem can seem so overwhelming that it will rob us of all our adult coping skills. Suddenly, we feel about five years old and want our parents to scoop us up and tell us everything is going to be OK.

When Scott, thirty-two, was told by his wife that she didn't love him anymore, he began to panic: "She keeps telling me, 'That's the way I feel and nothing can change my feelings.' I beg her for another chance—but nothing changes. I've tried coming home earlier from work, fixing up a babysitter, doing more about the house, but she still says her feelings are the same."

In effect, he was doing everything to *fix* the problem with instant solutions and when none of them worked, he became increasingly anxious and kept firing off questions—"Why do you feel like this?" and "Why won't you work at our marriage?" and "I've done all the things you've asked but you won't even give me a glimmer of hope"—all in a desperate attempt to blast his way through her defenses. He had even started threatening her: "You're going to ruin our children's lives." I had a picture of Scott as a small child pulling at his mother's sleeve to get her attention and I knew from experience that it would push his wife, Kirstie, further away.

"I feel he doesn't listen to me," she explained, "and to be honest, I don't think he can change." In effect, the more Scott looked for instant solutions, the more pressure he put on Kirstie (and himself), the more she withdrew and wanted to end the relationship.

So I tried to break this downward cycle by negotiating a truce where, for one week only, he would try to live in the moment and concentrate on improving their day-to-day communication—for example, who would pick up the children from school—and not to worry about the future. As a whole week would be too long for Scott to go without asking about Kirstie's feelings, they agreed to set aside one evening in the middle of the week, where Scott could ask questions and Kirstie would do her best to answer them. I later discovered that the resolution had been broken within hours of leaving the session.

When Scott returned the next week, on his own, he explained: "We went for dinner and it started really well but I became despondent because nothing had fundamentally changed and we ended up having a terrible row."

"So you thought one session with me would transform everything?" I asked.

Sitting in my room, with his rational head on, he knew this was a tall order but, overwhelmed with anxiety, he had needed reassurance and had started to pressurize again.

Breakthrough Tip: Difficult situations are often made worse by imagining doomsday outcomes. For example, Scott worried: "I'll lose my children" and "I'll be so bitter that I won't trust women again—ever." No wonder the stakes were so high and he would "do anything to get her back." When we began to unpick these fears, and Scott stopped catastrophizing, we found many were ungrounded. "I have a good relationship with my children," he admitted, "and I don't know what the future will bring or how I'll feel about other women." Whenever, in the session, he raised his eyes off the next seven days, I brought him back to the present and slowly Scott's anxiety levels began to come down.

Past trauma

Many couples will be making good progress tackling their underlying unhappiness but find it hard to be mindful and live in the present because one partner will be repeatedly overwhelmed by images or questions from the past.

Despite her husband's affair ending fifteen months previously, Jeanette, forty-eight, found herself daily assaulted by images of what her husband did with a younger woman: "They are very graphic, completely horrible, and make me sick to the pit of my stomach. So we'll be having a perfectly pleasant time, lying in bed reading the Sunday papers, and I'll be suddenly gripped by this thought: 'He took her to an art gallery one Sunday while I was away visiting my mother. He can make the effort to take her out but he doesn't love me enough to do the same.' It's stupid because up to that moment I was enjoying unwinding and showing each other interesting articles. But I can't help myself, I'll start up on all the old questions—that get us nowhere—and we'll end up rowing, I'll have to beg him to come back (which is demeaning) and afterward I feel terrible."

These setbacks were particularly worrying because Jeanette and her husband, Jake, were communicating much better. He had become more forthcoming about his feelings and she had started to stand up for what she wanted (rather than try and please him). Despite their relationship being on the brink of becoming the best that it had ever been, Jeanette feared the past would always spoil the present and make their marriage untenable.

Breakthrough Tip: If you're stuck and don't seem able to reach a calm place, ask yourself: What are the benefits of these terrible fights? At first sight, this is a stupid question. Who wants rows and falling out? However, there are often side benefits. Some people enjoy the attention, even though it is negative attention and any reassurances gleaned in the aftermath of a fight feel forced rather than natural (and therefore less likely to fill your inner void).

If you can find no hidden benefits, the next question to ask yourself is: Am I punishing myself? Again this seems a strange question but many people who get stuck in the healing process are feeling angry—often with themselves. For example, Jeanette told me, "How could I have been so blind not to realize that if our sex life was disappointing and Jake felt constantly rejected that he'd be tempted? How could I be so wrapped up in my own little world? And I suppose I'm angry with myself for staying. I never thought I'd be a 'stand by your man' woman, but I love him." Once these feelings were out in the open, Jeanette could start working on forgiving herself.

Finally, remember the second maxim: What is this feeling trying to tell me? Not about the affair or the past trauma but about your wider life. When Jeanette looked more closely at her fears, she worried that her life was totally centered around her children and her husband. "My youngest is already a teenager and before I know it will be going off to university. What if Jake had an affair then, I'd be left with nothing?" With this insight, Jeanette realized that she needed to broaden her identity, to be more than a wife and mother, and she decided to retrain and get herself a job.

THE IMPORTANCE OF SMILING

One of the most important signs that someone is enjoying the moment is if they are smiling, but that's not all. Smiles can also predict future happiness. Psychologists Lee Anne Harker and Dacher Keltner, from the University of California, studied photographs of women in their college yearbooks and found that those who had a positive expression were not only more likely to be married by the age of twenty-seven but had a more satisfying marriage (as they were forty-three percent less likely to be divorced than their unsmiling colleagues).

When the research was followed up by Professor Matt Hertenstein, at De Pauw University in Indiana, he found that the same results held for men too. He asked people over sixty-five to provide photos from their childhood and his team scored each person's smile. He found that only eleven percent of the smilers had been divorced while thirty-one percent of the frowners had experienced a broken marriage.

What this research underlines is the importance of positive emotions. A smile shows that you are friendly and open and encourages positive emotions in other people. Even more importantly, it means that other people are likely to interpret some of your ambiguous moods in a positive light. Finally, a smile will lift your mood.

- So why not see what difference it would make if you made a conscious effort to smile more today?

- Monitor what responses you get from work colleagues, family ,and friends.

- What impact does it have on your enjoyment of the day?

- Do you feel that you are more focused on living in the present?

SEVENTH MAXIM IN ACTION

Within minutes of arriving in my counseling room, Catlin, forty-one, had been through all the time perspectives. As a young woman, she had wanted to be a competitive sailor but her father had stressed the importance of getting a job with career prospects and she'd joined a firm of city stockbrokers. "I haven't achieved anything of consequence in my life and time seems to be running through my fingers," she explained. Before I could consider the wrong turns in the past, she had hopped into today: "I'm separated from my husband because I'm so impatient with him, he seems to be squandering his life and he's away on business a lot and when he's back we're always arguing." OK, I thought, that's lots to work on but before I could ask for details, Catlin was into the future. "I've developed feelings for a guy who lives in the same village and there's no nice way to put this: we're having an affair. He wants me to tell my husband and for us to make a go of it—because all this secrecy is doing his head in. And mine too. You see I'm not just hurting myself but other people too. That's why I've given myself until Friday to give him a decision!"

So I took a deep breath and asked her to use my seventh maxim: **Can I cope with now?** The answer was "yes" but she was almost immediately on to what she would do on Friday (which was four days away). So we looked at what would help her make an informed decision and I sent her away with a pile of books to understand why love drains out of a marriage and the dynamics of an affair.

I hoped they would help her find a more balanced view of her past and her marriage (so it was not all past negative) and a more realistic picture of her affair so she was not projecting herself into some overly optimistic view of the future. (She believed her lover would be better able than her husband to support her because "he really wants to help me achieve my full potential.") However, I also wanted to take her out of the present fatalistic where she was just drifting along—responding to other people's deadlines and cresting on a wave of "love"—and to focus on what she could control.

GREEN SHOOTS

- There are five time perspectives—future focused, past negative, past positive, present fatalistic, and present hedonistic—and advantages to looking at the world through each.

- Sometimes it is important to stop thinking and planning the future or worrying about the past, and be truly present in what you're actually doing today.

- The seventh maxim to change your life is: "Can I cope with now?"

CHAPTER EIGHT

Taking Control of Your Past

Once you have developed everyday calmness and reduced the risk of deepening your inner void, you are finally ready to look at the past and start healing some of the old hurts. A lot of my clients are nervous. They think it involves confronting their parents or past partners. Don't worry, I'm not going to be asking for anything like that. My message is about compassion and the best place to start is with you.

EIGHTH MAXIM

One of the advantages of reaching this point in the program is that many of the important ideas have already been introduced. I've explained that we should aim for good enough rather than perfect; how perfectionism is often a way of protecting ourselves from shame (which is a natural human emotion and therefore unavoidable); and that trying to suppress something often gives it more power over us. So now we're ready for another part of the jigsaw: my all-time favorite quote and a personal source of comfort in dark times. Philosopher Immanuel Kant (1724–1804) wrote: "Out of the crooked timber of humanity, no straight thing was ever made." In other words, humans are not perfect and although it is fine to aim high, we should not be too despondent when we fall short. That's why my eighth maxim is:

I'm doing my best but I'm crooked timber.

I want to take this idea one stage further. When boats were made from wood, it was impossible to make a perfect join—because timber is crooked—but that didn't matter because they used tar to seal up any gaps and stop the boat from springing a leak. When we invented steel, it finally became possible to make a perfect join. However, there was one big problem. These boats sunk! Unlike the timber which could shrink in cold water and expand in warmer water, there was no give in steel boats and they cracked in two. In effect, the designers had to create an imperfect fit, so there was some movement between the steel plates. So, staying with the analogy, it's fine that we're crooked timber because it allows us to grow, learn and adapt.

If we can be compassionate toward ourselves—because we're crooked timber and doing our best—it is easier to be compassionate toward others. After all, they're crooked timber, too. It certainly beats the opposite approach that I hear time and time again: "I have very high standards for myself. I always give my best and I expect the same from others." Not only will the person have a critical inner voice—which is a real cross to bear—but they will be expecting other people to be perfect, too, and under that pressure their relationships are more likely to crack in two.

ACKNOWLEDGE THE IMPACT OF THE PAST

It is hard to have a balanced view of our childhood, but if you are going to move from a predominantly past negative time frame toward a past positive one, it is vital. Some people are quick to attack—normally only one of their parents—for letting them down, while others minimize what happened or deny the full scale of their unhappiness. As one of the central themes of this book is acknowledging pain and accepting feelings, you will not be surprised to learn that this is an important ingredient for taking control of your past, too.

Martina, thirty-eight, arrived into counseling in a state of panic. On the face of it, she had a perfect life. She had recently married her financially successful partner, Derek, she had a creative and rewarding job and they had a three-year-old daughter. "This is easily the best relationship I've ever had," explained Martina, "and after years of dating hopeless men I know I should be grateful to have someone as focused and committed as

Derek, but I've been gripped with, what I can only describe as, a cold anxiety attack. It's like my heart is being crushed under a layer of ice. I can't breath properly and I keep thinking 'What if I've made a big mistake and I don't love him after all.'" (Fortunately, she had read my book *I Love You But I'm Not In Love With You* and this had taken the edge off her panic.) However, when a client lists everything they have to be grateful about, I always wonder what is happening behind the glittering drape. So I asked about her childhood.

At sixteen, Martina discovered that the man she thought was her father was, in fact, her stepdad. "Everything immediately made sense, as he was never really that interested in us. There would be some nice family days at the weekend but on Monday morning he'd walk straight past my younger sister and I having breakfast in the kitchen without even saying hello or goodbye. Most evenings, he'd be in the lounge and we'd be in our bedrooms trying to keep off the radar. I don't think he wanted children, just our mother."

So what memories did Martina have of her biological father?

"I must have been about three when my parents split. I have some vague memories of my mother crying and then, later, I don't know how much, a removal van taking us to a new house and my stepdad being there."

I was struck by the fact that Martina's daughter was the same age as she had been when her father left. It was probably no coincidence that the cold terror had struck at this point in her life.

Although Martina had had counseling for anxiety attacks in her late twenties and early thirties, and made the connection to her childhood, she had not really fed this knowledge into her everyday life. She had not asked her stepfather how he felt about having a ready-made family or her mother why she had hidden the truth. In effect, Martina had boxed the secret away and had effectively "forgotten" it.

The next week, Martina seemed much calmer. What had made the difference?

"It really helped to make the link between my feelings today and the past?"

"You know how much a three-year-old understands because you're caring for one every day," I pointed out.

"How could my mother have lied to me?" Martina asked

"And until you acknowledge the full impact of their decision, you can't begin to deal with it or answer that question."

Ultimately, Martina decided it was time to talk to her mother and stepfather—not to accuse but acknowledge what happened and the impact on her life.

KEEPING A JOURNAL

When you're going through a crisis, it is easy to think you're not making much progress and forget the lessons that you've already learned. That's why I recommend keeping a journal as it has four important functions:

- **Somewhere to dump your thoughts:** Instead of thoughts going endlessly around in your head, they are down on paper or in your phone or computer. Instead of dumping everything—your fears and hopes—onto your partner, you can talk to your journal instead.

- **Facilitating a dialogue with yourself:** Asking yourself questions and trying to make sense of what is happening allows you to be more mindful of the moment and can almost be meditative.

- **Monitoring your progress:** When you're feeling stuck, turn back to earlier entries in your journal. You will find issues that obsessed you then have eased and realize that although you might have slipped backward, it's not as far as you thought.

- **Validating your key insights and lessons:** When you're reading this book or something else—there's a reading list at the back—you will find some ideas really catch your attention. Put them in your journal and ask yourself: Why did this resonate? What does this say about my situation? Any key insights, write them in your journal. They could be your own maxims to live by.

IMPROVE YOUR RELATIONSHIP
WITH YOUR PARENTS TODAY

When you're a child, your parents have all the power and you have to go along with their rules, sulk, and try to undermine them, or throw a temper tantrum and stage a revolution. However, when you become an adult —and financially independent—there is the potential for an equal relationship. Time and again, I find that if clients can improve their current relationship with their parents, it goes a long way toward filling the inner void from their childhood and helping them move from a past negative into past positive time frame.

Esmé, thirty-one, who we met in Chapter Five, came into counseling because she was unable to form lasting relationships: "Sex is either a feast or famine and I find myself attracted to immature men rather than anyone my equal." It soon became clear that her parents' split at nine had had a profound effect on Esmé. The subsequent divorce was so painful that even twenty years later, her mother and father could not be in the same room or speak on the telephone to each other. Esmé was still angry with her parents for not protecting her from the fallout of their divorce. She felt neglected by her father (who remarried and had more children) and attacked by her mother. It was no surprise that intimacy made Esmé anxious.

"I see no point confronting my parents because my father will deny it was that bad, and when I did try and talk to my mother once, it degenerated into me shouting and her sobbing 'I'm sorry'—which just made me angrier," said Esmé.

"I couldn't agree more about confronting," I said, and Esmé looked up from her tissues. "This isn't reality TV. I never want someone to *confront* their parents. Talk to them by all means. Ask your mother and father to retell the story of what happened from their viewpoint—so you can understand better. Apologize for your part in any problems after the divorce—because I'm sure a frightened and hurt nine-year-old was not all sweetness and light. Explain how their inability to communicate affects you today—e.g. 'How can I get married if two people I love can't be in the same room together.'" Esmé was relieved but even these lower-risk options felt dangerous and difficult. So I suggested looking at her everyday communication with her parents and improving that instead.

I mentioned Transactional Analysis briefly in Chapter Four, but now I want to look at one of its central ideas—that everybody has three parts to their personality: Parent, Adult, and Child. When Esmé "confronted" her mother, she was in Critical Parent mode (complaining about everything she did wrong) and her mother was in Child mode (trying to deflect by agreeing too quickly, making apologies that she did not really mean and generally trying to "please" her daughter). As with many Critical Parent/ Child arguments, Esmé and her mother had repeatedly swapped roles backward and forward. For example, Esmé's mother had gone on the attack and become Critical Parent herself—complaining that Esmé did not understand and was ungrateful—and Esmé had responded in Child mode by sulking and slamming doors.

Fortunately, there is an alternative: switching into Adult mode. This is the rational part of our personality which asks open-ended questions— "how" or "why" and "what." For example, Esmé's mother could have asked: "What would help you feel better?" and Esmé could ask: "Why does the divorce still hurt so much today?," and they could both have asked: "How do we move forward?" This illustrates two other features of being in Adult mode: being focused on the problem today (as opposed to the past) and looking for solutions (rather than revenge or points scoring). The great advantage of using the Adult mode is that it encourages the other party to switch into Adult, too. Unfortunately, if you use the Child mode, the other person will automatically move into Critical Parent or if you use Critical Parent they will automatically become Child. As in the case of Esmé and her mother, it is easy to get stuck in this dynamic for years and years.

Esmé, however, decided to use Transactional Analysis, or TA for short, to improve communication over Christmas. Traditionally, she would spend Christmas Eve at her father's house and Christmas Day at her mother's. However, she was fed up with traveling back late at night from her father's so she could wake up at her mother's. "Normally, I would have sulked or been stroppy, but I just told my mother my plans. She got really upset but I calmly explained my reasons—it would allow me to have a drink—and promised to arrive nice and early on Christmas morning. Interestingly it was my brother who seemed the most put out; he phoned and started getting critical: 'You're messing everybody's Christmas' but I didn't rise to the bait and kept Adult: 'I'm sorry you've been caught in the crossfire.'" In the end, Christmas passed off peacefully and Esmé used this as a foundation for a better relationship with both her parents. When she had a minor operation a few weeks later, she was able to let her mother take care of her. (The other half of Parent in TA is nurturing parent.) "I wouldn't have allowed her to mother me in the past. I was too angry. However, I did this time and it was really healing," said Esmé. Although nothing was said directly about the past, ghosts were laid to rest during Esmé's recuperation, and mother and daughter were able to start again—as two equals.

TA IN ACTION

Everybody has three parts to their personality: Parent, Adult, and Child. While there are two types of parent communication (Critical and Nurturing) and two types of Child (Adapted—which is placating, protesting, or appealing—and Free—which is spontaneous, creative, and joyful), there is only one kind of Adult. We need all five modes as there are times when it is appropriate to nurture or criticize (Parent mode); to be in problem-solving mode (Adult mode); and to rebel, appease, or just enjoy the moment (Child mode). The problem comes when we get stuck or spend too much time communicating in one particular way. So how can you use TA to improve not just your relationship with your parents but all your relationships?

- **Week One:** Start by observing other people: when do they become critical parent ("I wouldn't if I was you ..." or "Why do you always ...") or are nurturing parent ("Let me help you" or "Don't worry"), and when do they become adapted child ("It's not my fault" or "I'm so, so sorry"). Look for the body language too: finger pointing (Critical Parent), nodding (Nurturing Parent), and downcast eyes, slumped shoulders, and pouting (Adapted Child). How does one person's mode trigger the other's response?

- **Week Two:** Look for a moment when you've been in each of the five modes: Critical Parent, Nurturing Parent, Adult, Adapted Child, and Free Child. The hardest to spot is Free Child; this is normally when you're laughing or excited (like playing sport or having sex).

- **Week Three:** Experiment with being in adult mode, which asks questions like "How?," "When?," "Why?," and "What are the facts?," and has a clear and enquiring tone and open body language that involves good eye contact and active listening. How do other people react? Do they switch into adult mode, too?

- **Week Four:** When you speak to or visit your parents, be aware of the critical parent and adapted child transaction—as this is by far the most common. If your father or mother is critical, do not people please or get rebellious, but switch into adult mode. You will be surprised at how quickly they will match you in adult and how much this will improve your overall relationship.

IMPROVE YOUR RELATIONSHIP WITH YOURSELF

My friend Kate had a difficult relationship with alcohol. Up until her late thirties, she had been able to drink, sometimes get really drunk, but stop herself from crossing over the line into destructive behavior. Unfortunately, the death of her much-loved father and the breakup of her marriage had turned something manageable into something that was slipping out of control. As problem drinkers go, Kate was a fairly glamorous and amusing one, and her drinking exploits were a source of great anecdotes: "I'd literally fall out of a trendy bar into the gutter. At the time, it seemed quite funny. Telling the story everybody would laugh, and nobody louder than me, but deep down inside I knew drink had the better of me." Fortunately, Kate used some of her inheritance to seek help from a private clinic which used a drug to block the urge to binge drink but allowed her to still enjoy a couple of glasses of wine. The program took three to four months and involved keeping a diary and writing about some of the underlying unhappiness that drink had been masking. Unfortunately, Kate's money ran out before she could complete the final exit interview with her supervising therapist. So I suggested that she come to my house for the weekend and, as a friend, I would help her review what she'd learned. I already knew the headlines: her mother had been unhappily married, and probably wanted to leave, but had become pregnant with Kate; how her elder siblings resented her and pushed her pram into the park pond and she had to be rescued by a passing stranger; how she had been sexually abused during her childhood by a relative. It was not surprising that Kate had a large inner void and that she had tried to fill it with alcohol.

I will always remember sitting in my garden on a summer's afternoon as Kate read out excerpts from her diary. Some of the images were so striking, I could see the small child in the woman in front of me. For example, her abuser would strike on Saturday morning before her weekly ballet lessons. Kate described what she would be wearing: "This little white ballerina dress and the little white shoes and I'd try and curl up and make myself as small as possible." Like most children in these circumstances, Kate was unable to tell her parents and tried to comfort herself "by pulling off strips of wallpaper and chewing on them." Kate's writing was so eloquent, I could see the angry child stomping around her ballet class, refusing to float and glide like the other girls, all crossed arms and "shan't." The treatment program asked Kate to write a letter to herself as a child. It was full of sympathy, understanding, and mothering—something that had been in short supply when she was growing up. I could almost see the small Kate look up from the corner of her childhood bedroom and unclench her fists.

The final exercise in Kate's program involved writing down her goals. However, this time the language was aggressive and angry. She wanted to "expunge" the past, stop the small Kate from "sniveling all the time," and "get on" with her life. I felt like I'd been slapped across the face and, when

I have such strong feelings during counseling sessions, I suspect they come from my clients. This time, in my garden, I knew that the pain really belonged to small Kate. Hopefully this won't sound too weird, but I could sort of picture small Kate shrinking away from us. All her hope from listening to the mothering letter, that things could be different, had been wiped off her face. Her shoulders had gone up and she'd retreated back into blank resignation. My therapy training encourages me not to question these images but to share them with my clients:

"It feels like one moment you want to hug small Kate and the next to punish her," I told my friend. "First it's 'Come here and I'll look after you' and then, this is a strong word, but it's what I want to say: 'I'm going to abort you.'"

Kate laughed and admitted that she couldn't have it both ways.

So we decided to look after small Kate but destroy all the paperwork from her program. Later that afternoon, we went down to the beach and found a few bits of driftwood to make a fire. Before she put a match to the diary, Kate said a silent prayer for small Kate. Afterward, we sat on the beach and watched the sun go down and the tide come in and carry away the ashes. Although this happened over ten years ago, Kate still reminds me of our impromptu ceremony and how cleansing it felt.

During my counseling with Esmé, I had explained the difference between self-medicating and self-soothing. Esmé understood self-medicating without any problems—in the past she had blocked out her feelings with both food and alcohol—but self-soothing was harder to grasp. One week, she told me about a dream where she had a hungry baby but had no milk in her breasts. Remembering Kate's inner child and how she cried out for mothering, I wondered aloud if the baby might symbolize Esmé as a small girl cut adrift by her parent's divorce. Could she soothe small Esmé?

'It's funny you should say that but I had a really hard day at work and I'd been recovering from some bug. Instead of going to my French Adult Education class, I decided to go home and indulge myself by watching a Lemony Snicket movie which just happened to be on the TV. It was just the right blend of childish fun and I felt a whole lot better by bedtime,' said Esmé.

"That sounds a perfect way of soothing yourself. You listened to the fact that you were tired and run-down and needed looking after, but you did not block out the feelings."

Next we looked at ways that Esmé could nurture small Esmé. She decided to have a stack of similar DVDs ready and, as she had enjoyed painting as a child, to get a box of watercolors and some artist's paper, so she could indulge herself.

"Previously, during counseling, when small Esmé entered this room," I said, "it seemed she was going to overwhelm you and she had to be pushed away as quickly as possible. Now it seems that you have the tools to look after her."

Fortunately, Esmé understood what I meant: "I feel I can manage the pain from the past rather than run away." At that point, I knew that Esmé had not only improved her relationship with herself but started to emerge from the crisis sparked by her boyfriend stronger, wiser, and happier.

Returning to Martina, she had to launch a new range of services for her company at a trade fair. She got to the exhibition center the day before, set up her stand, and got an early night. "I know everything will be all right but somehow my brain starts to panic," Martina explains. "I can literally lie awake all night worrying. In the past, I've taken pills which help me sleep but leave me sluggish and slow the next day, and I can't think quickly enough."

I had explained previously the difference between self-medicating (or in this case medication from the doctor) and self-soothing. Had Martina been able to use this knowledge?

"I know this is going to sound stupid but I imagined that I was a small child, just like my daughter, so I did what I would have done for her. I told myself everything was going to be OK, imagined holding myself, and gently rocking myself back and forth."

"It doesn't sound stupid. It sounds incredibly creative,' I said. 'You have learned to soothe yourself."

Martina continued: "I managed to fall asleep quite quickly and the next day everything went extremely well. If there were any problems, everybody turned to me and I was able to sort them out."

FIVE WAYS TO SOOTHE YOUR INNER CHILD

There are times when we need a break from being an adult and either to nurture our adapted child or give full reign to our free child. Here are five suggestions:

1 **Remember what you enjoyed when you were a child.** What was your favorite TV Show, movie, or book? Prepare a box of treats for next time you feel overwhelmed and need to soothe yourself with an afternoon of indulgence on the couch.

2 **Indulge your creativity.** When we were children, it was fine to draw and write stories—but somehow when we grow up, unless we are a professional writer or artist, we believe we'd be "wasting our time." So give yourself the same freedom: write a poem, draw the view from your bedroom window, or bake a cake—whatever you enjoyed when you were young or wished you could have done.

3 **Play sports.** Once again, children play to let off steam but adults have to be serious and compete. If you don't play sports anymore, remember your childhood pastimes and buy a set of rollerskates, book a horseback-riding lesson, or take a dance class. Exercise also blunts the brain's response to physical and emotional stress, reduces anxiety and provides an endorphin rush.

4 **Take a vacation from responsibility.** Adults have bills to pay, goals to reach, and places to be. Children have long vacations with no plans and go with the flow. So, instead of worrying about a particular problem or working through a mental list of "to do" items, take the afternoon off or plan a weekend away when you can put your responsibilities to one side for a fixed amount of time. If you feel them returning during the vacation, imagine pushing them away and saying to yourself, "I will think about that on Monday."

5 **Write a letter to your younger self.** When you've been imagining soothing your inner child, what age was this younger version of yourself? Start the letter: Dear ... I'm writing because I know life seems ... (describe your younger self's situation or outlook at this age). So I've got some advice for you ... (please be compassionate, loving, and understanding).

FORGIVENESS

The fourth and final strategy for letting go of the past is forgiveness. However, lots of my clients find it hard to forgive because of some unhelpful myths.

Christine, forty-nine, discovered that her husband had kept in touch with his former mistress. The affair might have ended fifteen years earlier but they had continued to exchange emails, met for lunch on a couple of occasions, and she had sent him pictures of her small children (she had subsequently married and had a son and a daughter). Although Christine's husband was adamant that he loved her and had no feelings for his ex, she felt trapped. She wanted to save their marriage—despite everything she still loved him—but was unable to forgive his repeated betrayal. When she contacted me, she was having trouble sleeping, her appetite was poor, and she repeatedly dissolved into tears.

Meanwhile, Angie, fifty-two, had been bullied by her brother when they were growing up: "He would pin me to the bed and slap me around the face—until I said how great he was or some other stupid thing. Once he even tied me to the apple tree in the garden and left me there. I was terrified of him." In fact, his bullying was so bad that she had hardly spoken to him since leaving home—beyond "pass the sprouts" or some other nicety at the occasional family gathering. "I hated the way I would be forced by my mother to go to—for example—his second wedding because 'What would people think if his own sister wasn't there' and I'd often have sleepless nights before such events." Although, these events had happened nearly forty years ago, they still had the power to unsettle Angie.

So what are the unhelpful myths about forgiveness that trap us in the past?

Forgiveness will let my parents, partner, friend, or whoever off the hook and excuse bad behavior. Stop and ask yourself: Who is really being hurt by not forgiving? In most cases, the other party has moved on or buried the issue but for you it is still alive.

If I forgive, they are likely to do it all over again. Stop and ask yourself: Is punishment the best way to gain cooperation? Otherwise, there is a danger of the other party labeling you bitter or twisted—and therefore being justified, in their mind, to dismiss your requests. Ask yourself: What would happen if I used a carrot as well as a stick?

I can only forgive if certain conditions are met. Stop and ask yourself: Does the other party know what these conditions are? Do I even know them myself? Does he or she have the necessary skills or self-knowledge to meet the conditions? In most cases, this myth leaves you trapped waiting for someone else to change rather than being empowered and acting yourself.

Forgiveness is a feeling and I just can't make myself do something that doesn't feel right. Stop and ask yourself: Is forgiveness really a feeling? Think back to previous times when someone has hurt you but you've consciously decided to let it go. In my opinion, forgiveness is an intellectual choice and therefore within your power.

How can forgiving help you move on?

If forgiveness is truly given—and not coerced—it allows you to let go of resentment, blame, and anger. Therefore, forgiveness is not just an act of generosity to someone else but a gift to yourself. This is because it frees you from the past, allows you to draw a line, and to start afresh. There are other benefits, too. With infidelity, not forgiving the third party keeps them in your life. While forgiveness allows you to purge them from your day-to-day thoughts. Better still, forgiving the person or people who hurt you±whether for infidelity or some other harmful behavior—makes it easier to forgive yourself for your own mistakes.

For example, when Christine decided to forgive her husband for being weak and responding to the other woman's persistent messaging, she stopped beating herself up for not noticing the signs that they had still been in contact: "Actually, I'm not surprised that I missed it because they spoke on the phone on only a handful of occasions—although she was a Facebook friend. What was I supposed to do? I didn't want to be one of those suspicious and bitter women who are forever checking on their husbands." She had finally started the road to healing.

In the following months, Christine found she could talk about the affair and the continued contact in a calmer and less anxious manner. Her husband was no longer frightened of setting off an avalanche of tears and opened up more. Finally, they could begin to work on improving their marriage.

During counseling, Angie began to look deeper into her relationship with her brother when they were children: "I was a terrible telltale. If I found him smoking, I'd tell our mother. I heard a rumor at school about him stealing from the stores and I told Mom that too."

"So what else might have fed his unacceptable behavior?" I asked.

"While I was closer to Mom, he was inseparable from Dad. They'd go hunting rabbits in the woods together and fishing too, but when we were thirteen and I was eleven Mom and Dad fell out, he disappeared, and we didn't see him again. Worse still, we weren't even allowed to talk about him. Just forced to pretend he never existed. Once I found Mom throwing away a birthday card that had come for me—before I got a chance to open it. I guessed the card must have come from Dad but Mom wouldn't talk about it, so I never knew for sure."

"So your brother, who had a more difficult relationship with your mother, must have felt even more powerless and angry?" I suggested.

"It must have been horrible for him. I missed Dad, of course I did, but I still had Mom and, although we had our differences, I had someone on my side," she explained.

Ultimately, Angie decided that she would apologize to her brother for telling tales as a child and repeatedly getting him into trouble. "Although he didn't directly apologize back, he did sort of refer to the bullying. I could tell in his eyes that he regretted his behavior and that, basically, was enough."

ARRANGE AN EXORCISM

If you are finding forgiveness hard because the physical pain is still strong, you might need some extra help. For example, Millie, thirty-five, discovered that her husband had taken his mistress to their holiday home and she felt the place had been violated. Although she had forgiven him for the affair, this extra betrayal seemed one step too far. "We had some really nice memories of that house—especially when the children were little—but I feel they've all been spoilt. I tried to spend a weekend there but I became horribly short of breath and had to leave," she explained. When we examined what hurt the most, Millie identified that she'd put a lot of herself into the backyard and couldn't stop thinking, "She saw this view, she's been here too." So I suggested an exorcism—not getting a priest to come around, but changing the place by adding or subtracting something. "In this way, you have taken control and reclaimed the space," I explained. After some thought, Millie decided to get a sundial for the center of the lawn, change the view, and thereby exorcise the ghost of the affair. Ideas for your exorcism include:

- Having a party, in order to mark the end of one phase of your life and the beginning of the next.

- Arranging a simple ceremony, perhaps reading a poem or an extract from your diary or letting go of a helium-filled balloon.

- Having a clear out of the attic or somewhere else where there is clutter. Although not everything will be connected with the painful event from the past, throwing possessions away will have a psychological impact and free you up for a better future.

MOVING FROM VICTIM TO SURVIVOR

It is much easier to take control of your past if your childhood was basically happy and your mother and father provided good enough parenting. It is much harder if you suffered neglect, your parents were overinvolved, or you were abused.

Returning to Greta from Chapter One, her mother had mental health issues and her father was an alcoholic. She was basically left to fend for herself—especially after her elder siblings left home: "I would try and spend as much time as possible around friends' houses—partly because I knew I'd get a meal but mainly to get scraps of secondhand mothering."

The more that I listened to Greta talk about her "latch key" childhood —how nobody seemed to worry where she was and what she was doing and the occasion when the hospital released her mother from a psychiatric ward but provided no backup to check if she really could look after her daughter—the more angry, I became.

"There comes a point where neglect becomes abuse. What was your father thinking? What about social services?" I told her.

Greta's reaction was complex. On one hand, she felt relieved: "Someone is finally on my side." However, on the other, she felt protective toward her father: "Alcoholism is an illness. He didn't choose to be ill. OK, he might have chosen to have a particular drink. Anyway, he's better now; hasn't had a drink in years. We have a good relationship these days."

Whereas previously, I'd worried that describing the neglect as abuse was too strong, I was certain that I'd found the key to help Greta put the past behind her. Let me explain more.

The drama triangle

This idea was developed by the TA (Transactional Analysis) therapist Stephen Karpman who outlined three roles that people play in difficult situations: Victim, Rescuer, and Persecutor.

If your parents were in some way neglectful, or expected you to rescue them or you suffered abuse as a child, you will end up playing out these roles in your adult relationships too. Worse still, the drama triangle is not stable; all the roles can quickly shift and you find yourself at a different corner.

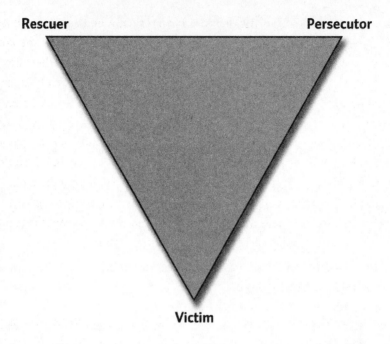

Returning to Greta, by identifying just how painful her childhood had been, I had started in the rescuer role with her father as the persecutor and Greta as the victim. Within seconds, Greta had stepped in to defend her father and become the rescuer. So he slipped around to the victim position and I became the persecutor who was attacking him.

Similarly, in the past, Greta had spoken to her mother about her miserable childhood—when they hired a holiday villa together in France— but the next morning, Greta woke up to find her mother sobbing her eyes out at the bottom of her bed. This time around, Greta had become the persecutor and her mother the victim ("you don't know how hard it was for me"). By choosing to come into her daughter's room to cry, Greta's mother was also inviting her to step into the rescuer role and offer comfort.

No wonder Greta found it hard to make lasting relationships. If she let someone get close, she risked being hurt all over again and, when she did make tentative steps into a relationship, she felt most comfortable rescuing people. Although that felt better than being trapped in the victim role, and not as destructive as persecuting someone else, it still left the triangle intact and prevented her forming an equal relationship (as opposed to rescuing lame ducks or mothering men who hadn't grown up).

Chelsea, twenty-eight, was an only child and for as long as she could remember her parents had vicious fights and they would do their best to draw her in and invite her to take sides. "Fighting was so much business as normal that it would feel strange if they were getting on," said Chelsea. "I remember setting off on vacation in the car and for once they were being nice to each other, so I deliberately needled them and within seconds they were at it again. Even at the time, it seemed stupid but I couldn't help myself." Once again, this is a classic drama triangle. Normally one of Chelsea's parents would claim the other was the persecutor and get Chelsea to rescue them. In this case, the triangle had swung around and Chelsea became the persecutor who picked a fight.

Breaking the drama triangle

If you suffered neglect or abuse as a child, the goal is to become a survivor rather than a victim and thereby dispense with the drama triangle altogether. But, first, it is important to "hold onto" the victim role because it allows you to acknowledge what happened, how it was not acceptable and how you were not responsible. It also stops the abuser or persecutor from slipping into victim ("poor me") or worse still making out that you were responsible ("you made me do it").

Greta decided that she would talk to her father about what happened and try and get some of her questions about that period answered. It was a difficult but productive conversation.

"He was upset and, many times, I wanted to reassure him, but that would have pushed me into rescuer. So I stayed quiet and just listened. I didn't really get much more information—after all he was drunk for much of this time—but I made my point and he acknowledged how I felt and apologized again," said Greta. "And you know what? I think that might be enough."

Next, you need to reinforce your boundaries and understand the difference between appropriate and inappropriate behavior. (I covered the importance of boundaries in Chapter Five.) This is tough, especially if your parents did not have adequate boundaries themselves. For example, with Chelsea, her parents should have resolved their own disputes—rather than embroil an eight-year-old. Instead, they broke the boundaries that should have been around their marriage (where serious husband and wife disputes remain private) and the one that should protect children from adults' problems.

In effect, perpetrators do not respect boundaries. They just do what feels right for them at the time and do not consider other people's personal space or interests. Therefore, it is not surprising that people who were abused as children find it hard to set appropriate boundaries and either have very low ones (where people walk all over them) or incredibly high ones (that nobody can breach).

Chelsea had set her boundaries too low. After her parents' divorce, she became "responsible" for giving her mother a vacation. "I do resent it because I'm twenty-eight and I'd rather go off with my friends, but my mother complains that she can't go away on her own." Instead of putting up an appropriate barrier—for example, a long weekend away together—Chelsea would moan but then give into her mother and book another two-week beach vacation: "It must be horrible stuck at home and never getting a proper break."

"Isn't your mother an adult? Should her daughter always be her 'plus one' for social events?" I questioned.

Chelsea went away and talked to her friends about what they considered to be appropriate and inappropriate requests from a mother to a daughter and decided to be more conscious of her boundaries in future.

Moving onto the winner's triangle

This next idea is credited to another TA trainer, called Acey Choy. She claims not to have invented it but rather to have found it (but she can't remember where). I like the concept because it provides not only clues about how to break the drama triangle but also a clear goal for the future. So what does the winner's triangle (next page) look like?

You will see the persecutor corner of the triangle has become assertive, the rescuer corner shifts to caring and the victim to vulnerable. So the winner's triangle looks like this:

Caring   **Assertive**

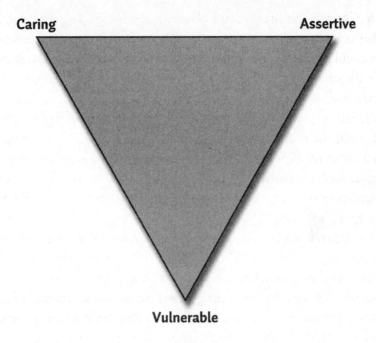

Vulnerable

When I did the winner's triangle with Angela and David, a couple in their early fifties, he immediately asked, "But isn't a rescuer going to be caring? I don't understand the difference." Angela was similarly perplexed: "I know victim and vulnerable aren't quite the same thing but I can't explain how or understand what the difference might be." They had come to see me after David had an affair with a work colleague and despite two previous attempts at counseling they were still trying to recover almost five years after he finally admitted to being unfaithful. They had found the drama triangle very useful because, when Angela was upset, David would try and take the pain away and make everything all right. In effect, Angela would start as the victim and David as the rescuer.

"If only I could find a way to answer her questions about when and why the affair happened but it was so long ago, I can't remember when it tipped over from colleagues talking about 'what I did over the weekend' to discussing inappropriate things like 'my unhappiness with Angela' or what exactly I did say," he explained.

At this point, he would get frustrated with himself (for not being able to rescue) and with her (for asking for the impossible) and consumed with guilt (because he caused the pain and therefore felt responsible for healing it). He would act out his feelings by becoming angry and defensive. Returning to the drama triangle, he would become the persecutor—which would make Angela angry, too: "How dare he treat me like this, and I'd get upset about all the years I'd lost out of my marriage and I'd feel stupid for putting up with some of his bad behavior before all this started. Eventually, I would lose my temper and say spiteful and horrible things." At this point, David would switch off and withdraw—pursued by Angela. She had become the persecutor and, in his mind, David felt the victim.

"A rescuer is like a knight in armor who sweeps the victim off her feet and 'saves' her,' I explained. "But you can't 'save' her or 'make it all right' because some of the problems are in her box and about her and you're not responsible for her personal stuff." (For a recap of this concept, see Chapter Five.) "And you know my maxim 'It's not ALL about me' and if not ALL about you then it's not your responsibility to fix it all."

"Because lots of this is about how I feel about myself because the other woman was younger and prettier," Angela chipped in.

"In the winner's triangle, you just need to care—which doesn't involve getting frustrated and switching off," I explained to David.

Next, I turned Angela: "In many ways, your last statement begins to show the difference between victim and vulnerable. First of all, a victim blames other people—for example 'You destroyed my confidence' or 'You made me hate my body.' Obviously, this is a tough place to be. I picture it as down on the floor. Sadly, to compensate, people swing to wonderful: 'I'm a special creation' and 'Nothing can touch me.' I picture this as up in the air."

Angela nodded; she could recognize those two extremes.

"What I'm looking for is vulnerable rather than closed off and 'nothing is going to hurt me again,' which might be the polar opposite of victim but can be equally unhelpful. Essentially, there is a middle place between victim and untouchable. Vulnerable is being open to looking at your part of the problem and taking your part of the responsibility rather than simply blaming."

I also find some people in the victim corner are tempted to run away and start a new relationship, which at the time seems a solution but, more often than not, means finding a new rescuer and perpetuating the drama triangle.

Although, in the winner's triangle, vulnerable replaces victim, caring replaces rescuer, and assertive replaces persecutor, everybody needs each of these three attributes. Therefore, while switching positions on the drama triangle is destructive, switching positions on the winner's triangle is constructive.

The skills triangle

Now I've identified the problem (the drama triangle) and the goal (the winner's triangle), the next question is: How do we get there? You won't be surprised at my answer—because it's at the core of this book—you need skills. So let's have a look at them:

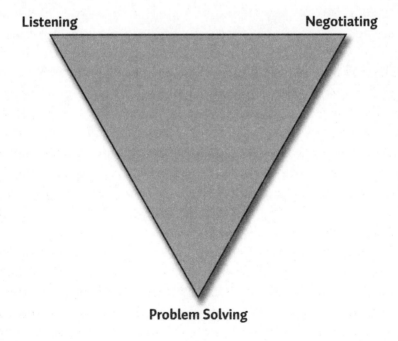

219

Hopefully, you'll have let out a sigh of relief because you've already begun to acquire these skills. We covered negotiating and listening in Chapter Six. In this chapter, I introduced the TA concept of adult to adult conversations—who, why, what, how questions—which is central to problem solving. In effect, adult to adult is an equal relationship as opposed to parent and child (which is fundamentally unequal) and can easily become rescuer and victim.

So, returning to David and Angela, David only had to listen to Angela to demonstrate that he did care about her feelings and was truly sorry for his infidelity. For Angela, instead of waiting for David to make her feel better, she could be empowered and start to look at how to solve the problem herself. Finally, they could be two equal partners in resolving their marriage problems.

Let's recap the three triangles and the journey of each particular corner:

DRAMA		WINNER		SKILLS
Victim	$\longrightarrow$	Vulnerable	$\longrightarrow$	Problem Solving
Rescuer	$\longrightarrow$	Caring	$\longrightarrow$	Listening
Persecutor	$\longrightarrow$	Assertive	$\longrightarrow$	Negotiating

If you're trapped in the drama triangle, you will have played every role, but there will one position to which you will naturally gravitate. Therefore, focus on that journey, the goal in the winner's triangle, and think about how you could improve the relevant skill in the final triangle.

LETTING GO OF THE PAST

Whether you suffered abuse, neglect, your parents had inappropriate boundaries, or you were just unlucky (for example, your parents had a bitter divorce), you need to find a story to tell yourself that makes sense of the past, and, most importantly, helps you move from a past negative to a past positive time perspective:

1 Take a piece of paper and draw a line down the middle. On one side write down all the negative things that happened and on the other the positive things.

2 Don't worry if it is harder to find positives—most people take the good things for granted. If you're having trouble, speak to your brother or sister, another relative or a childhood friend, and see if any of their positive memories chime with yours.

3 Think about the benefits of your childhood. I know this can sometimes be difficult, but even the most painful pasts provide some useful learning. (For example, Greta had become good at putting herself into other people's shoes. This ability to be compassionate had led to a career in Human Resources for a major company. Meanwhile, Chelsea's childhood had helped her become good at crisis management—an important part of her freelance business—and being an only child made her self-sufficient.)

4 Put your discoveries into the story about yourself that you might tell a new acquaintance or an interview board for a job: I had a difficult time because ... however, the positive side was that ... (For example, I had a difficult time at school because I used to be bullied. However, the positive side was that one of my teachers encouraged me to become involved with the drama society and that's brought me a life-long interest in the theater and music.)

5 In this way, you will integrate the past into your life today and instead of being a victim or something unpleasant, you are a survivor who has not been defeated by adversity but learned something or gained something important.

EIGHTH MAXIM IN ACTION

The aim of this maxim is help you to be compassionate toward yourself because **I'm doing my best but I'm crooked timber** and to encourage you to be compassionate to other people because they're doing their best but are crooked timber, too.

To demonstrate the difference adopting this maxim can make, I'm going to share two letters sent to my website. The first is from a woman in her early fifties whose husband was going through a midlife crisis and wanted a divorce:

"I can see that the roots of my 'rescuer' role are buried deep in my unhappiness at boarding school from the age of eleven. There were four years of relentless bullying going on within my eight-bedded dormitory. While I supported whoever was 'victim' at the time (my mothering and caring nature jumped in, which had been overdeveloped at home with three younger sisters), I found when the spotlight was finally turned on me, and I was bullied, not one of my dorm mates stood by my side, and it lasted for at least six weeks. Six weeks of being totally ignored (maybe this is why my husband totally ignoring me hits such a nerve within me), bed trampled on, unkind comments being tossed out in general conversation, etc., etc. There was no point in telling anyone because it would only have made matters worse.

"Ever since then, my coping strategy has been to lock myself away inside of me. I told myself that I had to cope alone. Telling myself that I didn't need anyone else, I couldn't rely on anyone else. I vowed not to get close to anyone else as I knew I would be rejected at some point in the future. (I recognize this as being useful at the time, as a child with limited resources, but that it has absolutely no use as a mature adult and needs to be addressed and laid to rest once and for all.)

"In order to continue engaging with people, however, I continued to do what I had discovered would keep them engaged with me, at least for the duration of them having a need for me, so rescuing became my role. Another tactic was to always keep people at arm's length, never really letting anyone have total access to my heart (and, if I am totally, totally honest with myself here, that included my husband), to protect me from getting hurt."

The second letter is from a woman in her early forties with two small children who does not trust her husband:

"He even takes his phone to the bathroom, seems terrified to leave it anywhere, and gets mad if I go anywhere near it. He says I have given him a phobia and this is why he explodes in a temper. He just bought a new one which has even more security and codes for everything (I know because, yes, I do try to look, but it's useless, there is no way I can hack into anything to put my mind at ease). The truth is I don't trust him. How can I??? I feel like I will one day find out what has been going on. I don't think he is having an affair, I just KNOW he flirts and chats with girls (or he used to), he probably sees them when he is out, maybe goes to their houses, I don't know!! I don't feel he is honest with me.

"I am miserable when I think about it and most days I just try to push it to the back of my mind and carry on but I worry I might be wasting my life. What if in three or five or ten years' time I find out he was betraying me all along, carrying on this chatting? A betrayal to me doesn't have to be sexual, but it may as well be for the damage it does.

"If he is doing anything, I want to know, I want to catch him because he isn't always a joy to live with anyway and I would hate to think I put up with it all and he was disrespecting me. I want to know the truth. He says I am crazy and jealous and have always been, about any girl. He has not looked after me like he promised to."

In the first letter, the woman accepts her crookedness and is compassionate to herself (and by extension toward her husband). In the second letter, the wife is firmly in the drama triangle. She sees herself as the victim and her husband as the perpetrator but wants him to rescue her (like he promised). There is a lot of blame and anger and no acceptance of the crookedness of human behavior and therefore she cannot be compassionate toward herself (it must be horrible to live your life under this cloud) or for her husband either (whose life sounds miserable, too).

GREEN SHOOTS

- There are four ways of taking control of the past. Acknowledge the impact of what happened—rather than wishing it away or minimizing it. Improve your relationship with your parents by changing how you communicate today. Learn to look after yourself. Forgive—not for the sake of the other person—but as a gift to yourself.

- You can shift out of the drama triangle into the winner's triangle by listening, problem solving, and negotiating.

- The eighth maxim to change your life is: "I'm doing my best but I'm crooked timber."

CHAPTER NINE

Discover Your Life Path

When you're in a crisis, it is important to know there's light at the end of the tunnel. So at the beginning of the book, I promised that change can be for the better. I hope by this point, you're not only feeling more optimistic but have started to take on board my maxims and let them sink into your daily life. My suggestion that this crisis could be the making of you is, hopefully, beginning to seem less fanciful. You should also be feeling more relaxed, have a better understanding of how you got into this mess and be more compassionate to your nearest and dearest—even if they are still behaving badly or don't fully recognize the changes you've made.

Although, for most of the book, I've tried to keep you focused on the next few steps, it's time to look further ahead.

NINTH MAXIM

The best way to live your life is to be in the present, with the past truly behind you, but facing forward. After all, without some sense of where you are going, it is hard to make the right choices today or to decide where your true interests lie.

One of my favorite authors is Jeanette Winterson and I want to introduce the ninth maxim with something she said: "Life is short and there's only one way to prolong it. Live for what you love. Don't give into indifference." It is a call to be more passionate—not just in our relationships—to find interests, pastimes, and work that inspire us. However, it begs the question: How do we know what is right for us?

The answer was inscribed over the entrance to the Temple of Apollo at Delphi, one of the ancient world's most sacred sites: "Know yourself."

The advantage of a crisis—and there has to be one because it's so painful—is that you learn a lot about yourself. Thank goodness because a clear sense of who you are and what you need is going to be your guiding star in the darkness ahead. So, when you're uncertain which way to turn or what to do, tell yourself:

Choose what gives my life meaning.

In this way, when you begin to emerge from the other side of your crisis, you will feel better orientated and better able to cope with life's ups and downs. I know from experience how helpful this maxim can be because it is easy to get sidetracked by something that seems tempting and exciting (but is not right for us) or to be seduced off our life path by someone else's passions or needs.

BEING FUTURE ORIENTATED

The importance of being future orientated is laid out starkly in a classic experiment by the psychologist Walter Mischel, who offered six-year-olds at Stamford University Nursery School a simple choice: Would they like one marshmallow or two? Obviously, the pupils all opted for two candies, but there was a catch. The children were sat at a desk with one marshmallow and a bell. The researcher explained that he or she was about to leave the room and if the children could wait, they would be rewarded and allowed two marshmallows. If they couldn't wait, the children should ring the bell and the researcher would return and they could eat the marshmallow on the plate in front of them. In other words, the choice was very simple: one marshmallow now or two later.

Between 1968 and 1974, Mischel tested 653 children, waiting fifteen minutes before returning, and recorded which children could resist temptation and which ones couldn't. What made this such a landmark experiment is that the team returned in 1982 and asked the parents of ninety-five of the original children to rate how well their son or daughter was doing both academically and socially. They discovered that children who could wait for a second marshmallow were most likely to be doing well at school, able to maintain friendships, and "cope with a problem of some importance." Meanwhile the SAT scores for the children who opted to eat the one marshmallow were up to 210 points lower. What was truly extraordinary is how waiting even a few seconds longer at six years old brought up their SAT scores, as teenagers, and closer to those that had resisted temptation.

Not surprisingly, low-delaying children turned into low-delaying adults, and when the team followed up the original subjects again, this group were more likely to have weight problems, issues with drugs, and to have been divorced. So why should being able to wait aged six for a second marshmallow be such an accurate predictor of future behavior?

DELAYED GRATIFICATION

As Oscar Wilde famously said: "I can resist everything but temptation." Just how hard it must have been for those children to wait for fifteen minutes is underlined in the many videos available on the Internet where people have recreated Mischel's famous Marshmallow test. Some children eat the marshmallow before the adult has even left the room, others keep smelling it or breaking off tiny bits to taste. Not surprisingly, the more focused the child is on the treat, the harder it is to wait. As Mischel explains: "If you're thinking about the marshmallow and how delicious it is, then you're going to eat it." However, if you can deal with a hot stimulus at six—a treat under your nose—you're also going to be able to choose to study for a test (rather than watch TV), think beyond your needs, *and* consider those of your partner too, and to save money for your retirement. This is why being able to delay gratification is so important: it allows us to balance our immediate and our long-term interests. So what makes the difference between the delayers and nondelayers? It wasn't about willpower or self-control. The children who waited found a way to make the situation work for them. They would distract themselves by kicking the table, singing songs, counting numbers, or twirling their hair. In effect, they knew how to shift their attention whenever temptation cropped up and become future orientated.

HOW TO RESIST TEMPTATION

At first sight, Mischel's research can seem depressing: our ability to delay gratification at six will influence our whole life! But don't worry if you suspect that you would have wolfed down the marshmallow before the researcher had even left the room. There was a fascinating subset in the original study of children who could *not* delay gratification at six years old but became high-delaying adults. So how could you pull off the same trick?

- **Think counterintuitively.** We imagine that concentrating on the reward will help us gain it. However, the researchers found the children could wait longer if they showed them small distraction techniques. For example, covering over the marshmallow with a piece of paper.

- **Think differently.** Mischel's team also taught the children mental tricks to switch off the hot aspects of the marshmallow (taste and smell) and concentrate on the cooler ones (shape and color). For example, the children were encouraged to imagine the marshmallow was a cloud or to view the candy as a picture surrounded by an imaginary frame.

- **Think past.** This technique comes from Alcoholics Anonymous rather than marshmallows but it is just as effective. For people with drink problems, one drink is never enough but two is too many. So AA encourages members to think past the first sip. So, instead of concentrating on how good it tastes, they imagine how good they will feel the next morning when they don't wake up with a hangover. Please think past the moment to something positive (like enjoying the birds singing outside your window in the morning) rather than something negative (like how much you will hate yourself). This is important because the latter can trigger shame and more destructive behavior.

WHAT IS THE MEANING OF LIFE?

What gives your life meaning? Why do you get up in the morning? What do you hope to achieve before you die? If you are unable to answer these fundamental questions, delayed gratification becomes pointless because we need a reason, for example, for studying rather than partying or going to work rather than going fishing. And although "I'll disappoint my parents" or "It pays the bills" might be a reason for doing something, ultimately it makes for a pretty empty or joyless existence.

Some people cite "pleasure" as their raison d'etre, but as the Austrian philosopher Ludwig Wittgenstein (1889–1951) wrote: "We are not here to enjoy ourselves or I don't know why we are here, but I'm pretty sure that it is not in order to enjoy ourselves." Others are seeking money, success or fame (or a combination of all three). If those things give your life purpose, that's fine. But what happens when there are setbacks, serious illness, your boss is talking about redundancies, you don't become a celebrity, or the paparazzi stops taking your picture? At a stroke, your life would be stripped of all meaning. And it is in these moments of crisis that we most need a reason for living, because as the German philosopher Friedrich Nietzsche (1844–1900) said: "He who has a *why* to live can endure almost any *how*."

So what is the meaning of life? Ultimately, there is no right or wrong answer and everyone has to find his or her own solution. However, there are five basic ways of making your life meaningful—read them through and see which chime with you.

Enduring something

Sometimes circumstances call on us to act and shape our future; sometimes we need to realize that we can't change events but must accept our fate. However, this does not strip our life of all meaning. Austrian psychologist Viktor Frankl (1905–97) lost everything that he had valued in the Holocaust. His father, mother, brother, and wife died in gas ovens and Frankl lost a manuscript (his life's work) that he'd hidden under his clothes while being transferred to Auschwitz concentration camp.

Despite enduring cold, hunger, forced labor (laying tracks for railroad lines), and hourly expecting death, he still found meaning even in these dehumanized circumstances. In *Man's Search for Meaning* (Rider) he explains why some prisoners gave up the will to live while others chose to survive: "Woe to him who saw no more sense in his life, no aim, no purpose, and therefore no point in carrying on. He was soon lost. The typical reply with which such a man rejected all encouraging arguments was, 'I have nothing to expect from life anymore.'" So Frankl decided to use his time to study what humans could endure. "It did not really matter what we expected from life, but rather what life expected from us." And let's be clear, even though we would rather shut our eyes to the cold hard facts, nobody can escape suffering, pain, and death.

So how can enduring something provide meaning? Like Frankl, we can use the opportunity to learn about ourselves and other people. (Not that we need to suffer to change, but sadly we don't learn much from good times.) We can grow spiritually ourselves or provide an example for someone else on how to bear a burden with dignity and fortitude. Even when we're old and sick, we can still be of service. I will always remember my paternal grandmother who worried about being a "burden" once she passed her ninetieth birthday. However, she was teaching me an invaluable lesson: if you are grateful for kindnesses given—rather than take them as of right—people will not only enjoy giving but give even more. Twenty years after her death, I'm still benefiting from her example and passing it onto you.

Creating something

Over and over again, I've had the opportunity to witness how being creative is not only incredibly fulfilling but allows us to leave behind a legacy. Katrina, forty-eight, was fighting breast cancer while her daughter was expecting her first child. She decided to use the time she was stuck in bed or on the couch: "I started knitting baby clothes of all shapes and sizes. Anything to keep busy and be productive and, when I'd knitted more than any one baby could possibly wear, I decided to make a tapestry for the nursery wall." Although Katrina's treatment was successful, the cancer returned a couple of years later. "I wanted to show my second grandchild that Gran-gran loved him. I didn't want him to say, 'So why didn't she make me a tapestry, too,' so I set to work and created this picture of the nighttime sky covered with stars. It took a lot of energy but, no matter what, I was determined to finish it." As Katrina shows, we don't have to be Beethoven, Leonardo de Vinci, or Shakespeare to create something that will be treasured by future generations. If you're not good with your hands or artistic, there are other ways of being creative (for example, starting a business, having children, or even becoming a great collector).

Doing something

Meaning is something that we create moment by moment. So sometimes we will have a short-term goal (like running to the park and back without collapsing) followed by a middle-term goal (completing a half marathon), and a longer-term goal (beating our own personal best time). Sometimes it will be a life's work. "Since I can remember, I've wanted to help adult survivors of abuse," explains my friend Kate, who is fifty-four. "It was partly why I decided to study psychology at university and why I became an agony aunt on TV and radio. I spent a lot of time helping others, but eventually I realized that I had to get well myself and I've been working hard on that these past few years. I'm making good progress but ultimately I'd like to run a retreat where people can step out of their day-to-day life, contemplate, and find a way to heal." This "something" provides meaning for Kate because it turns her own childhood abuse from completely negative into a source of strength and a resource to help others. As a journalist, I've interviewed people who have started charities after their child was abducted or campaigning groups to try and change the law after being injured. It does not always have to be something so public. As a therapist, I've counseled people who found meaning—for a section of their lives—by nursing their sick or elderly parents.

Experiencing something beautiful

It could be listening to Mozart's Clarinet Quintet or visiting fall in Vermont, but the power of beauty should never be underestimated. Josephine Hart (1942–2011) was a novelist—*Damage, Sin* and *Oblivion*— and a campaigner for bringing poetry into everyday life: "Stop depriving yourself of what is incandescently beautiful in life. To deny yourself that is voluntarily to starve your soul. And if your soul is starved, it is impossible to be happy. Modern life makes it hard for people to feed their souls. They're on a starvation diet." Her poetry events were always popular—as Hart explained: "They come out and they think: 'My God! This is a feast!'"

Encountering someone

For many people, it is their relationships that provide meaning to their lives. It might be with a lover, a child, or possibly a friend. (We often overlook the importance of friendship but for many people their friendships endure longer than relationships and provide a rock at important times—such as burying a parent or helping us celebrate all our landmark birthdays.) "I never thought I'd love again," explained Frederick, fifty-five, after his first wife left him for another man. "My children were very supportive, inviting me around for Sunday lunch and jollying me along, but my life was empty and meaningless until I met Anouschka at a gallery. We started talking about the pictures and we never stopped. She not only filled a huge hole in my heart but suddenly everything made sense again." For other people the encounter might be with someone spiritual—for example, a teacher or a priest—or it might be their relationship with God, Jesus, or the Prophet Muhammad.

COMPLETING A MEANING AUDIT

Look back over the past few months and ascertain what has given your life meaning.

- What have you created? It might be laying a new patio, baking a great chocolate cake, or compiling an insightful report for your boss. Write down everything no matter how small and insignificant.

- What have you done that has provided meaning? Have you tested yourself or achieved something that made you proud? It might be something small within the bigger picture of your life or the world in general (for example, rehoming an abandoned dog or cat), but if it provides meaning for you, write it down. If you can't think of anything, ask your family or friends what they have appreciated or any important acts of service (for example, listening to their problems).

- Which relationships are significant and meaningful in your life? If you're having problems with your partner look further afield. What about your parents, work colleagues, and customers? (Incidentally, if you are going through an unwanted divorce or your partner has told you that he or she doesn't love you, the fact that the relationship has stopped being meaningful for your partner doesn't mean it can't provide meaning for you. As Frankl writes: "What you have experienced, no power can take from you.")

- What has brought beauty into your life? It might be the color of your neighbor's new front door, the novels of Anne Tyler or the ceramics collection in the Victoria and Albert Museum, London.

- What have you endured and how might you have inspired other people? This might be a hard question to answer on your own, so ask your family and friends for their opinions.

- Which categories are particularly strong and which ones could do with a little attention? How might you rectify a significant deficit?

HOW TO FIND YOUR LIFE PATH

Time and again, I find that people who are depressed, anxious, or feel stuck have no direction and no sense of *why* and, without that, it is impossible to know *how* to live. Although we think of this as a particularly modern dilemma, the writer and statesman Michel de Montaigne (1553–92) summed up the problem: "It is an absolute perfection, and as it were divine, for a man to know how to enjoy loyally his being. We seek for other conditions because we understand not the use of our own, and go forth from ourselves because we know not what abides within us." So how do you know yourself and find your path?

Periodically review

For most people, what provides meaning at twenty could very well no longer work at forty. This was certainly the case for Alice, forty-six, when I asked her to look back: "At sixteen, I wanted to make my parents proud so I studied hard, got the grades and kept my nose to the grindstone. I was also interested in charity because my mother had always done a lot to help others." Unlike other teenage girls, she wasn't really interested in boys. "I was more focused on getting to a good university and getting a good job. My mother had always been very worried about money—my father's work was always precarious—and I didn't want to be beholden to any man." Although Alice had had a few relationships by twenty-six, her main focus was still on establishing her career. At thirty-six, she had rebelled and began to think there was more to life than work. "I took leave of absence and decided to travel, let my hair down, and find out what I wanted to do. However, first my father and then my mother became ill and I decided to nurse them." This had provided a strong sense of meaning for Alice: "I didn't like the idea of strangers taking care of them and my other brothers and sisters had families or important jobs. It was tough but I grew closer to them than I ever thought possible." At forty-six, Alice had returned to the city and, although her job was time consuming, it did not really provide a reason for living. She had a group of close friends who provided some opportunities for "encountering someone": "However they've all got husbands and although we all get on well and I'll go on vacation with one couple, it is not the same as having your own partner." Therefore, Alice decided to work on her relationship skills and make finding love her priority.

Don't deny your roots

One of the most straightforward ways of finding your path as a teenager is to rebel against your parents and strike out on your own. However, sometimes we throw out something important that we'll need later on our journey. It had taken Alice longer than most people to realize that there was more to life than her mother's insistence on a good job, sound finances, and not relying on a man. At the same time, she had forgotten her mother's interest in helping others: "Our firm has taken on a mentoring project for a school close by where there are a lot of disadvantaged kids and I get a lot of satisfaction from that—far more than my job.' Although Alice did not feel able to abandon her well-paid work, she did decide to volunteer more hours and give herself permission to gain satisfaction from this charitable endeavor (even though it did not pay her bills).

Another client, Marcus, sixty-six, had spent his whole career in the oil industry: "My family had, for generations, been basically peasants in Eastern Europe and took refuge here just after the war. My parents were determined that I was going to better myself and I did well—working all over the world." After a few years of retirement, Marcus found his life was empty and meaningless. "My kids are grown up and don't really need me. I love my wife but there has to be something more to life than drives out to the country and pub lunches." On one of these trips, Marcus discovered a smallholding for sale and was toying with the idea of buying it. "It seems like a lot of work and it certainly doesn't fit with my original plan of retiring and taking it easy." When I caught up with him a couple of years later, Marcus was right in the middle of the lambing season. He was exhausted because he'd been up half the night and he hadn't taken a vacation for eighteen months, but his life was full of meaning. "I suppose farming is in my blood. My family spent forever trying to better themselves and leave the land and, when I had money, the first thing I did was buy my own corner, start planting vegetables, and raising livestock."

On a personal note, my mother, my grandmother, and my great-grandfather and greatgrandmother were all teachers (and probably a couple more generations back, too). When I left university, I never wanted to be a teacher—nothing could have been further from my mind—but here I am, thirty years later, giving workshops and lectures, going into schools to teach creativity, and my books are all about passing on knowledge. Perhaps one of the advantages of reaching our middle years is that we become secure enough in ourselves to stop denying our roots and instead embrace them.

Don't shy away from what you fear

Tom Hardy is an actor who has appeared in many movies—including *Bronson, Inception, Tinker Tailor Soldier Spy*, and *Dark Knight Returns*—and battled alcoholism and a crack cocaine addiction in his early to mid-twenties. He is also interested in martial arts: "Ju jitsu is very Buddhist. All that we fear we hold close to ourselves to survive. So if you're drowning and you see a corpse floating by, hang onto it because it will rescue you." I find this idea inspiring because it is often fear that stops us stepping off the path laid down by other people or conventional wisdom and exploring the world for ourselves.

"When I lost my job in my late thirties, I had no idea what I wanted to do next," explains Jim, who is now fifty. "I'd reached the top of my profession and there were very few openings at that level, so I knew I'd have to start again or take a few steps backward down the seniority scale. One half of me felt compelled to get another full-time job and be certain of the bills being paid, but there had to be more to life than that. Fortunately, I had a small payoff and I was offered a few bits of freelance work, so slowly the panic that I'd never work again lessened. With a little breathing space, I had enough time to think about what I really wanted to do and took a writing course. Of course, I was worried that I'd never make my living that way, but one thing led to another and I've done better than I could ever have imagined. However, if I'd given into my fear, I would never have trusted that a way forward would emerge and that somehow I would keep my head above water. Sure, there have been some difficult times and I've had to adapt but I've never been more fulfilled."

Seek right working

We spend so much time at work, it is hard to find your life path if work is pulling you in the opposite direction. If you have an urge to work outside, it is soul destroying to be in an office all day. If you are a team player, it will be torture if you have to work alone. If your goal is to help people, it is probably not a good idea to sell something you don't believe in. However, most misfits between path and work are not so straightforward—especially as what is right working at one stage in your life might not be right at another.

In his twenties and thirties, Oscar worked for a city recruitment firm: "My work was challenging and exciting. I earned a lot of money, which was just as well because London house prices are astronomical—even though we lived in an 'upcoming area'—and we wanted the best for our children, so that involved private schools too." Everything changed for Oscar when he turned forty: "I found my element surfing waves. The fact that I was too old and being passed by teenagers and twenties was part of the challenge. I loved the feeling of being pressed down by tons of water, the light on the beach in the early morning and pushing myself to the limit. I started reading about older sports people—in what they called the roaring forties—who returned to competitions more focused and determined to win than before. For me, it started with a few competitions here and there—fighting my own incompetence and fears—and before I knew it I was completely immersed in the thrill of the wave."

Over the next few years, surfing went from a hobby to what made Oscar's life meaningful (doing something) and his job went from the center of his life to just something that paid the bills: "Then I had an epiphany: what if I moved the family down to the sea? It would cut down on hotel and fuel bills plus save all that traveling time. We could buy somewhere much cheaper and the kids could breathe in fresh air rather than car fumes." Fortunately, his wife was behind the idea and the children were at an age where they were about to move school anyway. "I got a job locally—with much shorter hours—and I often surf before or after work. Our quality of life is much better. I see more of my kids than ever before and my eldest son has taken up surfing, too. I wonder why I didn't make the change years ago," he said.

"Right working" does not necessarily mean a change of career or a dramatic shift like Oscar. It could involve negotiating to work from home on Fridays (so that you can miss out on the office politics), volunteering for a new project (because it is likely to provide more satisfaction), or just bringing some of your values from the rest of your life into your work (deciding to speak up when you see injustice in the workplace).

IMAGINE YOUR OBITUARY

Sometimes it's easier to make sense of our life looking back. I spent quite a lot of time with one of my friends while she was in a hospice dying from cancer. I'd always seen her as an artist and had been impressed by how, when she could no longer paint, she'd taken up sculpture, and when that became too taxing she worked on refining a children's story that she'd illustrated. At her bedside, I also had the chance to meet and spend time with several of her children. So I was surprised when she told me: "What I'm most proud of is my teaching. Looking back, my priorities were teaching, art and then being a mother." What a brave and honest thing to say! But what's the point of dissembling on your death bed? However, I shouldn't have been surprised that my friend considered herself a teacher first and foremost because many of the overnight shifts—keeping her company and getting anything needed in the small hours—were filled by ex-pupils, and I met many more at her memorial service. She had truly touched their lives for the better.

Fast forward from today and imagine picking up a newspaper or reading an online obituary about yourself:

- What headline about your life would be picked by an obituary writer?

- How would they describe you?

- What highlights would they pick out?

- Where does family sit in your obituary? Are they a couple of lines at the end—for example, X is survived by ... Or are they at the center of your story?

- Are you proud of your achievements or have they been marred by mistakes or scandals?

Like Scrooge, waking up after his visit from the "Ghost of Christmas Yet to Come," the good news is that you still have choices. Perhaps you're satisfied with the contents and tone of the obituary but would like a shift in emphasis. Perhaps you want to make some radical changes. Fortunately, it's not too late.

If you're finding it difficult to look so far into the future because you're in the middle of a crisis, imagine looking forward a year from now. What could you learn from your present difficulties? How might your current circumstances and the learning promoted by them become a turning point in your life story and the foundation for future happiness? In the words of Montaigne, "Whether the events in our life are good or bad greatly depends on the way we perceive them."

BALANCED LIFE

One of the themes running through all my books is the need for balance and that's what I want to return to for this last section. So what do I mean by a balanced life? It's more than getting the work/life balance right. There are eight different qualities within us that all need to be listened to and kept in harmony in order for us to be stronger, wiser, and happier.

Inner child: This is a concept that I introduced in the last chapter. Our inner child is responsible for fun, entertainment, excitement, and joy, but it is easily overruled by other parts of our personality.

Inner father: This is the manager who is responsible for budgeting, household duties, keeping us safe, and being responsible. Sometimes this voice tells us that we might be afraid or don't want to do something but we've simply got to get on with it.

Inner mother: This energy is about caregiving and is responsible for sustaining, soothing, and singing us to sleep. It balances out the father voice—if it gets too challenging—by accepting both our weaknesses and our strengths.

Inner brother or sister: This is about friendship and mixing socially and tells us to honor contracts, not to isolate ourselves, and to contribute. Unlike the father and mother, this energy is on the same level as us.

Inner lover: This energy is about honoring our sexuality, allowing ourselves to be sensuous, enjoying our bodies, and satisfying our appetites. It ensures that we allow ourselves nice things—like underwear—and indulge all our senses.

Inner hermit: Instead of hurtling from one place to another, one diversion to another, this voice asks for quiet time, contemplation, and truthfulness. It prepares us for personal growth and works in close collaboration with the next two energies.

Inner priest or priestess: This voice is about honoring our spirituality. Rather than "I want," "I need," and "I'm going to have," it considers other people's needs and connects us to nature and the larger world (beyond family, friends, colleagues, or even country). Our inner priest or priestess could lead us to an organized religion or developing our own sacred rituals.

Inner guru: Last and by no means least is the energy that helps find our life purpose and mediates between all the different qualities outlined in order to achieve balance and meaning. It is responsible for our identity, our moral code, and deciding whether our actions contravene them or not.

Don't worry if you find that some of these energies are better developed than others. Many people subcontract voices to other people. For example, their real father or their boss to provide the manager energy or to their own children to put us in touch with our own inner child sense of wonder. Some people subcontract out to organizations—such as churches (for inner priest or priestess) or supporting a baseball club (for inner brother or sister). However, you should *never* lose sight of your inner guru or you will start to feel controlled by others or risk being taken advantage of and manipulated by powerful organizations.

GREAT DEBATE OF TODAY

Being true to ourselves and following our life path brings us up against one of the thorniest of contemporary issues: What happens when our desire for personal validation or satisfaction comes up against the needs and happiness of other people? Of course we should have the freedom to make our life fulfilling and meaningful, but what if those choices strip someone else's life of meaning? How do we balance the competing needs?

Bruce, forty-two, had been married for almost twenty years and had two teenage daughters; he worked hard, paid the bills, had a good circle of friends, but his marriage was a source of quiet desperation. "My wife is very critical, so I've long since given up saying when I'm unhappy because she will have worked harder (so I'm not entitled to complain) and will have remembered the situation differently (so my grounds for complaint are shaky). I kept my mouth shut and just got on with it. Or as she would put it: 'Be a man and suck it up.' Well guess what? I've had enough, that's why I've moved out and rented a cottage in the next village."

His wife, Penny, forty-one, saw the situation completely differently.

241

"All our friends are in complete shock. As one of the wives said to me, 'You were the last couple I expected to have problems' and another confided that we were the 'gold standard for happiness.' We're Bruce and Penny. Penny and Bruce. I don't want anything else. Of course, we've had our moments—when we're tired or stressed—but doesn't everybody? Bruce has got two beautiful daughters, a loving wife who simply adores him and would do anything for him, I can't understand why he wants to throw it all away."

To make matters more complicated, since leaving home Bruce had become friendly with someone at the edge of their social circle and begun a new relationship: "Penny thinks I've betrayed her," said Bruce, "but we were on a break."

"You told me that you moved out for space, to get your head together, to give us some hope of sorting it out, not to look for someone else," replied Penny. "But, as always, it's what makes Bruce happy and damn the costs for everybody else." She turned to me. "He doesn't get to see the girls crying themselves to sleep. He doesn't get the calls from their form mistress after an 'incident' in class. Who picks up the pieces, yet again? Me!"

"Doesn't what I want count for anything?" Bruce snapped back angrily.

Another example of competing needs is William and Daisy. William was thirty-seven when his mother died. Their relationship had been intense and extremely close. He had been her only child and, beyond a brief fling with his father, William's mother had had no significant partners. Like many people who've lost a parent, William found himself questioning everything—his job, his life path, and his marriage. Over the previous eighteen months, William had become increasingly semi-detached—spending weekends at his mother's old apartment and signing up for a training course that would take him away from home. By the time William and Daisy arrived in counseling, he was beginning to question whether his marriage had a future.

"I love William with all my heart. I'm sorry that I wasn't more supportive when his mother was dying," said Daisy. "I thought I would back off and let him sort through his grief in his own way, but I understand now that was the worst thing I could have done. I've said I'm sorry and tried to make it up to William but he won't let me."

"I'm just tired, exhausted from forever talking about our problems, and need time alone. I'm beginning to think separating would be best for both of us," William replied.

"I want to be with you." Daisy turned away so William could not see her tears.

The problems had come to a head because William wanted to spend Christmas with his mother's family in Australia and didn't want Daisy to come too.

"It's partly because I can't go through the charade of pretending everything between Daisy and I is normal, but I need this time to think and get my head together. And when else, beyond Christmas, am I going to get long enough away from work?"

Meanwhile, Daisy felt rejected and overwhelmed by despair.

With Rosie, forty-eight, the conflict was between what was right for her and what was right for her children. She was born in a small town in Scotland and found the inward-looking nature of most of the inhabitants very alienating: "Half of them had hardly been to Edinburgh or Glasgow, while I wanted to see the world, meet different people, and have new experiences." The situation was further complicated because she had been abused as a child and her home town was forever associated with those memories. Like most people, Rosie had managed to find a way of living with her wounds and getting on with her life. She married and had two small children, but a chance encounter with her abuser brought all the pain back and highlighted other problems in her life.

"I should never have married my husband," Rosie explained. "I had done it to spite an ex-boyfriend and finally couldn't stay a moment longer. I had the offer of a great job, but it meant working in London from time to time." Over the next six months, Rosie spent more and more time away, but she didn't want to take her children out of their schools as they were only eight and ten. "I'd also hurt their father enough. I'd trashed all his dreams, I couldn't take his children too." However, Rosie found it harder and harder to return to Scotland. "I could breathe in London where nobody knew me and I could be myself. Except my daughter would be leaving messages—full of sobs—on my cell phone begging me to come back, wanting to know what she'd done. I tried reassuring her but what could I say?"

So how could Bruce and Penny reconcile their very different pictures of their marriage? What about William's need to understand what he'd been through and heal versus Daisy's desire to spend Christmas with her husband? And finally, Rosie needed to sort out her childhood problems and pursue her career, but what if it came at the cost of damaging her own children's formative years?

It is an almost impossible dilemma: should we think of the greater good and deny our needs or should we be true to our own life path despite what it costs other people? If you're currently facing this problem, there are three questions to ask yourself:

Can you be happy while causing suffering to other people?

I've spent thirty years watching couples grapple with this question and I honestly believe that it is extremely hard. If your partner or children are suffering, they are likely to be angry and lash out, normally at you (or your new partner). Of course, it's possible to blame others (like your ex for turning the children against you) or to close your eyes (everybody's coping very well), but self-deception is not a foundation for true happiness.

Indeed, Bruce's new relationship imploded under the pressures of step-parenting—between them they had seven children. He did talk about returning to Penny and they spent several months in therapy going over what had gone wrong, learning to communicate better, but decided it was too late to save their marriage. However, they were able to coparent effectively and Bruce acknowledged his daughters' hurt and slowly rebuilt his relationship with them.

In effect, by slowing down the breakup process (rather than rushing into his sparkly new future), genuinely examining whether the relationship could be sorted out (rather than dismissing everything he and Penny had shared), and giving everybody a chance to come to terms with the divorce (so it seemed a logical solution to the problem rather than imposed on them) Penny and the girls felt their suffering had been mitigated.

Can you find solutions by running away?

Humans are social creatures, so I don't believe that we can find solutions in isolation. Sometimes, stepping out of your normal life for a weekend or a few days away can provide fresh thinking. Especially if time out reduces the pressure and allows you to catch up on sleep. However, just taking yourself out of a difficult situation is not suddenly going to provide clarity (so you know what your next step should be), and whether you miss someone or not is not a reliable guide to planning your future.

I spent a session with William looking at boundaries (see Chapter Five) and how he either let Daisy walk all over his wishes (and organize a party for his birthday even though he didn't want one) or set his boundaries incredibly high (disappearing off alone for three weeks).

"Boundaries are negotiated incident by incident," I explained, "so that you can decide, for example, I'll have a few friends around for dinner but not a surprise party with everybody I know."

"But wouldn't it be different with someone else?" William asked.

"What about your mother?" I replied. "I bet she was a strong character who got her own way."

"There was no point arguing with her, she'd win in the end, so I just let her get on with it."

"Does that sound familiar?"

"Yes, that's how it can be with Daisy."

"And if you run away, rather than staying and trying to fix problems, you just take all the old habits and unresolved stuff into your next relationship."

Where is the middle ground?

Instead of thinking about a winning position (when you get what you want) and a losing position (where your partner or someone else imposes their decision), look for a compromise. For example, Bruce returned to counseling and he and Penny made a joint decision to end their marriage. William and Daisy discussed whether Daisy should come to Australia for Christmas Day, Boxing Day, and a couple of extra days and

William would spend the majority of the vacation alone. Meanwhile, Rosie decided to return to her home town, but only until both her children were old enough to go to university—and at that point she would consider them "grown up" and feel free to put her life path first.

If it is hard to find the middle ground, I would offer two pieces of advice. If your partner is considering leaving, it is very easy to think there is no middle path. Either your partner goes or he or she commits to working on the relationship. However, there is still a middle way: putting off making a long-term decision but trying to work on improving communication on a day-by-day basis. I know it is hard to cope with uncertainty—and so tempting to push for a bit of reassurance—but any pressure will send your partner toward certainty (and that will be leaving). Instead, concentrate on showing how life could be different. Not by trying harder or being sweeter, but by beginning to solve the small issues of everyday life and showing you can act differently. (There is more in two of my books: *My Wife Doesn't Love Me Any More* and *My Husband Doesn't Love Me and He's Texting Someone Else*.)

Finally, listen to your partner's complaints—as if it is the first time you've heard them. Try to understand why he or she is so upset and a middle way will slowly emerge that'll allow both of you to keep your dignity. Ronald Dworkin (1931–2013) was a law professor at New York University and Professor of Jurisprudence at University College London. He wrote in his book *Justice For Hedgehogs* (Harvard University Press): "Without dignity our lives are only blinks of duration. But if we manage to lead a good life well, we create something more. We write a subscript to our mortality. We make our lives tiny diamonds in the cosmic sands."

NINTH MAXIM IN ACTION

It is impossible to get through life without tough and horrible things happening. As we get older, people we love get sick and die. Our loved ones can be overwhelmed by their personal demons and act in a thoughtless and selfish manner. Much as we'd like it to be different, bad things happen—like car accidents, crime, and economic downturns.

If you know your life path and tell yourself **choose what gives my life**

meaning, you will find a sense of proportion about any adversity and make better choices about your future. Even if this crisis was not of your own making, and you may not want the wisdom that it's given you, it's still there for the taking.

Edward, fifty-two, came into counseling because something about his life wasn't working. On our introductory session, he told me: "I'm not certain if it's something about me or my relationship. I'm often worn down by my wife who can be negative and this has a drip, drip, drip effect. On one hand, I wonder if I still love her but on the other, I could be being unreasonable because life can't be all picnics and birthdays."

We discussed the dilemma together and Edward decided to invite his wife to join us for couple counseling. She was initially reluctant but agreed to six sessions and we worked on communication and balancing their priorities. Two years later, he returned on this own: "I know that I truly love my wife, and that's a big step forward, so I think the problem is my expectations and how I respond to her."

So I took him through the main elements of this program, helped him to notice his feelings, become more mindful, and challenge his thoughts. He also owned up to being anxious himself rather blaming it on his wife. However, the main focus was on what made his life meaningful: "I think it's about making a difference to other people—starting with my wife and my children and radiating out from there."

We went through the five ways of finding meaning and we immediately recognized "encountering someone" as important for him, but what about the other ones?

"With doing something, I've been learning to be more spiritual and meditate, but I'm not very creative," said Tony.

"Perhaps you'd like to challenge that idea? After all, you've created a business."

"I've been taking photography evening classes so I can take better pictures of the kids and I'd like to see where that takes me. I've also been interested in learning to play the piano—at the moment it's only my daughter who uses it."

"So that could also be experiencing something beautiful." (Some items can fit in more than one category.)

"I've also learned about myself and what's right for me," Tony replied. "The guy that fixes my appointments had put together a schedule of meetings that had me crisscrossing the city and would only have worked if there'd been no traffic. I would also have ended up on the opposite side of the city from home and not got back before my younger children went to bed."

"So you've also 'encountered' yourself?" I suggested.

"Previously, I would probably have taken the meetings because I didn't want to let clients down, but I thought **choose what gives my life meaning** and it's not lots of unnecessary driving. So I asked him to reschedule."

Obviously there is no right or wrong way to find meaning; it's up to you to choose the path that's right for you. However, in my opinion, the best ways to find meaning are through relationships with other people and benefiting society as a whole (which is open to everybody), as this provides a counterbalance to our modern obsession with success as the only source of fulfillment (which by its very nature is only open to a very few). But in the spirit of Montaigne: "What do I know?"

GREEN SHOOTS

- It is important to differentiate between passing distractions and what you really need.

- Finding your life path will, slowly but surely, fill up your inner void, and make you stronger, wiser, and happier.

- The ninth maxim to change your life is: "Choose what gives my life meaning."

Nine Maxims

Pythagoras stressed the importance of repeating maxims so the learning sinks into our brain and becomes an automatic choice. So let's look at all nine maxims together:

1. I need to explore and understand, before I can act.

2. What is this feeling trying to tell me?

3. Accept the feelings, challenge the thoughts.

4. What can I control?

5. It's not all about me.

6. I can ask, you can say no, and we can negotiate.

7. Can I cope with now?

8. I'm doing my best but I'm crooked timber.

9. Choose what gives my life meaning.

Look back over the maxims and decide which one (or maybe two) speak to you the strongest. To make certain it becomes your default position, put it somewhere that you'll see it on a regular basis. For example, the refrigerator door or as the wallpaper on your computer, or put a Post-it note on the inside of your wallet. When you're feeling anxious or stressed, repeat the maxim to yourself until you feel calmer and better able to cope. It might also be helpful to look at the relevant chapter again, so you reacquaint yourself with the knowledge contained in the maxim. When you feel the concept has become part of your default position, move onto another one of the maxims.

Further Reading

BY THE AUTHOR

What Is Love? 50 Questions About How to Find, Keep, and Rediscover It

Love is one of the most powerful forces in our lives. It's the reason we open our hearts to someone we hardly know and tie our destinies together. Unfortunately, when love runs smoothly we take it for granted so it's only when we hit a crisis that we ask: what is love, why does it go wrong and how do we get it back? Andrew takes 50 readers questions and uses them to illuminate a different aspect of love. They include:

- ♥ How do I make love work against the odds?

- ♥ Can I save this marriage alone?

- ♥ Should I stay in an okay marriage or look for something better?

- ♥ Can you love two people at the same time?

- ♥ When is it time to accept the inevitable and move on?

Resolve Your Differences: Seven Steps to Dealing With Conflict in Your Relationship

Love needs skills as well as connection and this book equips you with the most important one of all: how to disagree without being disagreeable and falling out. Andrew explains:

- ♥ What drives those petty squabbles.

- ♥ How to stop arguments spiraling out of control.

- ♥ The seven types of anger and how only one is productive.

- ♥ How to forgive and put issues behind you.

Heal and Move On: Seven Steps to Recovering from a Break-Up

Whether your partner left or it's you who has decided to end the relationship, breaking up is painful and sometimes overwhelming. Friends and family urge you to move on but it's hard unless you understand what went wrong, mourn the loss and, most importantly, heal. Andrew explains:

- ♥ The different journey for the leaver and the sticker (who wanted to make the relationship work).

- ♥ What will help and hinder your recovery.

- ♥ Helping your children cope.

- ♥ How to avoid repeating the same mistakes.

- ♥ Learning how to fly again.

I Love You But I'm Not In Love With You

If you or your partner has fallen out of love, this book will explain why and set out a plan for rescuing your relationship. There is more information about limerence, loving attachment, the stages of love, and love languages. It will also help you to . . .

♥ Argue productively and address the core of the issue.

♥ Employ the trigger words for more effective communication.

♥ Find a balance between being fulfilled as an individual and being one half of a couple.

♥ Take your sex life to a deeper level of intimacy.

♥ Create new bonds instead of searching for old ones.

Have The Sex You Want

If your sex life is more about going through the motions, something you only get around to a couple of times a year or is just another item to tick off your "to do" list, this book is for you. It will help you challenge the myths about sex that are stopping you from passionate love-making, break down the bad habits that have accumulated over your years together, and rebuild your sex life into something sensual and more plentiful. I show how you can:

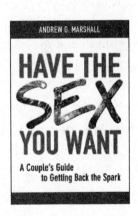

♥ Talk about sex with your partner without getting defensive.

♥ Deal with different levels of desire.

♥ Understand the three types of making love and how they can rekindle desire.

♥ Repair the damage from an affair by reconnecting again in the bedroom.

My Husband Doesn't Love Me And He's Texting Someone Else

If your husband has turned into a stranger, seems irritated all the time and nothing you say or do seems to make any difference, this book will help make sense of what's happening. It explains why men fall out of love and the three things every woman needs to know to protect her relationship. It is also full of practical techniques for coming back from the brink—like assertiveness—and advice on diagnosing whether your husband is depressed (plus what to do if he is). In  the second half of the book, I tackle what to do if you suspect or know there's another woman in the background:

♥ The six types of other woman, from "a spark" to "the love of his life."

♥ Tailored strategies for dealing with each type.

♥ Five worst and best reactions after uncovering what's really going on.

♥ How to keep calm even when provoked.

♥ How to combat the poison that she's slipping into your relationship.

♥ When to keep fighting and when to make a tactical withdrawal.

My Wife Doesn't Love Me Any More

If your life is in turmoil because you wife has just told you that she doesn't love you and your marriage is over, this book will bring a bit of sanity into your world. In my experience, more relationships end at this point not because women are determined to leave but because men panic and end up pushing their wife even further away. In 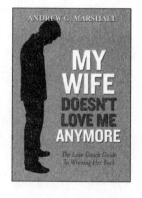 this book, I explain how to keep calm and listen, really listen rather than arguing, or trying to find a magic fix. I also cover:

- ♥ How to figure out why she's fallen out of love.

- ♥ Five things you think will save your relationship but should absolutely avoid.

- ♥ What her words and actions really mean and how to use them to win her back.

- ♥ What to do to instantly improve the atmosphere at home.

- ♥ How to prevent past mistakes from undermining your attempts to build a better future.

- ♥ Five pick-me-up tips when you're down and need to keep focused.

- ♥ When it's time to admit it's over and what factors indicate you should still fight on.

How Can I Ever Trust You Again?

There are few things more traumatic than discovering your partner is having an affair. However, it is possible to come out of an affair with a stronger and better marriage. I explain the seven stages from discovery to recovery and the main reasons couples get stuck along the way. There's more information about Transactional Analysis (TA), making a Fulsome Apology, and rebuilding trust. I also cover:

- ♥ The eight types of affairs and how understanding your partner's is key to rescuing your relationship.

- ♥ How to stop your imagination running wild and your brain going into meltdown.

- ♥ How the person who had the affair can help their partner recover.

- ♥ What derails your recovery process and how to get your marriage on track again.

I Love You But You Always Put Me Last: How to Childproof Your Marriage

One of the key reasons why couples become estranged is that they put so much energy into raising their kids that they neglect their marriage. However, you don't need to choose between a happy marriage and happy children, you can have them both. I explain how to parent as a team and raise an emotionally healthy family. Packed with tips, advice, and compelling examples, this book will equip you to turn your marriage around. I explain how to:

♥ Ask for the support you need.

♥ Overcome differences in parenting styles and find acceptable compromises.

♥ Share household responsibilities effectively.

♥ Define what your children truly need from you.

♥ Rekindle your passion for each other and keep it alive.

♥ Avoid the pitfalls of raising "red-carpet kids" and give your children a strong foundation for the future.

Learn to Love Yourself Enough

If you're in the middle of a relationship crisis, it's easy to think everything would be better if only my partner would . . . However, that closes off one of the most powerful and effective ways forward: working on yourself. After all, if you are calmer and in a better place, you will communicate better and the dynamics of your whole relationship will change. In this book, I will help you step back, get to know yourself better and rebuild your shattered self-confidence. It covers how to:

♥ Examine your relationship with your parents: Discover the six types of child-parent relationships and how to accept the legacy of your past.

♥ Find Forgiveness: Debunk the two myths about forgiveness and discover what can be gained from negative experiences.

♥ Don't let other people put you down: Recognize the five phases of projection and how understanding our own projections leads to better and happy relationships.

♥ Reprogram your inner voice: Identify the three kinds of negative thinking that work together to undermine self-confidence and whether they are based on fact or just opinion.

♥ Set realistic goals: Learn how perfectionism undermines self-esteem.

♥ Rebalance yourself: Understand that problems lurk in the extremes and why the middle way is the most successful way.

♥ Conquer Fears and Setbacks: Overcome the day-to-day problems that life and other people throw at you.

BY OTHER AUTHORS

Thinking Fast and Slow by Daniel Kahneman (Farrar, Starus, and Girroux)

If you have an important decision to make, it helps to understand how your mind works. This book has lots of exercises to demonstrate the shortcuts that the brain takes and gets you thinking about whether they are helpful or not.

Philosophy for Life: And Other Dangerous Situations
by Jules Evans (New World Library)

The greatest minds from the ancient world onward tackle some of mankind's most enduring problems. The author worked through his depression using philosophy and he looks at all the major schools of thought and how their teachings could be applied today.

Daring Greatly by Brene Brown (Avery)

The importance of vulnerability for a fulfilling life and why shame is so toxic.

Wherever You Go, There You Are: Mindfulness Mediation for Everyday Life by Jon Kabat-Zinn (Hachette)

The father of mindfulness talks about letting go, patience, nonjudging, meditation and, of course, cat food bowls left in the sink. The book is a series of short and easily digested articles but each one has a profound lesson.

The Heart of the Buddha's Teaching by Thich Nhat Hanh (Broadway Books)

Kabat-Zinn is a pupil of this author and the book provides some of the intellectual and spiritual underpinning of mindfulness. I owe a debt of gratitude to his teachings on calmness.

Man's Search for Meaning by Victor Frankl (Beacon Press)

Frankl was a psychiatrist and a holocaust survivor. Part one of this classic book covers his experiences as an inmate at Auschwitz and other concentration camps. Part two explains his therapeutic and philosophical outlook.

How to Live (A Life of Montaigne in One Question and Twenty Attempts at an Answer) by Sarah Bakewell (Other Press)

A biography of the Renaissance French nobleman, the questions he asked and the answers he explored.

About the Author

Andrew G. Marshall is a marital therapist with more than 30 years experience. He originally trained with RELATE (The UK's leading couple counselling charity) but now leads a team in private practice in London, England, offering the Marshall Method. He is also the author of 15 other books on relationships and contributes to *Mail on Sunday, Daily Mail,* and *Sunday Telegraph.* To date, his work has been translated into over 20 different languages.

You can follow him on Twitter (@andrewgmarshall) and Facebook (Andrew G. Marshall-Author) and to receive regular updates about Andrew's books, articles, and events, subscribe to his newsletter at www.andrewgmarshall.com

MORE TITLES BY ANDREW G. MARSHALL

ANDREW G. MARSHALL

ARE YOU RIGHT FOR ME?

Seven steps to getting clarity and commitment in your relationship

BLOOMSBURY

ANDREW G. MARSHALL

BUILD A LIFE-LONG LOVE AFFAIR

Seven steps to revitalising your relationship

BLOOMSBURY

ANDREW G. MARSHALL

HEAL AND MOVE ON

Seven steps to recovering from a break-up

BLOOMSBURY

ANDREW G. MARSHALL

HELP YOUR PARTNER SAY 'YES'

Seven steps to achieving better cooperation and communication

BLOOMSBURY

ANDREW G. MARSHALL

RESOLVE YOUR DIFFERENCES

Seven steps to dealing with conflict in your relationship

BLOOMSBURY

ANDREW G. MARSHALL

LEARN TO LOVE YOURSELF ENOUGH

Seven steps to improving your self-esteem and your relationships

BLOOMSBURY

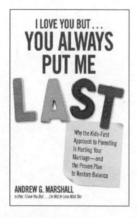

I LOVE YOU BUT...
YOU ALWAYS PUT ME LAST

Why the Kids-First Approach to Parenting Is Hurting Your Marriage—and the Proven Plan to Restore Balance

ANDREW G. MARSHALL
author, I Love You But...I'm Not in Love With You

BLOOMSBURY
ANDREW G. MARSHALL

How Can I Ever Trust You Again?

INFIDELITY:
From Discovery to Recovery in Seven Steps

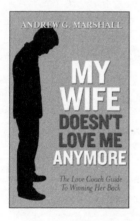

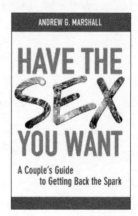

I Love You But I'm Not In Love With You:
Seven Steps to Saving Your Relationship

The Single Trap: The Two-Step Guide to Escaping It
and Finding Lasting Love

How Can I Ever Trust You Again?
Infidelity From Discovery to Recovery in Seven Steps

Are You Right for Me: Seven Steps to Getting Clarity
and Commitment in Your Relationship

Build a Life-Long Love Affair:
Seven Steps to Revitalising Your Relationship

Heal and Move On: Seven Steps to Recovering from a Break-Up

Help Your Partner Say Yes: Seven Steps
to Achieving Better Cooperation and Communication

Learn to Love Yourself Enough: Seven Steps
to Improving Your Self-Esteem and Your Relationships

Resolve Your Differences: Seven Steps
to Dealing With Conflict in Your Relationship

Make Love Like a Prairie Vole:
Six Steps to Passionate, Plentiful and Monogamous Sex

My Wife Doesn't Love Me Any More:
The Love Coach Guide to Winning Her Back

I Love You But You Always Put Me Last:
How to Childproof Your Marriage

My Husband Doesn't Love Me and He's Texting Someone Else:
The Love Coach Guide to Winning Him Back

Have the Sex You Want: A Couple's Guide to Getting Back the Spark

What Is Love? 50 Questions About How to Find,
Keep, and Rediscover It